The Kaminsky Symphony

Paolo G. Grossi

spectrum books

Cover photo by Viorel Sima.

Cover designed by Scott Gaunt.

Paperback ISBN: 978-1-915905-69-7

First edition, Spectrum Books, 2025

Discover more books at www.spectrum-books.com

Paolo G. Grossi was born and raised in Milan. Thirty years ago he spent a weekend in London and decided to stay. Like most Italians, opera and the visual arts are his main passions. When not writing , you will surely find him attending a performance, visiting a museum or spending some time cycling in Berlin or around the Wannsee. He lives in London with his partner David.

He's the author of The Tiergarten Tales and Serafino da Ferrara.

To the people for whom the rainbow never shone

Every man hangs by a thread,
any minute the abyss may open under his feet.
And yet he goes, invents for himself
all kinds of troubles and spoils his life.

Ivan Sergeyevich Turgenev
Fathers and Sons

The Chapters

Odessa and Odesa

I started to write The Kaminsky Symphony three or four months after the Russian invasion of Ukraine.

Like most people, I am appalled by the criminal act of Vladimir Putin and his acolytes.

I'm also fully aware that the city of Odessa is now widely called Odesa, as the latter is the Ukrainian name for it.

In the book I refer to this splendid city by its Russian spelling. This is exclusively due to my slight fixation with authenticity. At the time of the action, the city was firmly under the control of the Russian Empire, as were Crimea and Livadia, where the Tsar and his family regularly spent their summer holidays.

I would like to make clear that my use of the Russian name is not misunderstood as any form of support for the Russian invasion and that I'm firmly behind the Ukrainian people's struggle to save their country from a despicable act of war.

I. The Gardens of Porta Venezia

He's tired of gesturing to Teresina. Her tempo is too fast and the end of the opera is a very slow one. If anything he prefers it even slower than Maestro Verdi would have liked.

And, despite the title, hers is the starring role. It should have been called *Amneris*. An ambiguous character, torn between love, power, anger and revenge. Aida is, after all, a good-hearted Ethiopian slave, her love genuine, her plight moving. And boring.

Teresina Cason is a last-minute understudy from La Fenice and has failed to seize the opportunity. Carlo Alberto detects the murmurs up in the Loggione, that diabolical top gallery where careers are shattered by vengeful youths and unforgiving critics.

His left hand keeps telling her to slow down, but she isn't even looking and, hearing the murmurs and the occasional whistles, she's now a nervous wreck. He's had enough of slowing his orchestra down. The first violin occasionally looks up in wonder.

'Alma adorata.'

At the curtain call she's booed off the stage in tears. A handful of tomatoes splatter on the floor behind her, thankfully missing the distraught lady. Carlo Alberto hugs her but he feels like reproaching her too: 'My hand. Did you see my hand? What was the rush? This isn't Rossini.'

For him though, the usual standing ovation. And flowers for Aida. The boring one.

In his dressing room he dries the sweat off his neck and forehead with a soft cotton towel while letting the white tie loose. He dries and combs his luscious moustaches, contemplating his handsome features in the mirror.

Carlo Alberto Mandelli, Count of Castagnino, is barely in his mid-thirties. His physique is still slender, sinewy, almost bony. The complexion is pale, the always finely combed hair light chestnut, the moustaches a resplendent golden during the sunny days of a Milanese summer.

When the great Toscanini left in 1908, he was appointed to the post the very same day. Carlo Alberto had paid him a visit the day before for an afternoon tea at the Grand Hotel et de Milan and the Maestro had informed him that he would succeed him.

'Isn't it for the director general to decide?' He had retorted in genuine puzzlement.

Toscanini had repositioned the cup on the saucer with his usual calm and had smiled with a sardonic grin.

'The director general does what I tell him to do.'

It's late and he's tired. Having to accommodate an inexperienced understudy has sapped his energy and he's ready to walk home for a light supper and the soft covers of his four-poster bed.

Signor Brambilla bursts into the dressing room holding his top hat and stick in one hand. The cape and the long white scarf float mid-air over his evening suit. Mandelli greets him with a "Good evening, Count Dracula", as he does every time he sees him in his gala attire. The wisecrack doesn't go down very well, but Brambilla's need to flatter his client is stronger than his vanity.

'Carletto! My dear friend! Usual top performance. Crowd outside waiting for you as always. Allow me to introduce Contessa Invernizzi and Marchesa della Fontanella. Devoted admirers, of course.'

Two sumptuously dressed ladies suddenly fill the not so large dressing room, and Maestro Mandelli stands up to kiss their hands.

'Table is booked at Savini. Upstairs, so we won't be disturbed by the fawning populace.'

'Amedeo, I'm very tired. The understudy was hard work tonight, and the Loggione weren't happy, as you might have heard. I'd rather…'

'Nonsense! Ladies, you must excuse Maestro di Castagnino, he's of the home-loving type lately. But a glass or two of champagne will restore your energies, young man!'

He stoops to whisper in Mandelli's ear.

'As your agent, I strongly recommend you come along. These ladies sit at the top of the city's aristocratic order; I wouldn't be rude if I were you.'

Carlo Alberto lowers his gaze in resignation, humbly nodding while grabbing his cape, hat and stick from the coat hanger.

'Very well… could you do my tie up again, please?' He tenderly smiles to the ladies. 'Not sure if I have the strength…'

He enjoys the cool brush of the snowflakes against his flushed face. The pavements and the roads are already thick with a white, silvery powder. Carriages and cars proceed at a snail's pace to avoid crashing into the gilded entrance doors of the theatre.

He looks up to the grey, heavy sky while adjusting the scarf around his neck to protect himself from the searing cold. The fog prevents the foursome from even discerning the entrance to the Galleria. They stroll through, Contessa Invernizzi gliding her gloved arm under Carlo Alberto's.

When they finally grace the marble pavements of the glitzy arcade, the fog dissolves, allowing the late-nighters to recognise him. Heads bow and compliments flow across the wide passage until they reach the glittering doors of Savini. The maître d' knows them all very well, and he's far from surprised to see nobility and the arts together for a late meal.

They are ushered upstairs where a round table for four has been reserved for them in a secluded corner. The dining room is much smaller than downstairs but still packed to capacity, and the standing ovation at their entrance is all but inevitable.

Maestro Mandelli bows and thanks the diners, some venturing to shake his hand in congratulation, some commenting on the two beautiful young ladies on their arms.

When the bells of the Duomo strike one, he's exhausted. He detests caviar but Brambilla and Contessa Invernizzi have kept piling it up on blinis all night and passing them on to him. He had resolved that it would have been too rude to turn them down.

He had tried to pour water in the glass but the waiters were faster with the bottles of Dom Perignon incessantly landing on the table.

His agent always picks up the bill. In the dying days of 1913 ladies don't even get to see the prices - it would represent the ultimate act of rudeness - and Carlo Alberto is the artist.

'Artists create, managers look after the vulgarity of monetary rewards,' booms a rather tipsy Brambilla.

Contessa Invernizzi offers to share her carriage to take Maestro Mandelli home but he gathers the energy to decline, explaining that his abode is merely a ten-minute walk from the restaurant.

'Carlo Alberto is a city dweller and even the Gardens of Porta Venezia are way too rural for him,' shouts Brambilla, now visibly inebriated.

Marchesa della Fontanella, who has turned out to be as sharp as an oyster spoon, laughs with a puzzled expression.

'But… they are only around the block from your house, Maestro.'

'*Yes, that was the…*' But the repartee never leaves his lips. She wouldn't understand that either, he concludes.

The slow walk along Via Manzoni is the only pleasant part of the evening. The conducting was hard work, the late dinner akin to torture. He doesn't even mind that his shoes are now soaked after plodding along in what is now almost two feet of snow. The peace, the solitude.

He turns right onto Via Bigli and stops in front of a big wooden door. He pulls the bell chain and a middle-aged man in butler's livery appears.

'Maestro.'

'Oh, Tonio, I told you not to stay in your livery until late, it's really not necessary.'

The butler takes the cape, hat and stick, doing his best to shake off the excessive snow.

'I thought you might want some supper, Maestro.'

'Oh God, no. They've fed me like a goose ready to be slaughtered for a portion of foie gras at Savini. I'm positively ready for bed.'

'I've left the fire on all evening in your bedroom, sir. And some hot stones under the blanket.'

'Always thoughtful, Tonio. What would I do without you and Cecilia? I hope she didn't stay up?'

He sends Tonio to bed, telling him not to rise for an early breakfast. He will have some coffee and pastries around eleven.

Before heading upstairs, he stops by the grand piano in his study. In a drunken haze he peruses the scores scattered on the floor before sitting and playing the last few bars scribbled on the paper in front of him.

He shakes his head. Try to compose when drunk? He slowly walks up the stairs. His instinct is to crash on the bed, evening dress, white tie and all, but Tonio has kindly warmed it up with the stones and Cecilia and the younger maid have changed the linen that very morning; he can tell by the fragrant smell of lavender.

He manages to undress and put his nightshirt on. When under the covers, he stares at the ceiling and then at the empty side of the bed. He touches the pillow with his fingertips. One day, perhaps one day a human being will be there. Wishing me goodnight. Perhaps with a kiss.

Nonsense. Dreams. Not in this world.

The coffee and the pastries lie on the round table by the French window. In his velvet dressing gown and with his head still spinning from too much champagne, he sits on the chair and starts nibbling at the croissants while taking small sips of the coffee.

Cecilia and Tonio run the three-storey house with a gentle, slow efficiency. The young maid helps them with the cleaning. There is no garden, but a square loggia overlooks Via Bigli on the first floor. An awning shelters his reading time in the hottest months of the year, when La Scala is closed and he can relax, dedicating more of his time to books and composition.

Tonio is a well-built man in his late forties. So well-built in fact that he struggles to fit in the butler liveries. He went into service with the Maestro when, upon obtaining a permanent contract with the theatre, Carlo purchased the house. Cecilia, always dressed in long black skirts, is a skilled cook, though the work patterns of their employer don't allow for many slow and quiet dinners. He's also not fond of entertaining. 'They're entertaining me quite enough as it is,' he often remarks.

He made the mistake of mentioning his attempt at a symphony to his agent, and Amedeo's eyes immediately started rolling with *Lire* signs. He then had to cool his enthusiasm by explaining that being an outstanding conductor didn't necessarily lead to being a genius in composition.

Maestro Puccini had paid a visit while in Milan and

had darted towards the scribbled scores scattered on the rug by the piano, his curiosity getting the better of him. He had then sat on the stool and tried a few movements. Carlo Alberto had nervously perched on a chair, listening to his work played by one of the greatest.

Puccini, always the Tuscan, didn't mince his words.

'Carlo. My dearest friend. Why a symphony? They are going out of fashion, at least in Italy. And abroad… well, Strauss and Schoenberg? Those two dogs are viciously talented. Are you sure you can compete with them?'

'I'm not.'

Puccini had turned again to the piano and played a phrase.

'Here. I love the sudden melancholy. I do that often. It strikes the senses. The sadness. As if something were missing…'

Then Giacomo had stared into Mandelli's eyes with his piercing gaze.

'It is, isn't it, Carlo? Missing…?'

He strolls to the theatre after a simple lunch. He takes a little detour to stop at Cova for a *macchiato*, trying to keep the hat down and the scarf up to his nose to avoid another round of fawning congratulations.

No chance though. As usual, the barman greets him with a thundering *'Buongiorno, Maestro!'* which makes all the punters turn and bow their heads.

The rehearsal of *Cenerentola* goes well with no incompetent understudy to contend with: all seasoned professionals who seem to know exactly what he demands. He's walking out of the side door with some members of the orchestra and sees young Matteo and Alessandro across the road, almost as if they had been waiting for him. They are wrapped up in thick coats and scarves and have their viola cases on their shoulders. They look up at the sky from time to time while frantically clapping their gloves hands, trying to keep warm. It has started snowing again.

Mandelli crosses the road and greets them with paternal affection; they have only recently joined the orchestra.

'Good afternoon, young men.'

'Good afternoon, Maestro.'

'I hadn't had the chance to talk to you, mostly because the violas were doing really well. I'm very happy with your contribution, keep it up.'

'Very kind, Maestro.'

'Well, free evening for a change; take the opportunity to go out and enjoy yourselves a bit. Don't spend it practising, it can get obsessive.'

Matteo seems to have been chosen to do the talking.

'We will, sir. In fact, we wanted to ask if you would like to join us. We are going to a party.'

At this sentence the young men turn to each other, their gaze questioning, as if not entirely sure they should proceed with the invitation.

'I might be too old for your type of gathering; I'm starting to be rather home-loving these days.'

'Oh, it's for all ages. But, well… mainly for gentlemen.'

He freezes while maintaining a certain composure.

'For gentlemen?'

'Yes, kind of exclusively for gentlemen… who prefer the company of other gentlemen.'

He notices the boys' faces going slightly crimson, possibly afraid of having picked up the wrong signals.

'I see.'

Alessandro finally puts a word in while apologetically bowing his head.

'But forgive us if we have misunderstood. It wasn't our intention to offend you.'

'You haven't. But I think I will postpone the acceptance of your invitation. Another time maybe. I wonder what made you think of me for such a party?'

Alessandro hasn't raised his head. He stares at his right boot, nervously sweeping the snow left to right.

'You are a handsome man, sir.'

Matteo turns sharply to his mate while kicking his ankle.

'Alessandro… '

'I'm ever so sorry, sir. That was out of order.'

Carlo Alberto smiles, eager to relieve the young man of his discomfort.

'Not at all, Alessandro. I'm flattered. I will see you tomorrow at the rehearsal. Enjoy the soirée.'

He squeezes Alessandro's arm with his hand, making the young man nod, half relieved but sad at the Maestro declining to join them.

He takes a detour to Cova for some tea and a piece of cake. Once seated at his usual table he can't help pondering over the conversation.

They know.

And heaven knows how long they have known for. It could be just intuition, or they may have followed him. Where though? It might be his gestures, too feminine or perhaps just a little too delicate and unmanly. He catches himself staring at the mirror while lifting the cup. The movement is definitely not lady-like. He doesn't smoke and maybe that stands out. All gentlemen do, whether it is pipes, cigars, or roughly wrapped up tobacco for the less affluent classes.

But they know.

A plethora of speculations revolves in his worried mind. Matteo and Alessandro are a decent pair of lads though, passionate about their music, good viola players, respectful, polite and always on time. They come from well-to-do families and won't need the money that blackmail would generate. And Alessandro is clearly attracted to him. He's good-looking, a little cheekier than Matteo, an endearing half-smile always on his thin, northern lips.

But he might be upset at being rejected and do something stupid. And yet Carlo didn't reject him; he just declined to attend the party. In any case, blackmailing him for what? While vilified in some quarters or merely frowned upon in others, like the artistic milieu around him, it is not illegal. When still a student at the Conservatorio Giuseppe Verdi (freshly dedicated to the Maestro after his death), he secretly and avidly read all the reports about the Wilde affair and was shaken by the wanton cruelty of it all. He also became aware that the writer and his young lover had been able to freely indulge in their common vice in France and Italy, though admittedly he had found their drunken gallivanting a little distasteful.

But the law of this kingdom is not interested in his tribe. The monarch and his ministers wilfully ignore the subject and they are not interested in pursuing individuals practising the love without name; they are non-persons. Hardly a satisfactory arrangement, yet one which at least doesn't dispatch you to languish - and die - in Reading Gaol. He's composing a symphony in his study, not writing a ballad in a musty cell.

Why didn't he accept the invitation? He regrets turning it down now. Alessandro is handsome and they might have held hands, perhaps kissed. He's so clearly an affectionate boy, seeking kindness.

Now exhausted by the grinding thoughts, he calls for the bill and set off for home. After a steaming bath, diligently prepared by Tonio, he sits at the dining table, lovingly set up by Cecilia. The fare is always light. He eats enough complicated food when dragged to Biffi and Savini by Amedeo and several other hangers on.

He lulls in the comfort of the sparsely furnished

room, the soft texture of his velvet smoking jacket, the delicate taste of the *minestra di verdure.*

The townhouse is on three floors and tastefully decorated. Not for Maestro Mandelli the remnants of frilly and over-designed Victorian furnishings. It's a new century and a hint of modernism is starting to appear. A few years earlier he had travelled to Vienna for a brief spell at the Kaiserliche Oper and had ended up spending all of his free time perusing Klimtesques furniture in the most *avant-garde* shops. The Persian rugs covering the parquet floors of the house are expensive, but he always chooses the less garish ones at his favourite dealer. He occasionally browses in antique shops, but he's reluctant to clutter the rooms. Maestro Puccini was visibly enchanted on his first visit; Toscanini had been critical of the style, but he was prematurely starting to turn into a grumpy old man.

After supper he retires in the study again, trying to correct a difficult passage he had composed the day before.

It's not even eight. He walks up to his bedroom and after standing at a window, peering down onto the deserted Via Bigli, he returns to the door and pulls the bell rope to summon Tonio.

When the butler enters the room, Carlo Alberto is at his desk. No words are exchanged. Tonio approaches the desk and the Maestro opens one of the drawers, hauling 120 Lire from it.

Still without any conversation he hands them over to Tonio, who swiftly puts them away in his pocket.

'The extra twenty are for you.'

Tonio turns to gaze at the window.

'Maestro… it's snowing hard and it's probably zero degrees. I'm not sure there will be anyone in the Gardens.'

'It won't be the end of the world if you return empty-handed. Thank you, Tonio.'

The butler nods and leaves, shaking his head as soon as he finds himself in the corridor.

The three servants nurture a simple affection for their quiet, kind-hearted employer. He's a gentle and undemanding artist, paying for a doctor when they need one, telling them to go to bed and not stay up when he is late from performance nights or the usual *soirées*.

Tonio wraps himself up in his heavy coat, scarf and felt hat before opening the big wooden door. He starts ambling slowly towards Porta Venezia, negotiating the snow which hasn't been swept, still shaking his head at the slight madness.

'A wife. That is what Maestro Mandelli needs. And children. A happy household. Not this.'

He tentatively passes through the entrance gates. The night watch has just turned off the oil lamps, though the white sheet of snow covering all the vegetation reflects the lights that are still on in the adjacent street.

He more or less knows the more popular spots. Shades of wandering human creatures start to flutter between the chestnut trees: careful, suspicious, perhaps afraid.

The rough ones he ignores outright. Not his Master's taste. He knows that by now.

Obviously everyone is over twenty-one years of age. Obviously. Everyone is also slightly forgetful and leaves their identity papers at home. And they are all out on their way to meet up with their fellow students at their local *taverna* for a good glass of Barbera. Just passing by. As they do.

He approaches a young fellow with dark blond hair. It is the only discernible feature as everything else is buried under layers of wool.

'Buonasera, young man.*'*

'Buonasera.'

Tonio points to the scarf to indicate that he would

like to see his face before making an offer. The boy complies.

'Would one-hundred lire be a fair offer?'

'For?'

'An hour or so.'

'More than fair.'

Tonio nurtures an odd soft spot for these youngsters. He is a man for the ladies and fully conscious of his unfortunate lack of beauty. As if wanting to relieve the lad of his dejection at the incipient ordeal, he hastily lays out the details.

'Not me. My Master. At his home. Not far from here. At least you'll be warm. He's a handsome man.'

'God, anything to get out of this weather, it's freezing my guts.'

They walk in silence towards Via Bigli; when they reach the door Tonio turns with a sharp movement. A blade shines in his hand.

The knife is now against the throat of the terrified young man.

'Whether you recognise my Master or not, you keep your mouth shut, understood? I will find you if you don't.'

The lad is shaking.

'M-my mouth?'

'No blackmail. I know your lot. You're scum.'

'With all due respect, sir, I'm a student, actually. I'm no scum. I have no money, that is the truth. But if I blackmail your Master, no one will ever touch me again. Why would I do that?'

'Fair point. But I've come across some real scoundrels.'

'I'm sure you have, sir. But I'm not one.'

When Tonio moves the knife away from his throat, the youngster massages his neck with his hand, still visibly trembling.

He makes him clean his shoes when in the hallway and leads him upstairs without uttering anymore words.

He knocks at the door and walks in with the lad in tow.

'Sir, this is…'

He turns with a questioning stare.

'Ehm… Danilo.'

'Danilo. Or so he says.'

Carlo stands up.

'Thank you, Tonio. Have a good night.'

'And you, sir.'

He darts a warning glare at the boy on his way out, making him retreat with his hat in his hands.

'You have to forgive Tonio, young man. His manners can be a bit rough.'

Danilo again touches his neck with his hand.

'Not just the manners…'

Carlo Alberto takes Danilo's hands in his.

'Heavens, it must be freezing outside. Come and sit in front of the fire, I wonder if you would care for a glass of wine?'

'I could do, sir, very kind.'

He places his hands closer to the fire, sighing in pleasure.

'It's so warm in here. The Gardens are terrible tonight; the pond is all frozen. I thought I was going to pass out.'

He passes a crystal glass full of a good Barolo to the boy who thanks him with a bow of his head.

'What made you brave this weather tonight?'

'Rent is coming up and the cupboards of my room are empty.'

He notices for the first time that the boy is indeed handsome, though on the side of scrawny, the complexion a rather anaemic white. The soft, thin skin under his eyes reveals a worrying purple shading.

‘I can ask Tonio to bring up some soup and a bit of bread. Would you like that?’

‘You’re ever so kind, sir. I prefer not to have anything in my stomach when I do this. I mean… in case you want to… you know what I mean.’

Mandelli reddens. He does.

‘We don’t have to do that, no. It’s not indispensable. I hope other things are acceptable to you.'

‘Kissing?’

Carlo stares into his glass.

‘Some of your mates refuse outright.’

Danilo takes a good sip.

‘Ah! We know the type. They’re not into gentlemen. They like the ladies, but men are the ones who pay. The most beautiful ones sometimes land themselves an old countess or the bored wife of a rich merchant. Not sure if that is any better than men. But I’m not one of them and, well, you’re quite a looker, sir. I think we will enjoy ourselves rather.’

He smiles while he gets up. He leaves the glass on the table by the armchair and slowly approaches Carlo Alberto.

Danilo’s right hand caresses his cheek while his lips gently land on the Maestro’s mouth; his tongue unhurriedly searches its way inside.

They slowly undress each other and, unexpectedly, the boy kneels and lower Carlo’s undergarment. He looks up with those youthful pupils before taking possession. Mandelli feels the lips around it and gasps while laying a hand on Danilo’s head, softly stroking his rebellious blond hair, looking down at his eagerness.

Once under the fluffy covers the last piece of clothing flies out onto the floor and the hug is tight. Carlo feels the pleasure of being desired. Beside the financial transaction he can tell the boy is enjoying the evening.

He knows because he can always tell when they are not.

Danilo's head is resting on his tight, muscular chest, kissing his nipple from time to time. They always find the thin and fluffy hairline running down the middle of his hairless chest unbearably attractive.

'You are a very sensual gentleman, sir. I still have the shivers.'

Carlo ruffles the lad's hair.

'It did sound like you were having a good time.'

'A great time, sir.'

He looks up at the wall and finally notices the pictures of opera houses and some of their programme.

'You're Mandelli, aren't you? Maestro Mandelli.'

'Di Castagnino, yes. I try not to add the aristocratic nonsense.'

'My fellow students and I are more for taverns and music halls but I've seen your picture in the *Corriere della Sera*. Besides, we can barely afford to eat, let alone go to the opera.'

'Sometimes you might be listening to better music in your haunts, believe me.'

They both laugh. When they stop, Danilo kisses him on the cheek.

'You don't have to worry. I keep my mouth shut. And your butler is going to slash my throat open if I let any of this out.'

Carlo laughs again.

'Oh, he won't. He couldn't harm a fly. It's all a melodramatic piece of theatre to protect me. He's a good chap. But glad to hear of your discretion.'

They rest a little while, then Danilo speaks with a soft voice, almost afraid of what is going to ask.

'Would you like me to stay the night?'

'I'm not sure I have anymore money left in my wallet, I can ch…'

'No, not for money.' He laughs again. A cheeky,

youthful laugh. 'For the heat! My bedsit is damp and freezing. Only the cockroaches seem to be able to survive. I think the rats die too. And, well, wouldn't mind a little cuddle in the morning, sir.'

He kisses Danilo's hair.

'Of course. My pleasure. And Tonio will bring up a nice breakfast too.'

'I very much look forward to that, sir. I haven't eaten for… well, I've forgotten how long for.'

They hug and disappear under the covers, Danilo in ecstasy. A handsome, caring and kind client. And the warmth of wealth.

On his way to Amedeo's office, he's still thinking about Danilo. When he instructed Tonio to prepare a parcel of ham, cheese and bread for the lad to take home, he was embarrassed by the grateful bows. Danilo too is on his way home, riding the horse-drawn trolley. And thinking. Thinking about how good would it be to have Carlo Alberto as his Lord Protector, allowing him to continue his studies without dying of hunger before graduation. And of course, enjoying the passionate nights.

Carlo reaches his agent's office in good time, though the secretary lets him through straight away. Maestro Mandelli is the most profitable of his artists.

Every time he comes to visit Amedeo he can't help noticing new expensive-looking antique pieces, furniture or recently acquired fine leather armchairs or sofas.

'Amedeo, why do I suspect you are making too much money out of my trade?'

Signor Brambilla laughs out loud.

'Not as much as you do, Carletto. The difference is that you don't spend it, you old *avare.* Coffee?'

'Yes, please, it's still so cold outside. And I am actually younger than you.'

'The roughest winter I can recall.'

Once the coffee has been served by the secretary, Amedeo picks up some papers on the side of the desk.

'So, my friend, as you know, your contract with La Scala is coming to an end in a few weeks. They have already written to me with an improved offer. Let's not beat about the bush, you're the best show in town.'

The smile is sardonic.

'I'm not sure that I care to be classified as a "show". And I was kind of hoping to be the best in the country at least. Especially now that Arturo has gone abroad.'

'You know what I mean, old friend. Well, the offer is exceptionally good. However I did put out a word after your somehow bizarre request.'

Carlo Alberto lays the cup on the table after a long and restorative sip.

'And?'

Amedeo opens his arms in his usual melodramatic fashion.

'I was literally inundated.'

Mandelli smiles.

'Glad to hear it.'

'The Colon, Berlin, the Garnier, His Majesty's Theatre, the Met. I can go through all of them if you'd like.'

'No need. I was hoping for some more interesting locations, though.'

Eyes open wide.

'More interesting than London, Paris or New York?'

'They won't be much different from Milan.'

'Well, they would. Their houses are vastly inferior to La Scala, for a start. But… let me see… Ah! Here we go. A few days ago I received one of the most hilarious proposals ever. I had to stop laughing while reading it.'

'I'd like to laugh too then.'

'I had this hand-written letter from the Odessa Opera House; you know, on the Black Sea…'

'I know where Odessa is, Amedeo.'

'Well, they had the effrontery to offer a three-year contract as a sole chief conductor. I had to smile at the naivety. They said they can't offer much money, but they are able to let you live rent-free in a villa in the centre of the town. Also a maid and a butler - God knows how cheap they are over there - and allowances for food and furniture. The sheer cheek. The most revered Maestro in the world!'

'After Toscanini… '

'Well, you say that. Anyway, no more of that joke, we were saying…'

'Do they specify which language the musicians speak? I don't speak Russian.'

Amedeo's eyes open even wider, possibly reaching the limit of their extension, before squinting in concerned theatrical astonishment.

'Sorry?'

'You heard me.'

'Yes, I did, and I'm starting to worry.'

Mandelli sighs.

'Well, worry not and tell me what language they speak.'

'I… I believe… let me have a look… yes, they all seem to be fluent in French as it seems to be very common among educated people in Russia. Carletto, you are not seriously entertaining the idea of… '

'I speak excellent French, as it happens. How many members?'

'I believe it's a full complement, but honestly I don't think… '

'I'm definitely warming up to the challenge. I will take the offer home to peruse the details, if you don't mind.'

Amedeo's eyes re-open in disbelief.

'What?'

‘May I have the offer? It’s still in your hands, Amedeo.’

‘What? What offer? Ah, yes, of course, here it is.’

Carlo Alberto puts the papers in his bag and stands up.

‘Carletto, that thing is probably not even an orchestra, likely no more than a peasants’ brass band. Are you going mad?’

‘Well, in that case they need help to improve, don't you think?’

‘They do? Who? Yes, yes. But why you?’

‘Who else? Have a good day, my friend.’

‘I wish I had kept my mouth shut.’

‘We both know that you are unable to do that, Amedeo.’

The premiere of *Cenerentola* is a stunning success, and after the usual congratulations and general fawning, he manages to fend off Amedeo's invitations.

‘I’m going to have a beer at the music hall by the canals of Porta Ticinese with one of my players. Good night, Amedeo.’

Signor Brambilla storms off, gesticulating and rambling to himself: ‘Odessa! A music all on the Navigli. What is the matter with him?’

He hails a carriage and lets Alessandro jump up first. Once inside, they exchange a tiny, tentative smile.

‘I thought the music hall and a healthy dose of rowdy youth would be a good alternative to the usual empty-headed aristocrats I have to endure regularly. Though, to be fair to him, Amedeo isn’t stupid. Boisterous and annoying perhaps, but not stupid.’

He takes his gloves and hat off.

‘I am so very sorry for not letting you into the news before announcing it to the orchestra. You kept staring at the floor after that.’

Alessandro keeps looking ahead. A heavy late afternoon fog surrounds the carriage, the horses canter their way to the party venue between piles of swept-up snow.

'Why Odessa? What's in Odessa? Who's in Odessa?'

'Who? No one. Well, the opera house that has hired me.'

Alessandro smiles.

'My apology. My damn jealousy having the better of me.'

'That bad?'

'Worse.'

They drop into an embarrassed silence, Mandelli not knowing how to alleviate the boy's pain.

'I… I'm not very good with this sort of thing. I don't recall anyone falling in love with me before. And I am so much older than you.'

'I'm twenty-five, I'm not a child.'

'Still. I think what you see in me isn't a lover, Alessandro. And I'm no paternal figure, I'm afraid. If anything, I'm a little immature myself. I won't be any good.'

He stares at the fog outside, enveloping everything: the buildings, the roads and the boy's heartbreak. Carlo stares uncertainly into his hat.

'Not sure that's going to help.'

'I will get over it. Let's enjoy the party. I'll cry later. Alone.'

But you have no control over when and how your heart shatters into jagged fragments. It happens. And at his age he has yet to build any defence against life's delusions. Alessandro draws both curtains closed and lifts Carlo Alberto's arm. He snuggles under it, his cheek against the soft white woollen scarf. Carlo Alberto kisses his hair.

'I am so sorry, young man.'

He takes his glove off and with his thumb starts wiping the tears off the boy's cheeks. After a while he grabs his handkerchief and lets Alessandro blow his nose in it.

'I've been dreaming about the two of us. Me practising the viola, you correcting me. And then a nice dinner and tucked up in bed. Just the two of us. And so many kisses. Caresses. You holding me all night. Telling me off for little things.'

A little laugh breaks the emotional torrent.

'I am an idiot, am I not? Maybe I really am a child.'

'You know there are plenty of gentlemen out there. And you are such a handsome boy.'

'Men. Rarely gentle. And most of them with a huge issue with what we are. I understand that. But it isn't easy. This world isn't for the likes of us. I remember when you bent over my shoulder to show me what you wanted the violas to do during my first rehearsal. I remember your hand patting my back in encouragement. And your smile. I froze. I thought I was going to kiss you in front of everybody. Matteo had to endure hours of me telling him how wonderful you were while at the same time refusing to admit that I had developed a huge crush on you.'

'Yes, I remember. You were shaking like a leaf. That night I told myself that perhaps I should be less scary.'

They both laugh. Lightly. Two sensitive souls struggling to comprehend why it can't happen.

'How long have we got? Before you go away forever, I mean?'

'I'm going to pay a visit to the Empress Dowager first. Then I shall head to Weimar to stay with Ernestina for a while. She's my sister and we've always been very close.'

'The Empress?'

'Mother. Head of the famous Mandelli di Castagnino empire. Spanning the eastern shores of Lake Como.'

'I see.'

'Won't be pleasant. That is as assured as the air we breathe and the fog we can't see through.'

'Worse than making love to me?'

'Oh, come on. You very well know that if we do that it would only make it worse. For you.'

Alessandro smiles, almost happy.

'I knew it. You might not be in love. But you care. You do love me.'

II. Mothers & Sisters

As predicted, Amedeo wanted to hire one of those new motorcars with private *chauffeurs*. Of course Carlo Alberto can comfortably afford one of those, but he insists on making him book a seat in a first-class compartment on the daily train service to Lecco.

'My mother's driver will pick me up at the station with her carriage. The drive along the lake shore is quite scenic, I remember it from my days at the Lecco *Conservatoire*.'

'A carriage? What century does your mother live in?'

'Certainly not this one.'

Tonio and Cecilia have packed the trunks and a big leather bag with piles of scores. The old Countess never disposed of the old grand piano on which he studied assiduously in the early years of his life, and he plans to make good use of the melancholic pace of life at the villa to make progress on his symphony.

Tonio rings the station master in the morning as the night has brought even more snow and he fears they might arrive at the station to find all trains cancelled.

The old man assures him that the ten-thirty service to Lecco is running and the reservation is confirmed.

After storing the luggage in the carriage, Tonio negotiates the long boulevard leading to Stazione Centrale. It has been swept with Austro-Milanese efficiency and they arrive in good time. The porters take charge of the luggage and Carlo Alberto is ushered into the warm luxury of the first class cafeteria, where a cappuccino and a brioche alla crema are promptly served on his table.

When his train is called, he dons his heavy coat,

gloves, scarf and hat and walks slowly to the platform. He finds a gentleman and a lady in the four-seats compartment. After giving his coat, hat and scarf to the carriage attendant, he takes his seat by the window. He loves travelling by train and he asked Amedeo to specifically book a window seat facing the direction of travel. With the flat countryside between the city and the south-eastern tip of Lake Como under a blanket of snow and veiled by a light fog, he looks forward to a quiet, contemplative journey, eager to immerse himself in his thoughts.

If only.

Once he nods to the couple, not being sure that they are a couple, a Sartrean hell breaks loose. An inferno of other people.

'Well, I'm damned! Maestro Mandelli, no? Of course you are. Alfonsina, Alfonsina! This is Maestro Mandelli!'

He shuts his eyes in dejected sorrow. *Oh no.*

He politely nods. He was hoping for the train to go slow and allow him extra time to take in the calm of the surrounding fields and villages. Now he wishes he had taken up Amedeo's offer of a motorcar. The dam breaks.

'Now, we were at the last *Bohéme* at the San Carlo in Naples. No good. No good at all. What do you think, Maestro? My wife didn't think much of it. You didn't like it, Alfonsina, did you? Alfonsina, tell the Maestro that you didn't like it.'

She leans into his shoulder. A screeching voice pierces his right ear.

'No. I didn't like it at all. Not at all.'

'See? She didn't like it. Told ya. I wonder what Maestro Puccini thinks of a disaster like that. The lady playing Mimí couldn't sing the high notes. She couldn't, I'm telling you. Alfonsina, tell the Maestro that she couldn't sing the high notes.'

She leans even closer, her breath fuming into Carlo's nostrils.

'She couldn't sing the high notes.'

'Well, I wonder what you think of such a catastrophe?'

'I… I wasn't there, sorry.'

But it is all in vain. He distractedly turns and looks at them. Their vulgarity and garish over-expensive garments offend him, their loquacity in the Milanese dialect he can barely understand hurts his ears, their opinionated rants give him shivers of suppressed rage. Alfonsina's perfume is so overpowering that he feels like opening the window despite the minus five degrees temperature.

He answers in monosyllables, hoping that some kind of message will get through. But they don't even listen to themselves, why would they listen to him?

The train jolts and moves. He gets up.

'I hadn't a chance to have a coffee this morning. With your permission, I will decamp to the bistro carriage. Excuse me.'

'But this is first class! They can bring it here! I'll call the attendant, Maestro.' He slams the compartment door open and shouts at the top of his raucous voice. 'Attendant! Attendant!'

'Really no need. I fancy a little wander, but thank you all the same.'

He doesn't wait for the answer. He just darts through them and reaches the bistro where he sits for the whole journey ordering several cups of coffee. A few minutes before reaching Lecco's station he walks along the aisle and passes the compartment. The couple looks at him and nods, probably thinking how rude he has been, their self-awareness on the side of non-existent.

He retrieves his garments from the attendant, detecting a vaguely apologetic expression on his face. Perhaps the poor man had to endure the couple's complaints and rants, all in the loudest of voices, of course.

The day is still misty, that typical haze of the Northern Italian lakes. The platform is almost deserted, and he immediately spots Timoteo waving at him with a sunny smile.

'Signor Conte, *benvenuto!* What a pleasure to see you again, you are in such a good form, Maestro.'

'Thank you, Timoteo, very pleased to see you again too. How is your family? All in good health, I hope.'

'All well and good, sir. The children are too lively, though. They are driving my poor wife mad.'

'I hope they're taking up an instrument of some sort.'

'Filippo likes the violin but the lessons are expensive.'

'Good to hear that he's showing an interest. I'll see what I can do for the lad.'

He takes a longer look at Timoteo's uniform, his brand new leather gloves, the goggles and the flat cap.

'Very smart new uniform for a carriage, Timoteo.'

The driver leads the porter across the station concourse to the big revolving door opening onto the square. Once outside he proudly lifts his right arm to point at the other side of the road.

'We have a car, sir!'

'My mother has bought a car? Seriously?'

'She has indeed, sir. I was shocked when she instructed me to travel to the main Lecco dealer to order one. She gave me a budget but no instructions as she doesn't know anything about automobiles. I hope you like the choice, sir. I went for a brand new Mercedes Knight; it can be opened up in the hot days of summer. Your mother loves to be taken for long drives in the sun, but I have to drive ever so slowly otherwise she shouts at me. Sometimes even the carriages honk at us!'

Carlo smiles while winking and patting Timoteo's shoulders.

'That's the Countess we know, dear fellow.'

Timoteo stows all the luggage and opens the door for Carlo before settling into the driver's seat.

Mandelli enjoys the drive. The road caresses the sinuous shape of the lakeshore, the views spectacular even in the midday haze. Without the Countess in the car, Timoteo indeed seizes the opportunity to drive a bit too fast, making Carlo smile while slightly worrying about ending up in the frozen waters of the lake at every hairpin negotiated by Timoteo with the customary and legendary Italian confidence.

After opening the gates of the villa, the driver jumps back in the car and honks repeatedly to announce their arrival. The butler and all the other servants promptly emerge from the front door.

He's greeted with bows and respectful hand-shaking. He has always been popular. Polite and kind even as a young boy, never shouting at them, always enquiring about their families and wellbeing. The old Countess had always been more remote and severe, frequently disapproving of her son's intimacy with the staff.

He shakes the butler's hand.

'Your mother wouldn't wait for your arrival to have lunch, sir. She is very fond of her routine. We can prepare something for you right away.'

'Thank you, Amilcare. Just some cold cuts, cheese and bread. I never eat a big lunch. How is the old lady?'

'In great form, sir. Looking forward to seeing you.'

'I'm never sure whether that is the case, Amilcare. In the drawing room having coffee?'

'Indeed, sir.'

'Some habits never change.'

They both smile and Carlo makes his way along the long corridor which leads to the drawing room. It is spacious and tastefully furnished, with plenty of antiques on consoles, large mirrors with gold frames and fine paintings on the silky wall-papered walls. An oversized square carpet covers most of the parquet floor and the sofas are positioned in order for all the prospective guests to enjoy the breathtaking views of the lake, contoured by the occasional cypress and flowerpots on the bannisters of the large terrace. The tall French doors are closed, but the curtains are all open. The Countess is sitting upright in a corner of the biggest sofa, sipping coffee from a small porcelain cup, holding the saucer underneath with her left hand.

Her frame is small, her black dress buttoned up to the chin. The grey hair is immaculately arranged in a bun. Her light complexion is still fresh, hardly showing her fifty-eight years of age.

She doesn't turn when Carlo enters. He approaches and leans over to place a tentative kiss on her cheek, the cup and the saucer still in her hands.

'Good afternoon, Mother. How are you today?'

'Good afternoon, Carlo. Just had the most terrible of lunches. The new cook is no good. We had to let Giuseppina go a few months ago and since then it has been a disaster. You'll see for yourself at dinner. Why did she have to stop working?'

Carlo frowns.

'She had become too old?'

The Countess replaces the cup and saucer on the small baroque coffee table.

'That is not an excuse. She had an assistant who did all the work. We paid her well. At least Amilcare still makes the coffee; we ought to thank the Lord for that.'

'Yes, Amilcare always made good coffee. Mother, give her a bit of time, she will learn on the job. Don't send her away too soon.'

'It's a man. A trained chef, apparently. Trained in overcooking ravioli, I say. And the sauces are too watery. The meat is burnt and tastes like cardboard. He's more of an arsonist than a chef. The risottos are tasteless. It got so bad, I thought he came from England at first.'

'Has he improved a bit?'

She sharply turns away in dissembling annoyance.

'A little bit.'

'See, Mother. Give people a chance.'

Amilcare comes in with a tray laid out with cold cuts, some cheese and a decanter with red wine. The Countess thanks him with a nod.

'At least he can't ruin a good ham, I suppose. Thank you, Amilcare.'

Carlo, now rather hungry, start tucking into the food and taking a few sips of the wine.

'How are things in the big city?'

'All well and good, Mother. I do have some news. My contract with La Scala is coming to an end. I have accepted an offer from the Odessa Opera House.'

'Odessa?'

'Odessa.'

'Rather far away. What is the appeal?'

'Precisely that it is far away. A new culture and a challenge. I think they need some improvements in the orchestra.'

'The local band needs an improvement too.'

Carlo smiles at the silly remark, still not entirely sure whether his mother knows the difference between a band and an orchestra.

'I am sure they do. I still love it here, Mother, you know I do. But I could not stay here for the rest of my life. That I cannot do.'

'No. You and your people need to go somewhere all of the time. There is always somewhere else to travel to.'

Carlo lays the glass on the coffee table with a sigh.

'My people - as you are so fond of calling them - sometimes have to escape their places of birth in order to survive. Please let us not get into that again. You know

I've always been grateful to you for not hating me.'

The Countess turns, her expression between offended and surprised.

'Hating my son? What a rather uncalled for thing to say. That is for mothers of dubious heritage who give an inordinate and unwise amount of affection to their children, only to take it all away when the little princes and princesses don't turn out the way they wished. I still disapprove… but… hating my children?'

'I'm sorry, Mother, I did not mean…'

'No more of that. Your brother is joining us for dinner tonight.'

'Good news! I look forward to see Guglielmina and the boys too.'

'He is coming alone.'

'Ah, that is a shame. Are they all in good health?'

'I will let him explain. Your old room is ready. *Aperitivo* at seven in here, you know the routine.'

'I shall work on my symphony in the afternoon.'

'We hadn't had the old Bechstein tuned since you left. No one is playing it.'

'It might make my work sounds better. Why don't you let Timoteo's children play? There might be some talent we don't know of.'

She opens her hands in genuine puzzlement.

'He never asked.'

'Mother, he's your driver. And a polite gentleman. He's never going to ask. I'll arrange that. Apparently Filippo likes the violin. I will give him my old one. It'll be nice to know that it will be put to good use.'

'Always too soft with *les domestiques*, Carlo. You'll never change.'

'Neither will you, Mother.'

He changes into a comfortable, moth-eaten jumper still hanging in his old wardrobe and spends the afternoon at the grand piano. He's not very knowledgeable about tuning but he still has some tools in his old desk and he gives it his best shot.

By five, when Amilcare knocks at the door carrying a tea tray and a couple of *pasticcini*, he has made considerable progress and plays the last passage just scribbled on the score while the butler sets the tea on the coffee table by the sofa.

Once he has finished his task he turns on the oil lamp by the window, dusk now well on its way. Carlo turns from the piano.

'Thank you, Amilcare, I definitely needed a break.'

'The *pasticcini* are fresh. The bakery delivered them this morning. Chocolate and cream. I hope your tastes haven't changed, sir.'

Carlo smiles with affection.

'They certainly haven't. When it comes to chocolate and cream, I'm still a young boy.'

'Glad to hear that, sir. I have prepared your suit for tonight, if you could please be so kind as to inform me of the best time to run the bath.'

'About six, I would say. I like to linger in the tub a little bit too much. That's another boyish habit which hasn't gone away. Don't tell me it's white tie, Amilcare.'

'I'm afraid it is, Maestro. Your mother, the Countess…'

He says it with a little movement of his head to convey everyone's resignation to the inflexible routine of the grand old lady.

After blissfully lingering in the tub, he's dressed by Amilcare with his usual fastidious attention. The most infinitesimal speck of dust is brushed off his shoulders.

When he enters the drawing room no one is there. Upon being served a glass of champagne, he opens the French doors and walks out onto the terrace, taking in the crisp evening air, contemplating the silent stillness of the small village beneath the grounds of the villa. All covered in a pristine two or three feet of snow. A few lights dot the surface of the lake, some fishermen foolishly braving the cold winter temperature.

He enjoys this moment of quiet and peace immensely, but it is of brief duration. His mother's voice resonates imperiously across the terrace.

'Carlo, please! You are going to catch a chill. You're only in your evening suit. If you plan to stay outside I'll tell Amilcare to bring your coat, gloves and scarf.'

He speedily beats a retreat and shuts the doors behind him.

'It was only for a few moments, Mother. Do not fret. The view is still so beautiful. I've always loved it so much.'

'Yes. You were a hopeless romantic, even as a boy. A dreamer. Unlike that tropical hurricane, your brother. He broke so much stuff in this house.'

'Vittorio was a born and bred soldier from the start, Mother.'

'Well, not much porcelain has survived his early war manoeuvres.'

Vittorio walks in just in time to hear her comment. He smiles and kisses her cheek while Amilcare brings two more glasses of champagne on a silver tray.

The two brothers shake hands in a firm but friendly way, holding each other's forearm for a brief time.

'It is so good to see you, Vittorio. You look in great form.'

'And you, little brother. Always looking so much younger than your age. Some people wouldn't believe there is only one year between us.'

'If I remember well, congratulations are in order. Last time we saw each other you were due to become Captain Mandelli di Castagnino.'

Vittorio coughs in embarrassment, taking a sip of champagne. The Countess gracelessly interjects with not too subtle a sneer.

'He's still a lieutenant.'

Carlo feels the general discomfort and rushes to apologise.

'I am ever so sorry. I was under the impression that it had already been decided.'

Vittorio puts on a brave face.

'I was overlooked for promotion, I'm afraid. As Mother says, still a lieutenant.'

'I don't want to pry, but I find it highly unfair. You are an outstanding officer.'

The Countess almost shouts, waving the hand not holding the glass.

'Temper! His temper! Still the same as when you two were mere little boys. Always this flaring temper. You would think that by now he would have learnt to keep his mouth shut.'

'Mother, I can't just stand by when injustices or even blatantly illegal practices happen right under my nose.'

Countess Di Castagnino is having none of it.

'This is the Kingdom of Italy, Vittorio. We eat injustices, unfairness and blatantly illegal practices for breakfast. We dunk them in our caffelattes. To expect its army to be exempt from such an ingrained way of running things is to be a fool. And one passed over for promotion.'

Carlo takes a sip and nods in reluctant approval of his mother's crude assessment.

'She has a point, Vittorio. You know how things are run here. Sometimes it's better to go with the flow. I myself had to overlook some members of my orchestra recommended for, let's say, "romantic" reasons. One valiant lieutenant is never going to change the rot. This isn't America… '

Vittorio's eyes dart with a warning between his mother and his brother. The Countess turns away with an expression of revulsion. He whispers to his brother.

'Never mention America in front of Mother. Have you forgotten?'

'Oh God, still the old thing.'

Vittorio rushes to return to the subject. An unpleasant one, better still than the mere mention of America.

'If nobody ever does anything about it, nothing will ever change. Call me an idealist…'

'I call you a simpering fool, son.'

Carlo turns in irritation.

'Mother!'

Amilcare conveniently enters the drawing room to announce that dinner is about to be served, severing an exchange which, due to the Countess' frankness, was in danger of descending into a shouting match. She stands up while nodding to the butler.

'Well, let us taste what culinary catastrophe that young man has concocted for us tonight.'

She takes Vittorio's arm. Always led into the dining room by the eldest, escorted out by the youngest. A protocol neither brother has ever dared to question.

Over the *vichyssoise avec creme fraiche* he feels obliged to ask.

'I hope Guglielmina and the boys are in good health, Vittorio. I confess I was looking forward to seeing them tonight, though I know you object to them staying up for supper with the adults.'

The Countess and Vittorio exchange worried looks; Carlo notices them while bringing the spoon to his lips. He lays the spoon back in the plate with a slightly dejected movement. There seems to be only bad news coming from his brother tonight.

'Is… is there anything I should know?' He raises his hand to stop the Countess in her tracks. 'Mother, please. If there is, I would like to hear it from Vittorio.'

His brother wipes his mouth with his napkin.

'Guglielmina has left me. She has gone back to her family in Padua and she has taken the boys with her. Of course we cannot divorce, but it is what it is.'

Carlo stares into the half-finished soup with sadness. All he's doing tonight is apologising to his brother.

'I am ever so sorry to hear that. But... what happened, if I may ask? I have always thought of you as a normal, happy family. I don't understand.'

The Countess signals to Amilcare to take away the soup.

'Just tell him not to put so much salt in next time, please.'

Amilcare nods and leaves.

'Excessive discipline for my grandchildren and the usual temper again. She had enough. I have told him several times that a lady and a family are not a barracks of rough and tumble soldiers to punish and flog at every other infraction.'

Carlo turns in mild rage to his brother.

'You didn't beat the boys, did you? Vittorio, I strongly object to such behaviour. Father never laid a hand on us.'

Vittorio, unsettled by all the berating in his direction, snaps and bangs on the table.

'Discipline is important if they are going to be good officers. I was fair and just all the time.'

'You did beat them, didn't you? I'm ashamed of you. And who's to say that they are going to be officers? What if they aspire to become something else? Why do they have to follow your career, which, by the way, doesn't even run in the family history?'

'Father wouldn't have made a good soldier of the realm for sure. And for uncle Giulio, well, no more said.'

Carlo is starting to shake. He somehow knew dinner was going to end on the fields of Austerlitz.

'I would be grateful if you'd leave Uncle Giulio out of this. He's a fine gentleman. And please, enough of this idiotic mourning of father. He isn't dead. Mother, you should stop wearing black. It is utter nonsense.'

The Countess slams the glass of Barolo back on the table with visible force. Some drops of the fine vintage spill on the white tablecloth.

'Your father left for America with a *soubrette* from the Paris *Variété!* He is as good as dead to me. Your affection for him is misguided.'

Carlo stares at the glass in front of him while holding the stem with nervous force, trying to contain the usual anger when confronted with his mother and brother's maddening habit of blaming everyone else but themselves.

'So now we shouldn't love our father anymore? I do not condone what he has done for a moment, but we are human and we make mistakes. He has made sure through Uncle Giulio that you do not want for anything. The villa, the servants, the car. Everything is taken care of. You're still a countess, that *soubrette* never will be. My education and Vittorio's military career have been funded with no questions asked. And I know for a fact that he might indeed have had some questions about your career, older brother.'

Vittorio erupts while holding the edge of the table with his now trembling hands.

'Well! I am deeply sorry if I have offended father's sensibility by not becoming a world-acclaimed conductor, soon to be a world-acclaimed composer. I do apologise for not being able to tell the difference between a violin and a cello. But I am serving His Majesty the King, and I would like my sons to follow in my path, if it isn't too much to ask.'

Carlo is about to explode.

'It is if they don't want to follow your plans. They will be very unhappy if they are forced into the army against their wishes.'

Vittorio slams the napkin on the table.

'We have spent the last few centuries being invaded left, right and centre. Don't you think you should have more respect for the army that protects you and your career?'

'I am not being disrespectful towards your army, army; I'm just saying that one shouldn't literally beat children into joining it.'

Vittorio's fist hits the table, making the plates clatter.

'It isn't my army! It's the army of your country!'

'With all due respect, the genocidal waste your fellow officers laid to Tripolitania and Cyrenaica wasn't done in my name.'

'A European power needs colonies.'

'And what for, if I may ask? What do you need them for? To fill your coffers with more stolen gold?'

'This is socialist drivel and…'

Amilcare, who had forecast all of this, having witnessed much worse family brawls in his long and loyal service, wedges himself between the two brothers with the decanter full of Barolo and leans over the table by the side of Carlo.

'More of the wine, Maestro?'

'Thank you, Amilcare. I certainly need it.'

The butler turns swiftly to Vittorio with the same offer while snapping his fingers at the footmen who rush to clear the remaining empty plates and deliver the first course. He makes the explanation of the dish as long as he can possibly stretch it out, hoping it will give pause for reflection to the warring members of the fissiparous Mandelli family. When it comes to unhappiness, they would give the Karenins a run for their money.

The cunning butler's plan works, and over the first course, Carlo decides that it's no use antagonising either mother or brother further. He adjusts his tie with a light cough to compose himself.

'To change the subject, I have some news too, Vittorio. As already announced to Mother, I have accepted an offer from the Odessa Opera House, starting with the next winter season. It will be a challenge, but I feel I'm up for it. Fresh air!'

Vittorio nods.

'The Romanovs have no quarrels with us, I believe. And they detest the Austro-Hungarians. When the time comes to take back Süd-Tirol they will stand by us.'

Carlo is determined to avoid another argument.

'Well, the politics or the military aspect of it is of no importance to me. It is an artistic and life decision above all. As I have plenty of time before the start of the season, I have decided to live a bit in the meantime. I will visit Ernestina in Weimar and spend most of the spring season there. Then I will take the waters in Carlsbad before boarding a steamer from Trieste, which will take me to Constantinople. I believe there is then a regular crossing to Odessa from there. I hope to have enough time to work on my symphony.'

Vittorio nods in a silent and sombre mood.

'You and Ernestina have always been close.'

He knows his brother resents their closeness. But it happened naturally. Carlo and Ernestina's spirits were much the same. The uptight and at times pompous character of their older brother inevitably pushed them away from him.

The Countess cannot help a snarky comment though.

'Is she still running her *"salons"* for gentlemen of all sorts?'

Carlo bites his lips while darting his eyes to the enormous Murano chandelier hanging over the dining table like the sword of Damocles. How many times as a boy he had hoped the twinkling ball of lights would crash down on all of his siblings, splashing their soups on their faces. And forcing them to lay down their weapons.

'Not "gentlemen of all sorts". They are artistic gatherings, Mother. Musicians, painters, writers and poets. Weimar is bustling with them. Your tone implies that she is at the head of some improper circle. It is not the case, Mother. And I resent you thinking in such a way. Schoenberg and Strauss are regulars there. Ernestina is looking forward to introducing us to each other.'

'Still not married. People do talk about you and your sister, you know?'

'Let them talk. I have no time for silly gossip.'

'That is because you no longer live here. People enquire about you and Ernestina. And now they will enquire about Vittorio's wife and sons' disappearance. What am I to say about all of your shenanigans?'

Vittorio is about to reply but Carlo, detecting the onset of his brother's well-known temper, gently lifts his hand, asking to let him speak. In this family alliances switch at astonishing speed.

'As much as I disagree with Vittorio about his conduct, things happen, Mother. We should not care about people talking. As for me and Ernestina, marriage and children are not the only options in life. There are others.'

'Like gallivanting in some sordid Constantinople joint?'

Carlo sighs again, signalling to Amilcare the saviour to come over to clear the plates.

'Well, why not? If it will make one of your children happy, it should make you happy too.'

Holding the cup of camomile in his hand while taking tiny sips, he stands on the balcony of his old room in his pyjamas and dressing gown, taking in the crisp evening air. He was prepared to the usual sparring. It has been the same for years and it will never change. When his father packed up and left with the *soubrette* for Boston, all three siblings were reluctant to hate him and, despite their resentment at being left alone with their mother, they all still loved him. Vittorio perhaps a little less than Carlo and Ernestina, and naturally more severe in his judgement but still not too condemnatory.

Then ebullient Ernestina left for Weimar. Father purchased a villa for her to start her *Salon des Arts*, making her promise to write to him frequently all about it. It enraged the old Countess and more heated arguments ensued.

And it seemed that the causes to ignite new rows never ceased to land at the door of the villa. Against Ernestina's advice, who was made party of Carlo's weakness for the company of gentlemen in their early years and had loyally kept her mouth shut while loving her brother even more, one day he politely and elegantly announced to both his mother and his brother that he would never marry and that the reason for it should be obvious to them. His brother felt betrayed, and he expressed that feeling in the most offended of ways; Carlo struggled to understand why as they had never been best of friends anyway. If their mother had remotely entertained the idea of wearing anything else but black, that was now out of question. Both her husband and younger son were now dead to her.

A very sombre, extremely difficult period ensued, plunging Villa Mandelli into a funereal haze, suddenly interrupted by blazing rows and angry slamming of French doors (when Amilcare didn't get there in time to hold them open).

Then Vittorio became engaged. Guglielmina met Carlo and warmed to him a great deal. Vittorio announced that, due to the presence of his fellow officers, his brother's attendance at the wedding would be unacceptable, and Guglielmina stormed out of the room with an equally uncompromising ultimatum: 'Then there will be no wedding.'

Vittorio travelled to Milan alone and asked to meet Carlo at his house. Standing martially in front of him, he extended his hand, locking his grey-blue eyes firmly on his brother's stunned gaze.

'I needed time to think. My fiancée is right: you are my brother, and that is something that should not be renounced.'

Vittorio then found himself fuming at the wedding reception while observing his brother's unexpected popularity among his regiment's comrades, with some of the more inebriated ones judging it entirely appropriate to hug Carlo's shoulders in the midst of some scurrilous banter.

As she had made clear in the drawing room that night, the Countess could not hate her children, despite disapproving of most of their choices. Up until the revelation, Carlo had always been the most affectionate of the three, impervious to the aura of coldness surrounding his mother. When he had become a teenager, it took the governess a few long hours to press into his puzzled head that his mother, as a countess, should no longer be hugged and that a light kiss on the cheek would suffice.

After a ban from the villa lasting several months, a ban which hurt him more than he thought it would, he received a terse card from Mandello.

- *Please come home, Carlo. Mother.* -

In genuine Italian fashion she didn't mention anything regarding his peculiar nature, but she made clear that he was welcome back in her cold heart. Before letting him go back to his room to get ready for dinner, she surprised him by briefly holding his hand.

'I don't know anything about your people. Please, be careful.'

He hadn't taken offence. And besides, he hadn't even met any of "his people" yet. He just nodded and reassured her as best as he could.

After turning down the bed covers, Amilcare joins him

on the balcony.

'Maestro, it must be below zero. Shall I bring a blanket?'

'I fear that if I don't catch a cold I will seriously disappoint you all, Amilcare. I'm coming in presently. By the way, thank you for promptly intervening with various distractions. I must apologise for our behaviour at dinner. All that shouting is unbecoming.'

'Sir.'

'You don't happen to remember where I stored my old violin? I'd like to give it to young Filippo; Timoteo seems to think that he's quite gifted.'

'I have stored it away safely in its box and in a dry cupboard, sir. I will bring it to you tomorrow morning.'

'Always thoughtful, Amilcare. This household would crumble without you. I think my mother knows that.'

'Too kind, sir.'

At breakfast time he informs his mother that he will be visiting Uncle Giulio and that he will stay over for dinner. He was expecting her silence while she brings the coffee cup to her stony lips.

'Shall I give him your regards, Mother? They don't have to be kind, merely regards.'

'If you so wish.'

He tries to play the violin a bit, though he was never good at it and that hasn't changed. It is of course hopelessly out of tune, and he doubts he will be able to find anyone to tune it in the village. He tenses a few strings in the hope of making it sound better.

'It will have to do,' he says to himself.

Filippo is over the moon when presented with the gift. Carlo has asked about any teachers in the village, but of course there are none.

'There are some in Lecco, Timoteo. I will nag the old lady to let you use the car to take Filippo to the city for a weekly tuition.'

He goes down on one knee in front of the boy.

'One tuition a week is not a lot. You'll have to practise. Promise to your dad and myself that you will, Filippo.'

The boy nods with enthusiasm amid the thankful bows of Timoteo.

'Won't need the car today. I'm going to walk to my old piano teacher and then to Uncle Giulio's villa.'

He stuffs the score sheets of the symphony into his leather briefcase and ambles at a slow pace downhill, towards the lakeshore. The still dilapidated old coffee shop has miraculously survived the ravages of time and he treats himself to a slow cappuccino. He then walks along the promenade, thoroughly enjoying the sunny morning and the hazy silence, sparsely interrupted by the sound of the horses and carriages travelling along the cobbled road.

He rings the bell when he arrives at his old teacher's house, a modest but well-kept abode by the lake.

The old maid opens the door and he's ushered into the living room where a frail and petite old lady tries to lift herself up from an armchair by the fireplace.

'Please, Signora Tommasini, don't get up for me.'

'Oh, I want to give you a big hug, Carlo.'

They hug and over another cup of coffee they freely converse about the old days and his career, of which Signora Tommasini is very proud.

'I'm giving a shot at composition. A symphony. Would you like to hear some of the passages which I think are the best?'

'I keep the old Schulze & Pollman well-tuned as I still have some students. I struggle a bit at my age, but the pleasure of seeing them progressing is second to none. And their parents shower me with gifts. Not sure why, as I am not the one testing them.'

He laughs at the old Italian penchant for trying to corrupt whoever is in charge of your children's future.

'But that is because you're the best teacher!'

'Nonsense. Let me hear this symphony then.'

As he sits at the piano Signora Tommasini rushes behind him to adjust his posture.

'Still the same as when you were a young boy. Still bending too much forward. I hope you stand well upright when you conduct.'

'I try, Signora.'

He plays a few movements and he's very pleased when the old lady grabs a pencil and, squinting through her spectacles, corrects a few keys and quavers.

'Moving and powerful. That is what a symphony ought to be. Also very modern. Well done, Carletto.'

He reddens and thanks her for the corrections while feeling a blissful sensation of still being a boy, carefree and with music the only passion - and worry - in his life.

After strolling at a good pace up the hill, he reaches the gates of the second Villa Mandelli, a much bigger and way more sumptuous residence than his old family home.

The grounds are also vast and hilly. He finds himself a little sweaty when he reaches the main entrance, though, as always, awed by the breathtaking views of Lake Como.

Once in the hallway he leaves his coat, hat, gloves and scarf with the butler and walks to his uncle's study straight away.

A handsome gentleman with short, slightly grey hair, possibly in his early fifties, stands up from his desk and walks with open arms towards him. The hug is tight and lasting.

'Carlo. What a pleasure!'

'Uncle Giulio, how are you?'

'In splendid form, my boy. Splendid. And yourself?

How is life as a celebrity?'

'A great nuisance, since you're asking. You know me too well. I'm not for all the social aspects of it. My agent keeps dragging me along to these long and tedious *soirées* of his. Apparently it helps to raise my profile, he says.'

'You know that this your home. You can come and rest anytime you want, even if I am away. Let's order coffee.'

'I had so many cups already. I'll be a nervous wreck if I touch another one, Uncle Giulio.'

'Even better. Since it is almost lunchtime, a good glass of Lugana will gently lead us into the midday fare, which I believe will be ready at one. Your father tells me that in that funny continent he's now residing they eat lunch at twelve. At eleven even! I dare say some people are not even awake at such a horrid time.'

Carlo lets out an affectionate guffaw.

'Especially you, Uncle Giulio. Always the night owl, you are.'

'The evils of ageing are less visible in the hours of darkness.'

'Stop worrying. You are still such a handsome man.'

'You inveterate liar.'

He hugs his nephew's neck with his forearm, kissing the side of his head. At that time, without knocking, a young man of probably twenty to thirty years of age, flaxen hair and a pair of tiny northern sapphires where his eyes should be, enters the room. Before noticing Carlo he starts to speak.

'Giulio, I have some of the letters from the Banca Sella… oh… I am ever so sorry, sir, I thought you were alone.'

'Don't be silly. I am so glad to introduce you to my wonderful nephew. Carlo, this is Edine Pericauld, my new private secretary.'

Carlo and Edine shake hands with an already warm

smile.

'Please, no formalities with my nephew. Edine, you've been working all morning, join us for lunch, will you? Please.'

'I'll be honoured. I will let you enjoy each other's company beforehand, you must have so much to tell each other. I still have an hour to finish some letters.'

'Splendid.'

Edine and the butler carrying the glasses of Lugana cross by the door. When alone with his uncle, Carlo stares at the view through the French doors with a sighing smile.

'Edine?'

'Edine.'

'Will the time ever come when we will finally do away with "Private Secretaries", "Assistants", "Managers" and all these ridiculous euphemisms which no one is so stupid to believe? Will we one day be able to call them as they are? The people we love?'

They clink their glasses.

'Maybe one day, my boy. Maybe. But it would be foolhardy to swim against the tide. Mostly because people who attempt to do that usually drown. One lives in the times he's born into. It is of no use to keep trying to change them. This world, as currently designed, is not for us. And there are worse places to be born into, trust me. I have travelled extensively. Our fellow Italians will never send us in front of a firing squad; the lack of style would be unforgivable. But they will never allow us to join the squad either. All they want is lies, obfuscation, deceit and to look presentable in those churches of theirs on Sunday mornings. Do they believe our subterfuges? No, of course they do not. Backwards, yes; stupid they aren't. But if deception prevents them from persecuting us, well, I call that a result.'

'Cannot argue with so elegant an argument. Well,

what about Edine? Very handsome young man.'

'We met in the *ville lumiere*, in one of those Saint Germain taverns for colourful people. Before you ask, he's not a kept boy. His family is as wealthy as ours and rather loose on principles. The French often are. He's also a real accountant, he's graduated at the Sorbonne. He works hard.'

'I wasn't trying to imply any such thing, Uncle Giulio. He seems to be very charming. I'm so happy for you.'

The Count takes a sip and lays the glass on his desk before half-perching on it.

'How's the grand old lady? Still complaining about everything?'

'What do you think? She sends her regards.'

'She doesn't do anything of the kind. Stop lying. Despite Edine working day and night to manage two estates, all she does is moan about this and that. Your father arranges all the funds, but there is a lot to sort out and she doesn't want to do anything.'

'Better that way, trust me.'

'I do. My brother bolted and that wasn't a nice thing to do, I admit that. But all that wearing black; all that fake mourning. The *Miss Havisham* of Mandello del Lario. The Italian version, of course: without the cobwebs. He has no intention of divorcing her and she will keep the title. After all, we are aristocratic stock, not her. She should be more understanding.'

'You are asking too much of Mother, Uncle Giulio. I do have some news, by the way.'

After relaying all his plans to his uncle, he notices a slightly worried look on his face. The Count grabs the glass again and takes a good sip.

'Russia is starting to be in turmoil, Carlo. It's still relatively safe but I'm not sure for how long it will remain so. Could it be somewhere else? I approve of you wanting to get away from the rather stale and unexciting life here, but… Odessa?'

'I… I don't know. I was feeling a bit lost and… well, I don't know. Will you come and rescue me if I get into trouble?'

Giulio detects a sudden weakness in his nephew's misty eyes and pleading tone. He puts down the glass and hugs him tight. Carlo buries his face in his chest, his eyes welling up. The Count gently caresses his hair while whispering small words of encouragement in his ear. Carlo's face moves slightly out of the embrace and his lips reach his uncle's. The kiss is brief as Giulio gently detaches himself, extremely careful for his gesture not to be interpreted as a rejection. He kisses his forehead while holding Carlo's neck in his hands.

'Carletto, you are not a boy anymore.'

He lets his face sink in the warm chest of his uncle.

'I so wish I were, Uncle Giulio.'

Over lunch and dinner, he is pleased to discover how charming, intelligent and devoted to his uncle Edine is. He's learnt Italian and his conversation is witty, the manners warm and engaging.

After an exhilarating evening, the three gentlemen feel the pleasant sensation of being able to safely be themselves, with daring jokes and repartees free to cross the table back and forth. The things we can say when the righteous aren't in the room, perennially horrified at human happiness, flailing our merriment with their dissembling glances of disapproval.

He can't refuse his uncle's offer of having him driven back by his *chauffeur*. The wine and the grappa are making his legs rather wobbly.

He knew he was going to be late and he demanded the keys of the house from Amilcare, ordering him and the rest of the household to head to their beds once all the tasks of the day were completed. He insisted that he didn't want them to wait up for him.

Once in the main hallway he realises how thirsty he is, the drunken stupor slowly permutating into the onset of a hangover.

He unsteadily tiptoes to the kitchen where a lamp oil is still burning. While approaching he hears some toiling noise.

He enters and sees a young man of about thirty years of age holding the door of the fire oven; some screwdrivers and other tools disorderly lie on the wooden table.

The young man's white jacket is unbuttoned, his smooth muscular chest and defined ribs vaguely visible. Beads of sweat line his sculpted face.

'I'm sorry to intrude, I just wanted to get a jug a water and a glass to take up to my room.'

'No worries, *Monsieur*, I was trying to fix this old door. It's quite heavy.'

He lays the iron door on the table and walks towards Carlo, offering his right hand for a shake.

'You must be the Countess' son. The famous Maestro. Pleased to meet you, sir.'

'And you must be the new chef, I guess.'

'Correct, *Monsieur*. Anatole, from Gascoigne.'

Carlo shakes his hand and a sardonic smile appears under his moustaches.

'Only Mother could possibly criticise the cooking of a French chef.'

'*Bien sûr!* Your old lady is a difficult *Madame, Monsieur.* This and that. Tonight the soup had too much salt.'

'And tomorrow it will not have enough of it. Do not take it personally, Anatole. She will always find something wrong with your cooking. As a matter of fact, she will always find something wrong with anything.'

'*Pas grave, Monsieur*. I was in service with this

crazy lady, Mrs Dahlia Travers of Brinkley Court, *en Angleterre*. They loved my cooking but they were *très étrange, n'est-ce pas?* They also had this very dim nephew. Bertram, I think he was called. He caused all sorts of trouble. At least they never complained. They were distraught when I left.'

Anatole is not overtly handsome but sports a defined body and an engaging smile. And he keeps smiling at Carlo while chatting away.

'Do you need a hand with that door? It seems rather heavy.'

'I'm trying to put it back on its hinges. A screw came loose today while I had the snipes in the oven. *Quel désastre!* If we hold it up together I could try to screw it back with one hand.'

Carlo takes his coat and jacket off, unties his cravat, unbuttons the top of his shirt and rolls his sleeves up. With the door off its hinges and the coal still smouldering the room is positively roasting.

They lift the door together, and while Carlo holds it as close as possible to the oven, Anatole tries to secure it back with a rusty screwdriver.

They are very close. So close that Carlo can smell the food cooked today on the chef's body while Anatole inhales the fumes of a lethal Lugana, Barolo and grappa mix released from the Maestro's breath.

'Had a few *boissons,* Monsieur?'

Carlo nods with a grin. They manage to fix the door and, seeing the Count's hands now as black with soot as his, Anatole gestures to him to wait. He grabs a rag and plunges it in a bucket of water. Then he proceeds to wash Carlo's hands.

Mandelli smiles. Anatole's eyes are fixed on his brimming ones.

'Such a handsome *garçon. Un petit agneau.*'

'Thank y…'

Anatole's calloused hand is on the back of Carlo's neck, holding it either gently or firmly. He cannot tell as the ecstasy of the warm, watery kiss overwhelms him. The tongues knot around each other while a Gallic passion collides with a Latin one.

He's pushed against the wall and hands explore their now bare chests, stroking each other's ripped stomachs. Then Anatole's hand pushes him down, leading him to lick his hard nipples. The chef moans in pleasure. He's pushed down further to service him, aroused by such a dominant, confident act.

After a while, he's pulled up by Anatole's strong arms and their faces are once again close to each other's.

'Did you have a bath tonight?'

Mandelli, still in the throes of the wine and the grappa, frowns.

'What? Yes, of course… I… '

He's grabbed and pushed against the table. Anatole takes hold of his trousers and pulls them all the way down to his ankles. Without much ado, he kneels down and his face is quickly buried between Carlo's cheeks. He feels the Frenchman's tongue probing deeper and deeper. He feels like it's up to his stomach. He has never experienced a feeling like that, and he can't restrain the cries of pleasure. Anatole gets up and stuffs the rag into his mouth before returning to his job. Carlo hysterically grabs the edges of the table.

Then Anatole stands up and Carlo feels the tip of the Frenchman's member against the entrance. And the wanting fear. He takes the rag out of his mouth and turns his head back.

'Gently, please.'

'No worries, *Monsieur*.'

This time Anatole uses one hand to cover Carlo's mouth and the other to hold his body in a grip. The thrusts are gentle but regular, firm, skilled. Then, when they both feel ready, the chef floods inside him while he rains all over the tiled floor, the hand mercifully still on his mouth.

They slowly release from the embrace, breathing heavily. Mandelli turns and they lock in a long kiss, Anatole's hands encircling Carlo's head.

The chef ruffles his hair before proceeding to put his clothes back on.

'Such a handsome gentleman, *Monsieur.*'

'Thank you for this. I mean… you have no idea how much I needed this.'

'Oh, *bien sûr.* I did.'

He staggers upstairs and, beaten by the wine and Anatole's rugged passion, he undresses quickly and falls asleep exhausted under the fluffy covers.

He's woken up by Amilcare who, after laying the customary cup of coffee on the side table, proceeds to collect the evening suit from the armchair by the bed. He notices the ripped shirt but he tiptoes out of the room without so much as a single comment or murmur. The old butler is a man of legendary reserve and understanding. Besides, Carlo has always harboured suspicions of Amilcare: a reasonably handsome man who's never given so much of a thought to marriage. And he is never known to have entered any kind of courtship with any of the ladies of the small town, despite his position as a head butler with the Mandelli di Castagnino being sufficiently attractive to the less affluent families residing along the lakeshore.

Perhaps, Carlo had often reasoned in his mind, he has his *liasions dangereuses* in Lecco, Como or even Milan. But, as the intelligent and perspicacious man he is, he has concluded that a more meaningful relationship is not to be sought in such unforgiving times. Or, unlike Carlo, the physical drive might be absent or replaced by his unbending dedication to the running of Villa Mandelli. Many of us lead silent, mysterious lives.

After a still foggy breakfast, distractedly listening to his mother's complaints about Uncle Giulio always plying her son with immoderate amounts of alcohol, he shuts himself in the seclusion of the music room, working frenetically on the symphony.

He expects Amilcare to come in after a knock on the door, but Timoteo now stands in front of the old Bechstein, holding his old violin in his hand.

'Anything wrong with the violin, Timoteo?'

The driver's head is lowered. His body language betrays an uncomfortable nervousness.

'I don't think it appropriate for Filippo to play your violin, sir.'

Carlo frowns in genuine surprise.

'You don't? Has something happened, Timoteo?'

'It isn't for the likes of me to discuss it, Maestro.'

'Discuss what? Sorry, I'm at a loss here. I don't understand, Filippo seemed over the moon yesterday and eager to start with the lessons.'

'He still is, sir. I just don't think it's… well… appropriate.'

'You keep using this word, but I don't quite see what you may be referring to, I…'

He stops and notices that Timoteo hasn't been able to lift his head at all during the fraught conversation. He gets the point in resigned dismay.

'I see. I think I understand now. Please, leave the violin on the table. I will cancel the lessons.'

Timoteo carefully leaves the instrument on the coffee table and, still with his head bowed, opens the door to leave the room.

'I'm sorry, sir.'

Carlo doesn't reply. He's not angry with Timoteo but only with himself and his foolhardiness. And although he doesn't feel like he should be ashamed, he's distressed at the knowledge of having been seen in a rather humiliating situation.

He grabs the violin and walks to the kitchen where he finds Anatole imparting orders to the young assistant cook and other servants.

He gets close and pretends to enquire about the menu for the evening. When the opportunity of greater privacy arises, he whispers to the chef in the middle of the soup tasting.

'I'm afraid our encounter was witnessed last night.'

Anatole calmly replaces the ladle by the black cauldron bubbling on the large stove.

'By whom?'

'Timoteo.'

A very Gallic shrug of the shoulders ensues.

'*Pas grave*. I'm the *maître de cuisine* and you're the Count. He's the driver. I'm not exactly shaking in my pants.'

'I wasn't talking about the power dynamics. I know we aren't in any danger. And Timoteo won't say a word to a living soul. But allow me to be greatly upset at having a man I respect witness such an act. He's known me since I was in short trousers. It's demeaning and highly embarrassing.'

'Well, now he's seen you with no trousers. But he didn't have to watch. He could have walked away from wherever he was, *n'est-ce pas?*'

'I doubt he stayed long enough for the performance to finish under his eyes. He probably opened the door to come into the kitchen and saw us. We clearly didn't notice, entangled as we were. I thought it would be useful for you to know that.'

'Thank you, *Monsieur*. Quite likely he won't talk to me anymore. Well, I'm not going to lose any sleep over it.'

He's taken aback by Anatole's slightly irritating transalpine insouciance, but in a way he feels he's right in not accepting to be judged for something they both felt happened naturally and, in some kind of odd way, lovingly.

He nods in a sort of non-committal way and leaves the kitchen, slowly ambling outside, towards the gravelled area at the back of the house. He sees Timoteo polishing the Mercedes with nervous care. When in front of him, the driver bows respectfully and stays in that position.

'Timoteo, please, look at me.'

He raises his head reluctantly, fixing his gaze on the back of the villa. Carlo sighs.

'I understand your discomfort, Timoteo, and I do apologise. No one should have to witness such unbecoming behaviour. I am deeply sorry.'

Timoteo nervously toils with the fluffy rag in his hands while reverting to staring at the pavement.

'It's… it's a sin, sir.'

'Yes. And I am a sinner, I accept that. To some extent we all are at some point in our lives. Perhaps some more than others. But I don't see why young Filippo should pay for my sins. That is something I will do at some point in my life, I'm pretty sure of that.'

He lifts his arm, holding the violin case in his hand.

'I haven't cancelled the tuitions yet. Please take it back and give your son some joy. Perhaps you and your family can pray for my redemption?'

He nods and takes the instrument back.

'Thank you, Timoteo. I don't expect to be in your high esteem anymore. All the same I wish you and your family the best of luck.'

He turns to walk back to the house. He's halted by Timoteo's trembling voice.

'Thank you, Maestro. And I'm sorry too. We are

humble, God-fearing people, sir. We know little of the wide world. It's difficult for us. You've always been in our prayers and always will be.'

Carlo turns back with a gentle, tight-lipped smile.

'Thank you. I know how hard it must be for you, Timoteo. But it isn't easy for me either, believe me. Good day.'

The rest of the week is spent without anymore drama or illicit entertainment. Both Carlo and Anatole know that their wild tryst was a single and unrepeatable event.

He makes good progress with the symphony and the dinners *à deux* with Mother somehow become mellower and mellower as the days go by, Carlo slowly realising that the villa is not exactly swamped with guests vying for invitations from the Countess. The cantankerous and morose are invariably lonely souls.

Not all the old lady's bones are as cold as the Bering Sea on a winter night though. She often asks about her son's performances at La Scala, his favourite singers and the progress of the symphony.

The night before he is due to return to Milan, he almost chokes on the risotto as he hears her absent and vague question while staring in embarrassment at the plate.

'Perhaps… even you and your people value the advantages of a discreet, stable and durable friendship?'

He stares ahead, noticing the snowflakes landing on the glass panes of the French doors, neither of them able to look at each other.

'We do, Mother. We do.'

The preparations for Weimar and Odessa are long-winded and at times complicated. The visas are slow to arrive and at the last minute the Consulate of the Sublime Porte becomes suspicious of his decision to spurn the easiest and quickest option of travelling with the Orient-Express to Constantinople. He has to explain the leisure aspect of his trip to functionaries who will never understand the value of anything remotely involving leisure, let alone pleasure.

Tonio and Cecilia will remain employed and attend to the house which will remain empty but available for Uncle Giulio and Edine or Ernestina when and if they decide to descend on the grand old city.

By the time everything is finally ready, we are almost at the onset of spring.

The train journey on a Wagon-Lits sleeper is pleasant and comfortable, the on-board restaurant fare of superb quality and the company of fellow travellers not unpleasant either, after cleverly instructing the Maître d' to announce him to the occasional dining companions simply as *Signor* Mandelli.

When he finally alights on platform one of Weimar Hauptbahnhof, he is greeted by a crisp and bright early spring sun. He places his hand on his forehead as a screen to facilitate the search and, squinting, he initiates a slow scan of the pavement to locate his sister.

While still on the lookout, he feels two gloved hands from behind gently covering his eyes.

'Before you turn around, big brother, I must warn you that the words you are looking for are "*You are more resplendent than ever, little sister, and so beautiful and young.*" Any other kind of comment and I'll pack you back on that train and you'll never be seen again. Well, perhaps in St. Petersburg.'

He grabs her hands and kisses the palms.

'I have no intention of continuing my journey on to the imperial capital, my little sister. Though I thought you would have shed some of your shameless Italian vanity after all this time in a stern Prussian land?'

He turns around and they take a long look at each

other with beaming smiles of unbroken affection.

'Never! And I am too beautiful to be vain. That's for ugly people. Pretending. Mine is the truth.'

'Still the same mad lady, you are.'

They hug, laugh and almost cry with happiness at being reunited. Ernestina slides her arm under his brother's and they start strolling towards the carriages and automobiles waiting outside.

'You have no idea how happy I am to be here, Ernestina.'

'I can barely forgive you for not having visited before. Actually, you are still unforgivable! Half of Weimar knows everything about you - all good things of course - and the other half is waiting to meet you in the most frightful of frets.'

'Oh no. I forgot about your inability to keep your mouth shut.'

'You mean I shouldn't have talked extensively about my unbearably handsome brother? You will thank me immensely, trust me. I only informed the right people about your beauty, and they are all so eager to sleep with you. I dare say you are firmly in their fantasies while they do those things you boys do all of the time.'

Carlo chuckles.

'Your forthrightness hasn't changed one jot. Still about two hundred years ahead of our time.'

'I hope so, these times are frightfully boring. Of course they are about to become way more interesting soon. But not in a good way.'

'What if I don't want to sleep with all these beautiful boys of yours? I'd like to progress on my symphony.'

'Their loss.'

Ernestina's vanity is justified. She is indeed a remarkably beautiful young lady in her late twenties with a lithe yet sinuous frame, impeccably dressed in the latest - and most daring - fashion. Her reddish hair is long and soft, perfectly held up in a bun. When they were young children Carlo used to wind her up by stating that she wasn't a real Mandelli as no one in the family was born with red hair.

They board the open carriage.

'A carriage? It's 1913, Ernestina. Even Mother has bought a Mercedes. I am rather shocked.'

She snaps open her parasol after arranging her couture white dress around the seat.

'Well, don't be. An open carriage makes sure everyone will look at you. And it progresses slowly, allowing my admirers to dwell with long glimpses at their object of veneration. And now the ones who don't know that you are my brother will think that I have a new lover. Don't you think it's rather exciting to mislead people?'

The journey to the third Villa Mandelli in the family is spent exchanging news about brothers, mothers and uncles.

'I'm sure Mother still thinks I'm the *Violetta Valéry* of Weimar. Perhaps I should catch tuberculosis to confirm her suspicions.'

'Despite your bluster, I know you're nothing of the kind. I suspect Mother knows that too. It's just sadness at not having you there. Promise me you'll visit her sometime. She's getting old, and there is always Uncle Giulio and Edine to brighten your evenings in case it gets too heavy. Also, you're welcome to use my house in Milan. It will be empty for a long time.'

'Edine?'

'His new private secretary.'

'How old is Uncle Giulio's new "Private Secretary"?'

'Let's say he's legal. And most charming. Devoted to him. Not a hot head.'

Ernestina's face suddenly darkens with a worry.

'I am acquainted with a lot of politicians and big

shots of various types here, Carlo. They use my *salon* to discreetly meet diplomats and spies from the four corners of this cantankerous continent. Some of them have had secret meetings with this Lenin guy in Paris. He's determined to make his way to Russia one day. What we are sitting on in Europe isn't pretty. Don't go to Odessa. Please.'

'But I've signed the contract. And I look forward to my new post.'

'Always the dreamer. You'll never change. Always that maddening lack of interest in politics and the world outside your mind full of music and reveries. Russia is a powder keg, brother, and I fear for you. Do not go.'

He is taken aback by his sister's concerned foreboding. He knows Ernestina well and how well informed she always is, her connections with the higher echelons of society invariably solid and reliable.

'We can talk about this later, sister. What's the immediate plan?'

'A welcome ball. Tonight. Did you really believe that I wouldn't organise a welcome *soirée* in honour of the greatest living conductor?'

'What's Toscanini doing here?'

'He doesn't come to Germany. Not a fan, apparently. But arm yourself with the best defence of your composition. Strauss and Schoenberg are attending. They strongly believe any music composed yesterday to be frightfully obsolete.'

Carlo smiles, noticing strolling gentlemen turning to wave at his nodding sister while doffing their hats.

'I'm frightfully looking forward to meeting them.'

The third Villa Mandelli in the family is a well-maintained four storey limestone building in Erfurter Strasse, a quiet thoroughfare cutting across one of the wealthiest districts of the city. Apparently the fourth Villa Mandelli in downtown Boston has been built as the exact copy after their father requested sketches and blueprints from Ernestina.

- *Please, my dear daughter, they have no taste here* - he had pleaded in one of the regular letters.

Once in the elegantly wall-papered hallway of the villa, Ernestina warns her butler.

'Hans, my brother hasn't brought any servants with him. That is quite typical of him, I'm afraid. Sorry for Gotlieb and Leopold but one of them will have to look after him. If you know of any relative who would like to work as a valet for a few weeks at the villa, please send for him. With the ball and other forthcoming engagements we are all going to be frightfully busy.'

Carlo waves his hand.

'Please, do not worry on my account. I am perfectly capable of looking after myself without any help. All I need is daily laundry and a good brush to polish my patent leather shoes. I know how to make a knot with a white tie.'

Hans' reply lands in perfect and perfectly shocked French, elegantly leaving the salutation in German.

'Herr Graf Von Castagnino, you are planning to polish your patent leather shoes by yourself?'

Carlo feels like a schoolboy who has been sternly told off.

'All right. Maybe that is an effrontery too far. I will leave them outside the door. Is that acceptable?'

Hans looks at the Countess with a smile: 'My young cousin Wilhelm will be honoured to look after the Count, Your Excellency.'

Freed from the butler's presence, he chides his sister.

'You ladies cannot resist "mothering".'

'Rather impossible when your older brother is still a little boy, don't you think?'

She kisses him on the cheek and leaves him to settle in the blue room. Ernestina has of course allocated the best bedroom in the villa to her beloved brother, blessed as it is with a small terrace overlooking the square garden and the patio. He takes his shoes off and lies on the large bed for an hour or so, gently dozing off with the French doors half open.

He's woken up by a gentle knock on the door and the sudden presence of a tall, youngish man in a hastily arranged valet uniform.

After introducing himself, he proceeds to unpack Carlo's luggage and organise his wardrobe with fast-paced Teutonic efficiency. He then sends the evening suit and shirt downstairs for ironing before arranging for a shave and a bath.

Young Wilhelm is a lad of few words but he dresses Carlo with the skills of a seasoned footman and when he finally descends the stairs, following the sound of various minuets played by the small orchestra in the ballroom, he's positively gleaming.

His sister suddenly appears from one of the doors lining the long foyer in a light blue, gold-laced dress.

'Sister, you look absolutely ravishing. Thank you for Wilhelm. He's been wonderful'

'And so is the result. I can't wait to show you off, big brother.'

She slides her forearm under Carlo's arm and they slowly make their way to the ballroom where a few guests are already assembled and a continuous stream of elegant people keeps flowing in, glittering along the way.

They grab a glass of champagne and Carlo lets his sister guide him through introductions, bows, false smiles, real sneers and tiresome gossip.

As soon as they move on from a baron and his wife, he hears the consort whispering a little too loud in her husband's ear.

'Ernestina was right. What a handsome fellow. I told

you to bring our daughter along.'

His sister turns with a smile.

'Now that you're done with the boring, rich and thick, let's move to the music room where the ones who can read and write dwell. A very interesting gentleman has just arrived from Odessa, actually.'

As they grace the marble floor of the music room they are met by a slightly dishevelled middle-aged man who greets them in heavily eastern-accented French.

'Ernestina! This must be your talented older brother. What a pleasure!'

'Vassily, what are you doing here? Herr Berkovich is in the ballroom, busy chasing handsome young men and pressing my beautiful servants into attending rendezvous of a dubious nature at the far end of my gardens. But besides being a pest, he's also Weimar's most revered art dealer. Have you brought the painting we've been discussing? He is very interested but, like all art dealers, he's frightfully precious. Go and find him at once. I have informed him of your invitation and he has enquires about your work.'

'But I don't know what he looks like, Ernestina.'

'The footmen will point him out to you, if only to get rid of his hands on their backsides.'

After Kandinsky leaves in excitement, Ernestina turns to Carlo, speaking behind her open fan.

'A genius. But like all painters, all over the place. Herr Berkovich is not precious at all. He's dying to get his hands on his works. Now, brace yourself.'

They approach the piano with no further talking. A middle-aged gentleman of rather stern appearance, wearing an untidy evening suit and round spectacles, is playing the gleaming Blüthner between outbreaks of conversation. During the pauses, another man of younger age and with what appears to be a more forgiving attitude, joins the discussion with some other younger guests.

Taking advantage of yet another interruption, Ernestina authoritatively taps Strauss' shoulder with her fan. He stands up and kisses her gloved hand.

'And this is the famous brother. At last!' He turns to Carlo. 'Honoured, Maestro.'

Carlo bows with his usual innate and graceful elegance.

'The honour is all mine, Meister Strauss.'

'Allow me to introduce my fellow composer, Herr Schoenberg. Arnold Schoenberg. Not yet a household name but his score will be soon under your baton, Maestro. If dodecaphonic works don't offend your melodic ears, that is.'

While Schoenberg bows, Ernestina raises her eyes to the twinkling Bohemian chandelier while whispering behind her perennially open fan.

'That didn't last long.'

Carlo smiles while returning the bow to Herr Schoenberg.

'Oh, my "melodic" ears, as you so elegantly call them, are far more interested in your innovations than you care to believe, Meister Strauss.'

'Then why have you not cared to include them in your repertoire, Maestro?'

'Milan is a very conservative city and I'm still a young conductor. I still don't have Toscanini's dictatorial powers. I hope you can believe me when I say that I have tried.'

'But they just want Verdi, Rossini, arias, melodies, tunes and all that?'

'For the time being, yes. But you see, they were the most successful composers of the century we have just left behind. When you are as successful as them in the century ahead of us, perhaps even La Scala will give you a hearing.'

Ernestina waves the fan while throwing her head

back with a satisfied laugh. She then taps Strauss' shoulder again.

'*Touché*, Meister Strauss.'

'Success on the back of cheap, sugary melodies is not success at all. It's merely monetary reward for sensational drivel!'

Schoenberg, who's been staring at the floor visibly embarrassed, turns to Carlo.

'I hope one day you will conduct my work, Maestro.'

'I will head the Odessa Opera House for the next few years. I will try to cajole them into including your music in the repertoire.' He turns to Strauss. 'And yours, of course.'

Strauss waves his hand theatrically and points to the unoccupied stool in front of the Blüthner.

'But we hear that a revered conductor is in the midst of a composition. A symphony, I believe? Well, why not a little taste of it?'

Carlo shots a reproaching look at his sister: "*Can't you ever keep your mouth shut?*"

'It is my first work, Meister Strauss. Forgive my reticence, but I'd rather not…'

He's led away by Ernestina and they bump again into Kandinsky.

'I hear you're about to travel to Odessa, Maestro.'

'And I heard you have just left the city.'

'Indeed. You should have a rethink, Maestro. These are difficult times for my country.'

He turns to his sister.

'Have you started a conspiratorial plot to prevent me travelling to Russia? Everyone seems to be warning me about it.'

Ernestina shrugs while leading him around to meet yet more guests and some of the beautiful young men mingling with the crowd while being chased around by

Herr Berkovich.

They turn out to be on the shallow side and overtly fawn over him and other distinguished older gentlemen. They also seem to become upset and venomous when Carlo gives them the cold shoulder. He's once again rescued by his adoring sister.

'Thank you, sister. I think I'd rather endure Strauss' insults than give in to screeching young creatures determined to sleep with the greatest living conductor. After Toscanini.'

After the welcoming *soirée*, the days in the Thuringian city go by in a gentle and serene haze and he manages to establish a much-needed daily routine.

After breakfast he works on the symphony all morning before heading for lunches al fresco in Theaterplatz, taking advantage of the warm spring sun. The walks along the lime tree-lined boulevards are equally blissful.

From time to time he notices the same gentlemen in black coats and bowler hats turning the corner after him or overtaking him while pretending to read the Berliner Zeitung. Sometimes he spots them at the tables of the Café Reinhardt.

Over one of the rare dinners when Ernestina is not entertaining the great and good of Weimar, he squints his eyes in a mild inquisitive fashion.

'Am I being followed?'

Ernestina lays her empty glass on the table.

'Very likely. Everyone of any importance is being followed in Germany these days.'

Carlo opens his hands in disbelief.

'I am an orchestra conductor visiting my sister. Why would I be of any interest to the police? If it is the police. I haven't done anything and I'm not planning to. They must know I'm completely uninterested in politics.'

'Maybe they don't and they want to find out. Secret police forces are notorious for their paranoia.'

'The secret police?'

'Everything is secret in Weimar these days, older brother.'

'Talking about secrecy. I spotted you in the garden, confabulating with two rather shady gentlemen. Also not well-dressed and rather scruffy. Not your style, sister.'

He notices a little discomfort descending on Ernestina's expression.

'Black-marketeers. How do you think we get regular supplies of caviar, oysters and cigars? Down at the local market?'

'And here is me, thinking my sister wouldn't get into any trouble.'

'Weimar is trouble, brother.'

III. Zauberberg

After a few weeks of dinners and balls, frequently punctuated by Strauss' relentless sneering, he's ready to travel to Carlsbad to take the waters. He has stopped noticing gentlemen in black suits and bowler hats clumsily following him, reckoning that it can't be happening for serious reasons if they dispatch such inept secret agents.

Despite immensely loving his sister, he has always been aware of her untruthfulness in almost everything. Their close bond had never included not lying to each other. As Ernestina has been often and frightfully fond to remark: 'How boring it would be if we didn't have secrets. I loved it when I knew about your penchant for gentlemen before you revealed it to me. I loved your clumsy lies.'

Despite reserving the suite at the Grand Hotel Pupp under the title-free name of Carlo Mandelli, he's dejected at hearing the Italian-speaking Slovenian bell-boy immediately greeting him with a beaming *"Ben arrivato, Signor Conte"*.

The hotel director is the first to come out to explain how everyone is so honoured at the presence of the greatest living conductor - after Toscanini - and that the local authorities will be along shortly to welcome him with the city's keys.

When finally in the suite he sits on the huge bed and stares at the floor while still holding his hat and stick: *"Oh no."*

Luckily he's not asked to conduct local boys' choirs or brass bands in the ornate baroque stand in the park. The summer festival has already been long planned and all the concerts are fully staffed with local conductors.

He can't avoid meeting them, but they turn out to be rather pleasant fellows who are justly in awe of his fame. He's also relieved that when they meet up for tea in the park, they are keen to ask for his advice on conducting and are not interested in small talk. To his relief he ends up enjoying helping young colleagues with a few suggestions and the gatherings imperceptibly turn into joyous masterclasses, especially when some of the youngest suggest they dispense with tea and cake and move on to the local ales.

He manages to reserve the mornings for taking the waters at the Thermal Institute and progressing with his composition.

The splendid weather, the tranquillity of the small city and the slow-paced strolls along the tree-lined canal, surrounded by blooming flower beds and quaint cafés, do him a lot of good; he feels relaxed and creative. The symphony powers ahead.

Towards the end of the first week he realises that he's being followed again, though the young gentleman regularly sitting two tables away at the café in the park hardly looks like a secret agent. Rather, an aura of boyish vulnerability surrounds him, and his skills as a spy must be very poor since he repeatedly looks up to stare at him before lowering his gaze back to his newspaper when caught.

Despite his fondness for older gentlemen he can't help noticing how breathtakingly handsome the young man is: the small moustaches grace fully defined, chiselled features, the thin lips hardly ever open, the lean frame of his body slips effortlessly into an immaculately tailored morning suit. He always doffs his hat with an ethereal, distracted grace, and he never sees him slumping in the cushioned armchair outside the café kiosk.

Definitely not a spy but certainly following him and obviously wary of making any kind of contact.

After a few days he comes prepared. Having realised that the young gentleman is either too afraid of introducing himself or just a little too shy, he writes a note on the hotel paper before leaving the suite for his midday stroll.

I wonder if you would care to join me for a cup of coffee at my table.

I would be honoured if you accepted my invitation.

Carlo Mandelli

He dispatches the puzzled waitress with the note and he sees him getting up slowly before ambling towards his table. Once standing in front of him while blotting out the midday sun, he doffs and holds his bowler hat closer to his hollow chest with the usual elegance before bowing by only a couple of inches.

'Most grateful for your invitation, Maestro.'

Glad to hear the impeccable French, Carlo stands up and they shake hands. He notices that the young man doesn't take his white cotton gloves off before sitting at the table.

'My name is Kimmich. Walther Kimmich. From Berlin.'

'You seem to know who I am.'

'Who doesn't?'

'People who do not follow opera?'

The waitress approaches and takes their orders.

They stare in almost suspicious contemplation at each other. The young man's grey-green pupils pierce through Carlo's distracted yet intrigued gaze.

Once tea and cakes have been delivered and served by the waitress, Walther almost whispers between frequent coughing.

'What brings you to Carlsbad, Maestro?'

'I'm on my way to Odessa. The local opera house has hired me for a few seasons. I have visited my sister Ernestina in Weimar and I thought it would be beneficial to take the waters before boarding a liner to Constantinople.'

Walther's small eyes widen a little.

'Odessa?'

Carlo cannot help a mildly exasperated sigh.

'Oh, not you as well.'

The young man frowns.

'Me… as well… what exactly?'

'Forgive me. Everyone seems to warn me about travelling and moving to that city. I understand Russia is under some political strain but I'm getting rather tired of this worrying.'

Walther smiles. Carlo notices the small, perfect teeth, the youthful, tender parting of his lips. The lack of malice.

'I was only wondering why such an acclaimed artist would choose such a remote city. I acknowledge that the Russians can be very passionate about culture. Still, allow me to be surprised at such a decision.'

'I understand. You see, I was worn out by my existence. I can't be sure whether it was Milan or just my life in general. I suppose I will find out once in Odessa. It might happen that after the initial excitement everything will reverse to the same dreary routine.'

'If your issues were in your mind, they are travelling with you as we speak. But I agree that sometimes a breath of fresh air is necessary for us.'

Carlo returns the cup to the table and abruptly lifts his gaze towards his new young acquaintance.

'For us?'

Walther shyly looks away, his pale, sickly cheeks turning a shade of pink.

'Unless, of course, you happen to be them.'

His face nods in the direction of a family of four sitting at the next table, their children happily slurping a hot chocolate topped with an inconsiderate amount of whipped cream, half of it now on their tiny sailor uniforms. He turns in the Maestro's direction again.

'If that is the case, Maestro, I beg for your forgiveness first and your friendship later anyway. However, I am well aware that it might be difficult for you to bestow it on me. I won't hold it against you and I will politely bid you farewell. I hope I can count on your discretion as I am not familiar with the local legislation. Please, do not report me to the police. My present constitution would not survive even a few nights in an Austrian cell.'

At that point, as if brought on by a sudden mild fear, a bout of violent coughing prevents him from carrying on talking. He takes a clean handkerchief out of his pocket and fully covers his mouth. When the cough subsides he carefully folds the handkerchief, stands up, walks to a rubbish bin and throws the handkerchief away. Carlo is too polite to remark on any of these peculiar manoeuvres.

'You can count on my friendship and there's certainly no need for forgiveness. Not between us.'

The tender and loving smiles appear in unison, full of relief.

They agree to meet the following day in the same café, though they try to sit at a different table from the day before to make it look like a casual encounter.

Carlo remarks that such excessive prudence might be misplaced. Walther stares at the gravel of the patio.

'You weren't conscripted into the Italian Army, were you?'

'No. My grades at the conservatorio were too high. I was declared ineligible. Something to do with being too "useful" to the motherland in other ways or similar. I've forgotten the exact wording of the discharge. Don't mess with Italians and opera. A terrifying combination.'

'I see. I enrolled in the cadets of the Imperial Army at fourteen like my father did. Predestined to follow in his path. Though he left the army too.'

'You left?'

'I was discharged. Without honour. Though they kept it very quiet. The general of my regiment wasn't so lucky. He had a wife and a family.'

'I see.'

'He's no longer with us. I think they saw me as the seduced, which it wasn't true. But I was nineteen and he was thirty years older than me. They forced me to tell the full tale and I was so scared. I never had the strength or the nonchalance of my father. I managed to see the general for one last time and I asked for his forgiveness in tears. He hugged me, kissed me on the forehead and said that it wasn't my fault. In my naivety I proposed to him that once both discharged we could flee and live together somewhere in the countryside, just the two of us. We loved each other so much. He said that it was impossible. An impossible dream. Little did I know that they had already delivered the revolver and a note for him. I keep a picture of the two of us. A daguerrotype taken during a secret trip to a nearby village. He hired a cottage for a couple of nights but I dreamt that it would be forever.'

He takes the picture out of his pocket and shows it to Carlo. He looks at it on the verge of tears.

'I am so sorry to hear this. How old are you now?'

'Barely twenty-two.'

'It goes that your staying in Carlsbad is a much-needed breath of fresh air too?'

Walther's face freezes in a sudden expression of sadness.

'Much needed. Yes.'

Together with the afternoons at the café in the park, they

start having long strolls along the river, taking the waters together and revealing more of their lives to each other.

Despite not feeling any sexual attraction, Carlo starts fretting when Walther is slightly late. He invites him to dinner at the Pupp, but barely an hour before their time to meet for a cocktail he receives a small envelope from the bell-boy.

Dear Carlo,

I will not be able to attend dinner tonight. I am not feeling too well. I hope to be better tomorrow and will see you at the usual café. Please, forgive me.

With affection,

Your Walther

When they meet up he cannot fail to notice a paler complexion on the young man's face, but again he's too polite to ask, and he fears that he might offend him and lose him altogether. He also notices that instead of the usual coffee he orders a hot tisane.

'I am so sorry to have let you down for dinner. My sincere apologies. I tried to get out of my bed, but I couldn't.'

'I am so sorry. But I'm glad that after your note I can now finally call you Walther as you dropped the formal way of address.'

He nods.

'Forgive me, Walther, but did you say you couldn't get out of bed? Did you call a doctor?'

'I…'

A thin stream of tears appears on the young man's cheeks, leaving Carlo bewildered.

'In the damp and crowded barracks of the Imperial

Army, I contracted tuberculosis. That is why I am here. I'm due to travel to the Jánské Koupele sanatorium soon. Actually, I was supposed to report to their infirmary a few days ago but then I saw you in the lobby of the Pupp, and it was like a sort of lightning had struck me. I knew who you were and I was just happy to follow you discreetly. That's all. I will be going there in a few days.'

'What do the doctors say?'

'The usual lies.'

A bout of coughing strikes him and this time Carlo manages to spot the red dots on the handkerchief before Walther disposes of it. When he comes back to the table he lays his hand on his arm, feeling the boy shaking. As he lifts his eyes to one side he spots an old lady and her husband watching them while whispering to each other in stern disapproval. He feels his blood boiling, but Walther detects that he's about to stand up and walk over to their table to say something stupid and grabs his arm with unexpected force.

'No, Carlo. It is of no use. They will always win. Discretion is our only defence.'

He delays his departure to Jánské Koupele and they see each other more and more frequently, finally managing to have dinner together. Walther's health seems to be improving, perhaps helped by Carlo's company.

After ordering the entrées, Walther takes a tentative sip of the chablis.

'I haven't told you much about my family or how I ended up in the army.'

'I didn't want to pry.'

'We have time on our hands and I've never felt this comfortable with anyone before.'

'I'm much honoured you think this way.'

Walther stares at the empty plate in front of him.

'You don't have to worry about me having fallen in

love with you, Carlo. I'm lacking the time to become unbearably possessive. You can indulge me with no fear for the future.'

'Nonsense. People recover.'

Walther shrugs.

'Some do.'

He takes another sip before speaking again.

'My father was a certain Felix Kimmich, scion of one of the wealthiest landowning families of Brandenburg. He was one of us. The stronger type, that is. The type who would take on an unrepentant, hostile world with his guile, charm, beauty and an extraordinary strength of mind. I take after him physically, but that is all. Unlike him, the world, this world, frightens me. I often remember the first of my secretive glances at the other naked boys in the showers when I joined the cadets. It's terrifying to discover that you're a marked man and you'll always be so for the rest of your life. In a way, it came as a relief to learn that a life like that is not going to be long anyway.

'Improper desires aside, I was quite a happy boy. My uncle Walther, after whom I was named, isn't really my uncle. He was my father's butler first, then private secretary and, naturally, his lifetime lover.

'He looks after me and my three younger brothers better than any doting father would do. He runs the family estate with an iron fist and we want for nothing. After my father's death, to maintain the respectable facade, he married my mother. Her lover, Fräulein Kahler, still lives with us. It is a futile endeavour, if you ask my opinion: no one believes these lies.'

'What happened to your father?'

'It depends who you ask.'

'It does?'

'He fell down the main staircase of our Berlin villa. That version of events is for public consumption. But he was murdered by a gang of Polish youths in the Tiergarten. After what is believed to have been an open-air gathering of a carnal nature. He was found naked, all the money gone. The official story saved the family's name. Together with a ridiculous amount of money, of course. Again, I'm not quite sure how many actually believed the official report; attendance at his funeral was rather sparse and hardly anyone followed the hearse to the burial place.'

The natural slide to becoming inseparable leads to an unexpected happiness gradually surging in both souls. One evening, after a slow cocktail hour on the hotel terrace, Walther lays his tumbler on the table with unexpected determination and stares at Carlo with unprecedented intensity.

'Let us skip dinner tonight.'

Carlo freezes in apprehension.

'Are you feeling unwell?'

'On the contrary. I'm feeling an odd sense of energy. Would you invite me to your suite?'

The silence and the stares don't feel uncomfortable, and the reply is untroubled by hesitation.

'Of course I would.'

Once in the suite, Walther grabs Carlo's hand with his still gloved one and leads him into the bedroom. He takes two surgical masks out of his pocket and covers his and his lover's face with them.

'These and the gloves will stay on. I love you too much and I don't want to kill you.'

'Are you sure that it's that contagious?'

'No. But I want you to live. If it's enough for you, let's take our clothes off, slide under the duvet and hug. Hug until we can hardly breathe. That is all we can do.'

Carlo hugs him while softly kissing the young man's neck, detecting the shivers. Under the covers, without kissing, without almost anything else, they become one.

The sunny morning reveals a chatty and happy Walther once breakfast is delivered to the terrace table. And a good appetite too. Carlo sees the young man's complexion finally showing some colour.

Walther sips the coffee and gracefully wipes his lips with the napkin.

'Thank you for putting up with the lack of exchange of bodily fluid.'

'Well, at least we managed to safely release them.'

They both laugh out loud, careless of neighbours hearing their conversation. Walther gently frowns.

'Carlo, are you aware that you're being followed?'

Mandelli sighs.

'Yes. I was followed in Weimar too. Not sure if these ones are Austrians or still Germans or both. They might be Ottomans or Russians for all I care. I just ignore them now. I have no idea why they are following me. I'm an orchestra conductor and I take almost no interest in politics.'

'Maybe they were dispatched for your protection?'

'From what?'

'The Reich is paranoid. They have files on everyone, very likely on me too. The Austrians are fretting about your King wanting to invade Süd-Tirol.'

'My brother insists that we should take it back.'

'Difficult to take back something that was never yours, but I guess they want Italy to look good on the maps. Without the indentation.'

They laugh again.

'You're probably right. We like things to look good in general.'

Their naked feet caress each other, their eyes meet with renewed intensity. Walther looks over to the forest at the foot of the mountains.

'This lovely breakfast and the bright sun deserve a bath and a gentle stroll into town. But I propose to slip under the covers again and resurface when you're ready to travel to Odessa.'

'But that is days away.'

Walther smiles and winks.

'Even better.'

When he sees him almost running towards him, he smiles and would love so much to hug and kiss him right there in the gardens of the hotel where they are planning to have tea. The last few days have been spent in a sort of heavenly daze. Carlo has been busy composing at the grand piano in his suite, reassured by Walther's presence. The boy has been resting on the terrace, breathing the good air and basking in the increasingly warmer sun. He has noticed that the young man hasn't coughed up blood for days and his complexion and appetite have greatly improved.

When they sit at the table Walther appears in a fret. A joyous fret.

'I've spoken to my doctors. They were amazed at how good I look and feel. I will travel to Jánské Koupele tomorrow. I… I want to live, Carlo. I so much want to live now. I still don't know if you love me or not, but whatever happens, I understand now that maybe life is worth living. Because people like you can drop into it anytime. And it has just happened to me. Let's keep in touch. Please.'

'Of course we will. And I do. I do love you, Walther.'

The stare is intense.

'We have about twenty-four hours left. Let's go back to your suite.'

They pay the bill and almost run back to Carlo's suite. Once naked and standing in front of each other by the bed, Walther doesn't retrieve any masks from his clothes and softly takes Carlo's face in his hands.

'The doctors said we can kiss. You can't catch it that way. They said I should find a beautiful girl and kiss her.'

'And are you going to?'

'I have the most beautiful man in the world to kiss.'

And when their lips finally share their love, Walther abruptly moans, shaking violently. And a copious warm stream runs along Carlo's leg while he holds the panting boy's head close to the curve of his neck. The sobs are full of joyous emotion.

'I'm so happy, Carlo. So happy.'

He looks down at the mess on his leg with an affectionate smile.

'I thought we were going to last twenty-four hours?'

'Oh, we will.'

IV. Sur l'eau…

The arrival of the service from Vienna proves quite a chaotic experience. The station of Trieste Campo Marzio, an imposing Victorian building, is teeming with all sorts of fretting humanity: market sellers, relatives searching for their alighting siblings and hanger-ons.

Carlo slowly descends the steps of the first-class carriage and looks around for a porter to hire.

He's about to signal to a burly man standing by one of the huge marble columns when an emaciated lad of Eastern European appearance parades in front of him with a brand new cart lined with red velvet.

His uniform is impeccably ironed and the bell-boy hat is firmly positioned over his head. Despite the vaguely sickly look, his eyes are surprisingly alert. The manners are decisive and polite. He addresses Mandelli in perfect Italian.

'Your Excellency, the Count of Castagnino? Maestro Mandelli?'

'Yes. That is me. How do you know my name?'

'I'm one of the bell-boys of the *RMS Adriatic*, sir. The ship director was advised in your booking that you're travelling without a valet.'

'That is correct, yes.'

'That is why they sent me, sir. At your service.' He bows again.

'Very pleased to meet you. I wouldn't have known who to trust with my trunks. Some of the porters wear a uniform and some don't.'

'And some are not even real uniforms, sir!'

Mandelli laughs in approval while the boy lifts all the trunks and piles them neatly onto the cart. As they start walking, Carlo is pleased to be able to have some conversation in his mother tongue.

'Where are you from, young man? Are we sailing on a full vessel? What's the weather forecast? This is my first time on a liner.'

'I'm a student in Belgrade but wanted to travel to Trieste. I've paid my way by working as a bell-boy for the White Star Line. I will be disembarking at Dubrovnik. Full ship indeed but the forecast is for a smooth sailing, sir. And no icebergs either! They've assigned you the best suite. I'm too low rank to be made part of any important decision, but I'm sure it'll be the captain's table for you tonight.'

'I see. I was rather planning to retire early and read. Is there a piano on the ship?'

'Yes, sir, in the cocktail bar.'

'Perhaps not the best place to compose a symphony then. Are you Serbian then? Your Italian is excellent.'

'Thank you, sir. I'm from Bosnia. But I study in Belgrade for the moment. My hometown is currently and illegally occupied by these people.'

He shoves an Austrian officer away using the handle of the cart and with what Carlo detects to be clear, deliberate force and a hint of repressed anger.

'I bet you can't wait for your King to expel the remaining Austrians from your country, sir. You'll take Trieste back and we'll grab Bosnia from these low-lifes.'

Aware of having been followed by an array of German and Austrian spies, Carlo elects to ignore the angry comments and wisely reverts to silence. Revolutionary, hot-headed students come two-a-penny but he's nevertheless concerned about being overheard by any of the officers and sailors ambling around the Austrian port.

When they arrive at the embarkation steps, he stops the cart and turns to Mandelli.

'I will take all your luggage to your suite, sir. Then

one of the ship's butlers will unpack your trunks for you.'

Carlo extracts a few notes from the inside pocket of his jacket.

'Thank you, young man. And good luck with your studies.'

The student bows, takes the notes and walks away with the cart towards the steerage loading point.

He climbs the steps and he's greeted by one of the first class butlers who escort him to his suite. Spring has been slowing turning into an early summer and the heat has been rising. The *RMS Adriatic*, one of the finest vessels of the White Star Line, positively gleams by the dock. The black bow shines and the immaculate white upper decks reflect the sun's rays, almost blinding the best of Austrian and Italian society heading to their cabins.

He walks to the bathroom to splash his face with cold water while hearing three whistles and bell-boys loudly ordering visitors out of the ship.

This being his first marine voyage, he collects his hat and stick from the bed and makes his way up to the deck to enjoy the sail-away.

The exchange between the passengers and the crowd ashore is joyous and frenetic: relatives, friends and their children shout and wave small Austrian flags in festive excitement. Once the ship starts moving, he tries to navigate his way back to his suite, but he gets hopelessly lost. As soon as he mentions the number of his bedroom, a bowing bell-boy offers to escort him back. He asks for his keys and opens the door before standing to attention.

He walks from the drawing room to the bedroom to find all his luggage carefully positioned on wooden racks and ready for unpacking. That student was a good lad after all, he thinks. The doorbell rings with some insistence and he lets in what is clearly a butler who eagerly offers to unpack his luggage and send the used garments to the laundry with no further ado.

He's taken aback by the efficiency and he agrees to the butler's suggestion to have a relaxing stroll along the first class deck and admire the coastline fading into the distance.

He finds a quiet spot to enjoy the view of Piazza Grande becoming smaller and smaller until all he can see is the sinuous waves of the Adriatic forming a foamy wake behind the ship.

All dressed up in white tie, he enjoys one of those new American cocktails which seem to have become the *de rigueur apéritif* before heading to the dining room where the dreaded captain's table is waiting for him.

The French Maître d' and a few standing waiters bow in unison.

'Maestro Mandelli! What an honour. Captain Moorhouse has humbly requested your presence at his table. By his side. Guest of honour, of course.'

'I suppose it would be rude to opt for a small table in the far corner of the room?'

He's worried by the sudden panic appearing on their faces. Yes, it would.

'*Monsieur le Comte* is not feeling too well? We can send some supper to your suite, *bien sûr.*'

He smiles. He really doesn't want to cause any trouble for these lovely and fawning young men.

'Of course not. I look forward to meeting Captain Moorhouse's guests.'

He's never been a good liar but this one seems to have passed muster as a smiling young waiter makes way for him.

It gets worse.

As soon as he's shown the table, the captain and his guests rise in a standing ovation. The rest of the dining room, knowing who the important guest is, follow suit and the whole of the dining hall erupts in deafening applause.

When he's back into his suite at around midnight, he's beaten. He loosens his tie and heads to the balcony to take in the fresh night breeze of the Mediterranean. A few *lampare* dot the surface of the sea. Some are close enough to allow him to discern the sailors letting out the nets for the night fishing. The silence reinvigorates him and he's in dire need of it: every single guest had volunteered an opinion on singers, composers, the latest trend in opera, ballet and what else floated through their minds. An American had all but accused Giacomo Puccini of being a pederast: '*Cio-Cio-San is fifteen, Maestro. Fifteen!*'

During one of the rare moments of silence, Captain Moorhouse had almost whispered to him in despairing resignation: 'My dear fellow, I have to go through this every night.'

At some point, without realising it, he had replied to the excessively bejewelled woman next to him in an exasperated and off-hand way: 'I do not have an opinion on Maestro Wagner, Lady Astor. I merely conduct his music. I do not even have an opinion on his works, why should I have one on the man? Perhaps, if you make me party to yours, I could use it in my next conversation.'

The following day is entirely at sea, sailing at full steam to the port of Dubrovnik. As the *RMS Adriatic* heads south the temperature rises fast and he ambles along the upper deck promenade, bowing and lifting his hat at every greeting given by the star-struck guests.

When he reaches the end of the deck, he walks down the stairs and continues his stroll on the level below. He notices that the guests' couture has changed dramatically. More middle-class department store than Faubourg Saint Honoré tailors and dressmakers. But he welcomes the fact that hardly anyone recognises him and he's able to progress for more than a couple of yards without having to acknowledge admirers and their omnipresent daughters. Especially their daughters who are always nubile, they all seem to invariably "love" opera, have just come out in society and are ready to be married. He never fails to politely kiss their hands, hoping never to have to kiss anything else.

He stops to stare at the sea in the sun's direction. He has read somewhere that sunlight is good for your well-being and he tries to make the most of it.

A rather distinguished gentleman positions himself a couple of feet away. When Carlo turns he notices the understated yet rather faded elegance; no department store but well past its best and not well ironed either.

He lifts his Panama hat and bows his head slightly.

'Mandelli. Carlo Mandelli. *Bonjour*.'

The gentleman doesn't turn but the tone of his French is friendly and tinged with a heavy English accent.

'Everyone knows who you are, Maestro Mandelli.'

'It seems I can't escape that.'

'I see. You love the music but not the fame that comes with it. Correct?'

'More or less. But I'm glad in a way that it makes so many people happy.'

'That is not why they come to your performances, Maestro. They come to be "seen". That is all there is about it. To be seen is to be important. To be important is to have power. The only thing most people care for.'

'How refreshing to find someone more cynical than myself.'

The gentleman turns. Carlo reckons that he must be in his early fifties but in good shape. The ginger hair is combed neatly, the beard and the moustaches trimmed with fastidious care. He lifts his bowler hat.

'Pontus Dandeville. Lord Dandeville. I believe us to be fellow members of the aristocracy?'

'Delighted to make your acquaintance. I never make a display of being a count.'

'Oh, you should. It keeps people in their place. We English excel at that. We give the populace enough rope to avoid falling and drowning *dans La Manche*. But it is all an illusion. We exploit them thoroughly as everyone else, including our hectoring American cousins. You Europeans exploit the plebeian mob without pretending to give them any agency. You don't play cricket with your servants. That's a grave mistake.'

'Actually we don't play cricket at all.'

'That is even more inexcusable.'

'Thank you for your insights. I fear you speak the truth. Where are you heading, if I may enquire?'

'Constantinople, the city of hidden vice.'

'So am I. But I will continue on to Odessa.'

'Where the vices are not so hidden yet equally and delightfully despicable. I hope you intend to enjoy the full menu of Ottoman depravity. It might be skilfully hidden but widely available to our tribe.'

'Our tribe?'

'I'm not easily fooled, Maestro.'

'I see. Despite not being so young, my experience in such things is rather limited, I'm afraid.'

'Then we will have to make sure to expand it in the most elegant and debauched of ways. The two mostly go together anyway.'

'They do?'

'Oh, yes, my boy. Were you at the captain's table last night? Of course you were. You would be. All those respectable grand people. Half of them have mistresses or catamites on the side, most often both. God knows how much opium is smoked in those plush suites of theirs. There isn't a single bell-boy on this wretched vessel who can safely declare himself a virgin. Ladies or gentlemen. Boys never care of what is put in front of them. Or behind them. They love the novelty and the shillings which pay for their inexhaustible energy. Some may visit two or three suites every night. And the doctor in the morning, of course. You don't mind if I call you "my boy"? I could be your father.'

'Not at all, not at all.'

The frank and on the side of outrageous conversation is refreshing and welcome. He's fast warming to his new acquaintance and his shameless upper-class nonchalance.

'We Italians have very little sense of humour, I'm afraid. I hope you will make my crossing more enjoyable with a hefty dose of yours.'

Lord Dandeville throws a little laugh.

'You come from the land of love. And love is never funny. Most of the time it's a demented tragedy dressed up as happiness. A travesty. But I haul from the land of spite. And that, my boy, is always funny.'

They start walking along the promenade.

'I saw you on the dockside with the Bosnian lad pretending to be a real bell-boy.'

'Was he not? But my luggage has safely made it to my cabin.'

'Yes. With a pistol in it. They are Bosnian separatists. I saw them doing it. They used you to smuggle the weapon to Dubrovnik. They knew that due to your status your trunks would not be searched. Did the ship's butler appear as soon as you were in the room?'

'Yes, he did. He suggested a stroll while he unpacked the luggage and… oh, I see.'

'Do not worry. You're not disembarking at Dubrovnik therefore they won't use your services again.

You've done your bit.'

'You must think I'm a gullible fool.'

'Not at all, my boy. They are actually working for the White Star Line. But it's an excuse for trafficking all sort of stuff. The Balkans are a restless land. A powder keg.'

He's asking himself if Lord Dandeville likes his company. He could do with a witty and clever companion for the rest of the journey.

'Lord Dandeville, may I…'

'Apologies for interrupting you, my boy. Pontus would do. Or, as our ever-abbreviating American cousins called me while in that vast and vastly uncouth country of theirs, Ponty.'

'Well… Ponty, may I invite you to my table for dinner? It would be my honour and pleasure to dine with you.'

'I knew you were of the daydreaming type. You haven't noticed that you're on the second class deck, have you?'

Carlo turns left and right, realising the reason why everyone is dressed so "department-store".

'Oh, I am ever so sorry. I thought…'

'You thought, and are still thinking: why is an English Lord travelling second class. Aren't you?'

'I… I don't want to offend you.'

'No offence, my boy. A lot of English aristocracy have fallen on hard times. My family belongs to that lot. We're not destitute but, let's say, when it rains we have to constantly move the grand piano in the drawing room. A passage in first class was rather unjustifiable, though admittedly the savings could never pay to fix the roof of our country seat anyway. Second class is not that bad, if not on the side of tedious. All accountants, doctors, lawyers. Even mentioning them makes me yawn. Third class is far more exciting. That is where all the action is. They may be dirt poor, but also young and beautiful. You should see some of the boys. And they're so cheap. Even I can afford them. Your buying power would land you in a crowded room.'

Mandelli reddens and Dandeville guffaws.

'My dear boy, you definitely need a dose of Constantinople.'

'Well, I'd like to invite you, anyway.'

'Would they allow me upstairs?'

'Though I thoroughly detest my celebrity status, it does have its perks. They will do whatever I ask them to do.'

'It will be my pleasure to dine with the finest of gentlemen, my boy.'

As Carlo expected, the Maître d' is horrified at the prospect of having a passenger from the second class deck dining in the restaurant. His face lights up with relief at hearing that the gentleman is an English Lord whose London agent had tried in vain to secure a first class cabin on the otherwise full passage to Constantinople.

The lie passes muster, leading the man to suggest the best table for two in the house.

Rightly suspecting that the best table would place them at the centre of everyone's attention, Carlo suggests the most secluded one with another set of lies about the need to have some private business conversation of the utmost urgency and importance.

While he adjusts the white tie looking at himself in the mirror, he feels he relishes the impending conversation is about to have with Lord Dandeville, away from guests who kept asking him why had Toscanini gone to America. *'Why don't you ask him yourself?'*, he had replied, to the horror of Captain Moorhouse, whose hosts had been growing increasingly puzzled by the frankness of Maestro Mandelli.

As expected, Lord Dandeville may be travelling on the

lower deck, but his manners are, of course, impeccable, his knowledge of *haute cuisine* extensive and the suggestions about vintages and grapes invaluable.

After tasting and sipping a more than decent claret, Pontus slowly peruses the room and the array of diners around them.

'Impeccable couture in magnificent surroundings, Carlo. I must thank you again for the invitation.'

'The pleasure is all mine, Ponty. It still feels strange calling you that.'

'I could call you Charlie, if you'd like. Then we will both be abbreviated. So, tell me Carlo: Odessa. No, actually you can't tell me anything about that as it is in the future. I'm far more interested in your past. You see, I have seen those eyes before. They have cried and they will do so again. Unlike our fellow guests, who wouldn't cry if their mother dropped dead at this very moment. Though they would upon learning that they have been cut out of her will.'

'You're in for a disappointment, I'm afraid. My life has been pretty ordinary. But you're right about the unhappiness. That has featured.'

'Nonsense. Our lives are never ordinary. The moment we see a naked classmate in the gymnasium at one of those schools where parents send their children to become animals, we're done for. Then we're told that we are monsters and our lives become Shakespearean comedies; sometimes farces and almost inevitably tragedies. We only live the belligerent part of Tolstoy's lengthy ramble. We never get to experience the peace.'

'By God, that doesn't fill me with hope for the future.'

'There are other things to be filled with, given a willing boy. Hope for the future is so despicably American. They spend their lives hoping for a better future. Of course it never arrives. So, reveal Maestro Mandelli's wild ride so far. I'm confident the future will be even more sensational, deserving a footnote in some deceased Irish playwright's equally sensational diary.'

'I was actually a rather happy boy. I didn't turn into an animal at school, though others indeed did. The feral ones mercifully left me alone. A day-dreamer living in a parallel universe made of notes and quavers is no threat. A big bully boy took me under his protection. I think it gave him status to be the *Lord Protector* of an artist. He came from a wealthy merchant family and didn't expect anything in return. *"Mandelli is not touched"*, he declared one day. He probably saved me from a few beatings.'

'You were a prodigy then?'

'Not quite. I wouldn't have made it as a solo pianist or a singer. Definitely not as a singer. But score-reading came naturally to me and I even organised a small orchestra at the Mandello del Lario college. I conducted a few movements from Haydn's *Creation*. We were often out of tune, but it won me a place at Lecco's *conservatoire*. Do you know where Lecco is, Ponty? It's a sleepy little town.'

'Of course I do, my boy: at the southernmost tip of the less glamorous branch of Lake Como. The one that *"Volge a Mezzogiorno"*.'

'You've read Manzoni?'

'I have. His pretentious pomposity scarred me for life. The English professor who translated his drivel must have killed himself. I would have.'

Carlo bursts out into a loud laugh which attracts the disapproving attention of a few taciturn Austrian guests.

'That's a brave assertion in front of an Italian.'

'You're far too intelligent to approve of such sycophantic propaganda, Carlo. What about his French weepy fellow contemporary? Once I spent a night of sinfully romantic intercourse with a French officer who had considered applying for Mongolian citizenship after reading Victor Hugo. *Très misérable* indeed.'

'I must agree with you. But it was imposed on us. The boredom was borderline criminal. I fell asleep every time it was read in class. I still remember the ruler hitting my fingers: *'Mandelli! Always asleep! Always thinking about your music. This is Manzoni! Manzoni! You have no respect! I will write a note to your mother again.'*

'Why not to your father?'

Carlo lowers his head.

'He left us. He visited Paris far too often for Mother's liking, and she was right about it. He was having an affair with a *soubrette* from the Lido. They fled to Boston. They're very happy, apparently. Since then, Villa Mandelli has been in constant mourning.'

'Did you love your father?'

'Immensely. He understood me. The good and the bad things.'

'And you have forgiven him for bolting, haven't you?'

'To my shame, yes, I have.'

'Oh, there is no shame in bolting, my boy. And it all depends the characters or the situation one is bolting from. Mother?'

Carlo reddens with boyish embarrassment.

'Mother.'

'There is no shame in not loving your mother either.'

'You say that but, well, I am ashamed of it. And I do… love her. In my own sort of way. Which is, I admit, peculiar.'

They order their food.

'I'm very close to my sister. Mad lady she is. I just visited her in Weimar. We were and are so close. My older brother is really not one of us. In every possible way, I may add.'

'But the interesting part of the story is about how you survived the first shoots of desire. When unclothed men refuse to leave the deep and undiscovered alleys of your mind. When you suddenly dream of doing unspeakable things while attending mass. When you touch yourself but so wish the gardener or the ubiquitous athletic boys in your class would be doing the touching. When everything becomes wet. When Earth turns on its axis and you know that at some point all will boil over. Because it always does. But let us not digress. Who saved you? You are way too tranquil. Someone must have saved you.'

'Uncle Giulio.'

'Ah! Now I'm interested.'

'I don't know why but it is something I've never revealed to anyone. And somehow it feels right to reveal it to you.'

'That is because you have understood that I only judge people without a soul. If you have one, you're safe with me. And you do.'

'He sort of became the head of the family once Father left. His brother instructed him to look after all of us. And he did. He sheltered us to distraction. Not that Mother would ever thank him, of course.'

'Would your mother thank anyone? Ever?'

Carlo's eyes resignedly lower on the foie gras.

'No.'

'But that is not the way he saved you, am I right?'

'At the age of fifteen I was shuttling back and forth between Mandello and the Lecco's *conservatoire*. I loved it there and my grades were very good; always top of the class. But I was miserable. I was falling in and out of love with various boys in my year. Teachers too. Once a young gardener winked at me and I almost fainted. I was staying at my uncle's villa quite a lot. It was fun there. He was fun. Always joyful, always coming up with some silly game. My sister and I loved staying there. My brother, not so much.'

'Why am I thinking your brother is a miserable, hardened soul?'

'Because he is?'

'You're learning, Carlo. Go on. You're on stage, my boy.'

'One evening I felt like exploding. There is only so much one can do for himself after all. I sneaked into his bedroom and snuggled up to him in his huge four-poster bed. The rest is history. My history.'

'And you still love him dearly, don't you?'

'I do. For some obscure reasons young men seem to take a liking to me. Naturally that is flattering but it does nothing for me.'

'For them you are a safe haven. They are in the middle of the most violent of Aegean thunderstorms and your empathy lends them the comforting sensation of protection. And, not to discount it in the equation, you're on the side of adorably handsome. That never fails. But you're still a boy, aren't you? The boy who snuggled up in his uncle's bed.'

Carlo nods.

'I have some bad and good news, Carlo. The bad is that you will always be the boy who discovered the pleasure of the flesh, courtesy of dear Uncle Giulio. The good one is that there will be other uncles. The world is full of the poor things. Gentle, kind and compassionate. Not me, in a nutshell. You will find someone who will not be me. That is the best thing that can happen to you.'

The stopover in Dubrovnik is brief and the two men have just enough time for a sunny lunch at a taverna in the walled old town.

While disembarking they see the Bosnian student and his mate walking away from the ship. They smile and wave at Carlo and Lord Dandeville with a friendly grin.

'There will be a war, Carlo. And so many beautiful young men will die. Because that is what wars are for: to kill beauty. The waste, my boy, the insane waste.'

Their table is now reserved for the remainder of their journey. Carlo secures a couple of hours in the morning in the solitude of the cocktail bar, though he has to allow the cleaners to prepare the room for the evening. The white piano is slightly out of tune but he makes good progress on the symphony and as a result he's always in the best of humours when meeting Lord Dandeville for afternoon tea. Sometimes they have it in the second class foyer which Mandelli finds perfectly acceptable and much less formal than the one on the upper deck.

On the second evening of sailing to the Piraeus, after a hefty serving of Highland oysters, a young man suddenly parades himself in front of their table. Mandelli, realising that he's not one of the waiters, looks up in puzzlement. The youth ignores him and his eyes fix on Pontus. Carlo can't help noticing the raging blaze in them.

'Lord Dandeville. I do not believe you presence here to be appropriate. If you had any decency you would leave at once.'

Pontus wipes his lips and replaces the napkin on his lap.

'Lord Butterbuck. The pleasure is all mine. What brings you to sail on the Adriatic? The ship, that is.'

'I boarded at Dubrovnik and you have seen me at my table over there. With my fiancée.'

'You are confused, Lord Butterbuck. You see, my conversations with Count Mandelli are of such great interest and amusement that I pay scant attention to other guests. And none whatsoever to their fiancées.'

Carlo detects that the boy is about to explode.

'Well, my fiancée is greatly upset by your presence here. And upon enquiring, I have discovered that you're booked in second class. You should not be here and I am ordering you to leave.'

'I am so deeply sorry for your fiancée's discomfort. Could it be derived from the sudden realisation of having been deceived? As for ordering me to leave, perhaps you should have a word with my host. I urge caution. He's not only a fellow aristocrat but a rare one with a brain and a standing on this vessel which I repute to be far higher than yours.'

A few people have turned round, intrigued by the fraught tone of the conversation, though understanding very little of it. Most of the guests are either Italian or Austrian and the *lingua franca* is French. Most have little or no knowledge of English. When Lord Butterbuck shouts with renewed anger, the whole of the dining room turns in stupefied suspense, the ladies nervously covering their mouths with their fans.

'This is an outrage! I will have you thrown out!'

Dandeville calmly shakes his head.

'You're making a fool of yourself, my boy.'

'I am not your boy!'

'Not anymore. No.'

Mandelli stands up and, while parading himself in front of the young man, he snaps his fingers, summoning the Maître d', who in turn calls two waiters and now stands to attention.

'Jean-Luc, I have no understanding of this angry young man's ramblings. But they are upsetting my guest and attracting unwanted attention to our table. Please escort this gentleman away. My guest clearly has no intention of entertaining a conversation and his behaviour is rather uncivilised.'

Dandeville interjects.

'I will have to translate that for you, Carlo. You see,

they tried to teach French to Lord Butterbuck. But he was always more interested in estuary slang. He learnt that all right. What with all of his evening "expeditions" to the most Dickensian of the London slums?'

Jean-Luc has an accented command of English and orders Lord Butterbuck to leave the table in haste. The *RMS Adriatic* cannot countenance such scenes. Before he is escorted away, Dandeville points out his table to him with a slightly raised index finger.

'Your fiancée seems to have retired to your lodgings, my boy. Or, more likely, gone to the Purser Office to move out of them. I, for one, cannot blame her. Such a scene will prevent the pair of you from ever gracing the gilded entrance of this dining venue again. Or maybe you will anyway. The lack of shame in some of your ilk is remarkable.'

He's escorted away in furious silence. When he has completely disappeared from sight, they sit back down and breathe a sigh of relief.

'I must apologise in the most humble of ways. I had seen him entering the dining room yesterday but didn't expect him to throw such an unworthy tantrum. Though perhaps I should have predicted it. The boy has been bred with umpteen overdoses of arrogance and entitlement. Beside the most eclectic selection of bodily fluids, of course.'

Carlo guffaws behind his napkin and orders another bottle of petit chablis.

'The story you are about to tell me deserves another round of Scottish Highland slime, I trust.'

'Another round of oysters and chablis? I suppose I can't escape my duty to relay the full account to you? Can I?'

'In all of its most sordid details. Please.'

'Lord Butterbuck is an acolyte of that other despicable

scion of our blue blood: Lord Douglas, Mr Wilde's thoroughly unpleasant catamite. Our stories are almost similar though I lack the genius and have never written anything remotely successful. But the Irish storyteller and I converge on a wealth of other personal dealings. Except that he is dead, of course.

'I'm not sure whether you happen to have the same kind of establishments in your country, but in the East End of London all sort of entertaining humanity can be found. Occasionally even not so human yet still entertaining.

'Some of these *Maisons* are called Molly Houses and some of them are called nothing at all. It's safer. But the regular punters know exactly where to find them and are fully acquainted with the ludicrous hours at which to attend them. What happens in these secret and sacred locations is not for public consumption. Except when it is.

'I met Lord Butterbuck in one of these venues. "Met" is possibly not the right way to describe our encounter. You see, Carlo, you must have noticed that he is a very handsome young man. He's well in his mid-twenties, but we English tend to look pubescent until middle age, when the wrinkles and the sagging finally give the game away. Your boys tend to look like men at a very early stage. Must be the facial and body hair.

'A few years ago, Lord Butterbuck was the star of many an evening show, if we can call them that. He didn't notice me for a while when I entered the room by a small and creaky door. Well, how could he? They had mercifully laid some sort of blanket on the plank where he lay flat on his back. Two rather unwashed sailors were holding up his hairless, lily-white legs by the ankles while greedily slurping on his toes. At one point I believed I saw one of them swallowing at least half of his rosy foot. It can't have escaped you that Lord Butterbuck is quite a petite fellow. They had to hold him down with a degree of force as the pounding thrusts by the men taking their turn in the breeding process were fierce and determined. He was preparing them for the task. One by one. After leaving the welcoming crevices of his mouth, they would replace the ones who had spent himself inside the boy, and the gunning for England would restart in earnest. He's perhaps too skilled, I may add. Some of the sailors wouldn't make it to his other hole and relieved themselves in his never-satisfied throat. There were always two tongues circling his small, pink, flushed nipples. Another one would be enjoying a drop of the old gin in his belly button and a wandering mouth would be swallowing his manhood whole. Some of the men would also be too skilled with their tongues and I think I saw him in the throes of the most thunderous climax a few times. He sort of redecorated the walls. Not that it prevented him from continuing to enjoy being the centre of attention. The door kept creaking, letting an endless stream of users in and out. And in the end, of course, they had to pee on something…'

He notices Carlo's face flushing red.

'I wonder whether your sudden change of complexion is due to the oysters, the chablis, the tale, or all three? Should I abandon ship?'

Carlo downs a full glass.

'Absolutely not.'

'Eventually, whether because even his insatiable energy had finally been depleted or the establishment had run out of boys and men to satisfy his voracious appetite, a respite did happen and after somehow cleaning himself up, we struck a conversation on the bench of the tavern next door. It has always amazed me how we men can detach sexual activity from sentimental nonsense. We can please our newly seduced acquaintance and go for a pint with them after the event. Like that. As if nothing has happened. And perhaps that is the point. Most people believe that something happens but it really doesn't. It is all in the moment and afterwards it vanishes like drops of rain in a manhole. So to speak. It is remarkably non-eventful. It's a wonderful gift we have. I've always suspected the ladies to be ragingly envious of that. What with all the tiresome paraphernalia which disfigure their couplings? Engagements, *marriages à la mode*, children, illicit affairs. Our life is an illicit affair, don't you find?

'But I once again digress. As you have just witnessed, the lad is of the utmost unpleasant nature but it didn't stop me from desiring him for his devastating beauty. Because no one can resist beauty. The ones who claim so are liars.

'But that was just that. And he introduced me to the said Lord Douglas who was, if that is even remotely possible, more insufferable than him in his carelessly cantankerous way.

'I enjoyed a few nights of bliss. Given his activities in the East End, I was positively shocked to learn from my doctor that I had miraculously avoided being saddled with syphilis for life.

'But I soon tired of his effeminate and screeching posturing. The tantrums, the emotional blackmail, the childish jealousy. I put it to him that given I was more than twice his age, his possessive obsession was all the more preposterous. He was the young and beautiful one.

'But there is nothing like vanity scorned. And by an older and less attractive man. A surly constable knocked at my door one foggy winter morning. Butterbuck had reported me for soliciting his services and seducing him with payments and gifts. Which was, of course, absurd. Unlike Lord Douglas, he had no father to disown him. He had full access to his family funds, which, as I might have mentioned, are vastly bigger than mine. But there was no point in denying anything. No one would have believed me. We English love a good scandal. I also had

Mr Wilde's example in front of me as a warning against the very idea of fighting a losing battle against the judges, the savage press, the braying mob and a deranged little boy's accusations.

'I put up bail, ordered my accountant to transfer whatever funds they could to France and rushed to Victoria Station to catch the first train to Southampton. Don't even ask how I sneaked onto the *Carpathia.* I had to hide in third class for the whole journey to New York. There, no one cares about what you have done. They don't even care about what you do. Americans are only interested in what you will do. Well, that is what I'm doing. Running away from mad people.'

Carlo pauses and downs another oyster.

'It makes my life as a good Catholic boy look the most tedious ever.'

'Don't envy me, my good Catholic boy. There is no rest in running. Glamorous as it might look to you, it wears you out.'

The bottle of petit chablis lies empty in the ice bucket. Jean-Luc is soon over with a chilled replacement.

'The fiancée affair genuinely surprises me. Of all of his grotesque shortcomings, angling for spurious respectability is one I never suspected he would succumb to. And I bet the "excursions" to the dark underbelly of the East End haven't ended. They never will. He's enslaved to the sublime joy of unrestrained depravity. But he's a golden bachelor after all, and we English sleep in separate bedrooms when we marry anyway. Do you do that in Italy?'

'How would I know?'

They laugh with a loud guffaw, causing their exasperated fellow guests to turn again. Carlo leans over to whisper to Pontus in a conspiratorial fashion.

'I think they adored me when I boarded the ship but

they now positively detest me, Ponty. But I am presently so comprehensively drunk, I do not care in the least.'

He lifts his glass to the lady at the next table with a sardonic, intoxicated, spiteful grin. She turns away in horror, hiding her pearl necklace with her gloved hand. Dandeville lifts his glass too.

'That's the attitude, young man.'

In his drunken euphoria he doesn't even hear himself asking the question. He leans forward again. The adorable curiosity of a good Catholic boy.

'Ponty. Are there Molly Houses in Constantinople?'

'Ah! An entirely different game, my boy. Much more exciting. Beyond the wildest of dreams. You see, the Ottomans are very repressed. And repression is the mother of all aphrodisiacs. It laces your brain with recurrent, unspeakable thoughts. It leaves you constantly wanting to savour the forbidden. The raw possibility of getting caught makes your nerves shiver with intravenous fear. It sets you on fire.'

He winks at his charge, because that is now what Carlo is.

'And it burns you.'

V. The Blue Hammam

They spend the evening strolling along the narrow streets of the Greek capital after a long and exhausting climb to the Parthenon.

After several glasses of ouzo in the most ragged tavern they could find, they return to the *RMS Adriatic* thoroughly inebriated.

The passage through the Dardanelles and the southern half of the Bosphorus leaves them spellbound with its supreme beauty.

'I'm staying at the Pera Palace Hotel, Ponty. I only have three nights before my crossing to Odessa.'

'Where I am staying is irrelevant. What is important is where I will take you. This gentleman, Omar, runs the most spectacular of hammams. The Sultan is rumoured to visit it incognito when he tires of his harem. Which I reckon must be a recurrent occasion as ladies can never do what boys do. No customers have ever left the Blue Hammam unsatisfied.'

'Allow me to be generous, Ponty. My treat.'

'We will take in this extraordinary city tomorrow, my boy. Then we'll descend into Hades. Which will be heavenly, of course. For the fortunate ones who know how to gaze at it, there is no blue sky like the one in hell.'

They meet at the bolted wooden door of an imposing building not far from the Hagia Sofia Mosque, just behind the old Bazaar. There are no signs of any sort and no doorbells. The alleyway is deserted. Before knocking at the door, Lord Dandeville scans the adjacent streets.

'The Ottomans allow anything which cannot be seen.

Discretion and invisibility are welcome and required. No one here wants to hear what you do. They don't mind you doing it, they just don't want to hear about it.'

'It sounds a bit like back home.'

'The one thing all the cultures in the world have in common is scandalous levels of hypocrisy, my boy. They just do it in different ways.'

The door slowly turns on its creaking hinges. The man - they assumed he's a man - doing the opening is completely hidden behind it.

Once the door shuts behind them with a loud thump, he appears and bows without a word. He then points to a short corridor which leads to what seems to be a reception room or a coffee parlour, possibly both. A corpulent man in richly decorated garments is lying on a *chaise longue*, vaping from a *narghilé* standing on the carpeted floor by the coffee table. A young man of undefined age, barefoot and wearing only silky gold trousers, is fanning him with a feathered pole. Carlo notices his defined torso and his wiry, muscular arms. Another young man comes in with a tray of Turkish coffee. The big man invites the two friends to sit and they are promptly served the refreshment.

'Lord Dandeville, my old friend. You have come at the right time. We have acquired some new associates. Even I couldn't believe such beauty. And the manners. Pure gold.'

'I'm glad to be back in Constantinople, Omar.'

'And your distinguished friend?'

'Maestro Carlo Mandelli, from the Kingdom of Italy.'

Despite his size, Omar bows with surprising grace.

'Maestro, you don't have to worry about your real name being mentioned here. The house rules are very simple. None of my associates would dream of revealing a single word uttered in this establishment to the wider world. The streets of this city can become ever so perilous for boys with loose tongues. Now, Lord Dandeville, I detect that your dear friend is still not quite as relaxed as he should be. Perhaps it is his first time on the shores of the Bosphorus?'

Carlo nods with a reddening face.

'I thought so. Allow me.'

He claps his hands beside his face and another bare-chested young man in gold trousers appears through a beaded curtain. He kneels behind Carlo, gently takes his jacket and waistcoat off and lays them on a nearby sofa with the most delicate of manners. He then slowly unbuttons his shirt. When Carlo turns to see who is behind him, the young man tenderly smiles under his impeccably groomed moustache. Carlo notices his sculpted features before turning back to face Omar again.

'Kemal's hands are what this handsome Italian gentleman needs right now.'

Omar nods to the young man who gently starts massaging Carlo's neck before moving to his ears and scalp. Not before long his soft palms are massaging his back. When they slowly progress onto Carlo's nipples, he closes his eyes in ecstasy.

'Now, that is much better,' Omar declares with satisfaction.

Lord Dandeville takes an envelope out of his inside pocket and hands it over to Omar. He opens it and stares at Pontus with wide eyes.

'Lord Dandeville, my friend. This generous contribution honours me. You and your friend will leave my humble house wanting to live forever.'

'Omar, my companion has a weak spot for the more mature gentlemen. He's by all accounts still in his youth. I trust his taste will be taken into consideration.'

Omar laughs out loud. The booming sound jolts Carlo who was starting to drift away since the boy had begun sensually kissing his neck. His lips are so velvety, it took a few seconds for him to understand that he was being kissed.

'Lord Dandeville, if it weren't you, I would take offence at the impertinent insinuation that I cannot provide for my friends. The Italian gentleman will be led through the blue door. My more experienced associates will be thrilled to welcome him in their parlour. You see, they sometimes get a bit bored. Like yourself, most gentlemen prefer walking through the white door. My younger associates can become dreadfully busy. And the Maestro is so handsome. My guess is that they have already taken a good look at him.'

He points at several spyholes in the surrounding walls before summoning the boy with the fan. He whispers in his ear, the lad nods and walks through the blue door.

'Lord Dandeville, you know your way. Some gentlemen will be here shortly to lead your inexperienced friend to his beautiful fate.'

Pontus bows before disappearing, hardly noticed by a heavily distracted Carlo.

Two muscular men of around forty years of age enter the parlour and with gentle force lifts Carlo by the arms.

Omar nods.

'The boy will come with you, Maestro. As an indispensable accessory in your extraordinary journey. Leave your worries outside. These gentlemen know what to do. And there are others behind the door. Welcome to the Blue Hammam.'

He's led through a long corridor lit by torches hung on the walls. In a haze he wonders whether this could all be a hoax and, after taking his money, Omar has ordered the admittedly handsome men to throw him out into a dusty backstreet.

Unfounded fears. Both men must be in their late thirties or early forties. Their bodies are lean and muscular, either naturally smooth or shaved, their moustaches bushy but skilfully trimmed.

They lead him into a vast hall crowned by a spectacularly high dome. The temperature is high but the steam which causes it not to be very thick and he can see other gentlemen being attended to by Omar's associates of all ages. He instinctively looks out for Dandeville but his two escorts are now gracefully undressing him, passing his garments to the boy masseur who disappears with them behind one of the colourful curtains around the hall.

The afternoon light is filtering through narrow long windows in very thin slices. Once all his clothes have been removed, the more muscular man cups Carlo's flaming cheeks with his hands and lays his lips on his mouth while lowering his eyelids with his thumbs. Then he feels embraced by the other man who gently leads him to lie down on the marble slate while guiding his head to rest between his crossed legs. He's surprised to hear a few French words whispered in his ear: '*Effendi* will be washed. Then massaged. *Effendi* is handsome and many of our friends will love him. Over and over. You will be ours but we will be gentle. We know what *Effendi* likes. *Effendi* should not be afraid. Is *Effendi* afraid?'

Without opening his eyes Carlo shakes his head. The man gently kisses his forehead.

A few hands gloved with soft sponges soaked in warm soapy water start scrubbing his body vigorously. He jolts when they circle his aroused manhood and enter him afterwards. The man holding him between his crossed legs leans forward for another tobacco-flavoured whisper.

'*Effendi* is already happy. If *Effendi* needs to let go,

he should let go. We have all day.'

After another soapy intrusion he can no longer hold back and feels like an ocean wave exiting his body, the man's thumb in his mouth softening the cries of pleasure, stars twinkling in his still closed eyes.

'*Effendi* has paid us the highest of compliments with his youthful energy. *Effendi* loves our company. *Effendi* will rest now and fall asleep. Then we will love him.'

The breeze at the end of the pier where the *RMS Empress of Russia* is docked is rather fierce today. Carlo has to hold his hat in his hands to prevent it from flying away. He's anxiously waiting for Lord Dandeville. Their last goodbye before the crossing of the Black Sea.

He hears the horn announcing the imminent departure and keeps scouring the horizon to check for Pontus.

Finally he discerns a cab approaching the embarkation ladder at furious speed. It halts with a screech, and a flustered Dandeville emerges from it, wiping his forehead with a soaked handkerchief.

'My dear boy, I was detained by the most tiresome of issues. I couldn't let you depart without a proper farewell.' He takes a sweeping glance at the ship. 'You must be glad you have only two nights to spend on this rickety thing. Make sure you sleep by a lifejacket.'

Carlo chuckles.

'I'm sure it's perfectly safe, Pontus. They do have first-class cabins. And it's a rather elegant vessel, don't you find?'

'As elegant as they built them before Bonaparte invaded, I suppose. There must be some white paint left under all that rust.'

Another ear-piercing whistle blows from the deck together with an announcement in Russian which they guess must be the command for visitors and relatives to leave the ship.

Dandeville offers his hand.

'It has been my utmost pleasure to make your acquaintance, Carlo. A real gentleman. I wish you the very best in Odessa. Good luck, my boy.'

'I can only state the same about you, Pontus. Given our lives, we might not meet again.'

'By the by, I never got around to ask you about your day at the Blue Hammam?'

This time Carlo nearly laughs out loud.

'Possibly an out-of-body experience. Well, there were so many bodies, I struggle to remember which ones were in or out. I guess it was something which had to be tried once.'

A satisfied smile appears on Lord Dandeville's face.

'Farewell, my friend. Don't miss your passage to that most bizarre of countries awaiting your genius with bated breath. And bathed in beetroots, I fear.'

'Goodbye, Pontus. And try to behave.'

'Beware of the people who do, my boy.'

He slowly climbs the steps and he's greeted by an officer in Russian. All he can do is to show him the reservation for his cabin. A young sailor is ordered to accompany him to his cabin. He turns around to wave at Lord Dandeville but the cab has already disappeared. Only a few bystanders crowd the pier now and the the ship has started to move away.

After inspecting the cabin, he climbs up to the top deck and enjoys the slow sailing between the shores of Europe and Asia. When the Black Sea finally opens up in front of him under the uncertain early afternoon sun, he feels lost and afraid for the first time. No one seems to speak anything but Russian. People seem different and they appear to look at him with a curiosity one holds for the "exotic". He notices for the first time a pungent, lingering aroma of tobacco and alcohol, possibly vodka. Everything feels unfamiliar and odd. But it is indeed too late. He retreats back to his cabin to get ready for dinner and his new life. The cabin boy has diligently prepared his evening suit and left a note on the desk. He picks it up but again it is all in Russian. Well, adventure into the unknown is what he wanted when he left the safe and foggy alleyways of Milan.

And to the unknown it is. To Odessa.

VI. The Pearl by the Sea

The *Empress of Russia* gently manoeuvres to dock by the main pier in the morning sun. After an early breakfast he climbs up to the main deck to take in the city's seafront, an eclectic mixture of elegant townhouses and ramshackle buildings.

The temperature is pleasant. The air feels fresh, despite the *Empress*' funnels spewing out large quantities of fumes and tiny greasy specks of something similar to volcanic lava.

The cable told him that a clerk from the opera house had been dispatched to meet him and everything had been arranged to assist his arrival. The only worry was that the telegram had not specified whether the clerk spoke French or Italian. Therefore he's mentally preparing himself to communicate in gestures. He purchased a French-to-Russian old dictionary in one of the bustling bookshops of the Ottoman capital as he was told that an Italian version wasn't even in existence. The usual Levantine lie, he thought.

Once the docking is complete, he and other first class passengers are offered a priority disembarkation and he soon finds himself on the embankment, surrounded by porters, sailors and welcoming relatives. All he can hear again is Russian and it finally dawns on him that he might well be the only foreigner in town.

He keeps turning around, holding the cable in his hand, hoping to be recognised by the clerk. Finally he hears his name called out.

'Maestro Mandelli!'

He turns and sees a tall and skinny young man of possibly twenty-five approaching fast.

He notices that he's holding a battered leather briefcase in his hand and a small picture frame under his arm. The young man's attire is rather elegant though on the worn side; both suit and tie are of a slightly discoloured black. The white shirt is crisp and clean though. His eyes are a deep blue, his hair a longish but tidily combed blond.

'Maestro Mandelli, I suppose?'

'Yes, that would be me.'

'So honoured to meet you, sir. Allow me to introduce myself: Vassily Vassilievich Demidov, junior clerk at the Odessa Opera House. At your service.'

He's immensely relieved at the fluency of Vassily's French.

'Pleased to meet you young man, and, I must stress, relieved at hearing your excellent French.'

He notices a shy reddening of Vassily's cheeks.

'Thank you, sir. Most kind. I do apologise for the wait. I had to keep looking around and at your portrait at the same time. Always a big crowd waiting for the service from Constantinople.'

'My portrait?'

'It's a daguerrotype, actually. But we had it framed and hung in the foyer, sir. I hope you will forgive our impertinence as you have never conducted for us.'

'But I am about to! May I have a look?'

Vassily shows him the portrait and he smiles at noticing how much younger he looks in it.

'May I have your luggage papers? I will trace the porter and everything will be delivered to your villa, sir.'

He hands the papers over and they start ambling away from the pier. Vassily keeps drying his forehead with a crumpled handkerchief. Carlo is not yet quite sure whether that is because of the rising temperature or the usual nervousness his celebrity causes in new acquaintances.

When they reach the lower end of the Potemkin Steps, Carlo opens his mouth in wonder.

'The Potemkin Steps, Maestro. Your villa is right at the top of them, in Boulevard Primorskyi. One of the finest areas of the city, sir. We so hope it will be agreeable to you.'

Mandelli lays his hand on Vassily's forearm.

'I'm sure it will be. You can stop shaking, Vassily.'

More forehead-drying.

'We… we have never had a conductor of your status here in the city, sir. We are very worried. Please, if anything displeases you, I would humbly ask you to let me know right away. And… before telling my superiors, if possible.'

'I'm sure I will be highly satisfied with all the arrangements. I'm really not very demanding.' He turns to the Steps. 'So, are we climbing?'

Despite Carlo's friendly demeanour, Vassily seems unable to calm down. Mandelli suspects his superiors have delegated everything to the poor young man and would be furious with him if anything went wrong in settling the Maestro in his new city.

'What? Climbing? Oh no. We have a car for you, sir. Actually, this will be your car from now on, though admittedly the opera house is only a short walk from your villa.'

'I was looking forward to some exercise but a car is probably best for the moment.'

The dusty old black Yakovlev navigates the bustling city roads to finally reach the entrance of the villa in Boulevard Primorskyi, a leafy, near to immaculate thoroughfare, lined with townhouses, villas and high-end apartment buildings. As soon as they alight, he sees the horse-drawn cab with his luggage coming to a slow halt behind their vehicle.

'How did he make it here so fast?'

'They know their shortcuts, Maestro. The competition from the motorcar is fierce these days and they try hard to be ahead of the game.'

He doffs his hat and peruses the villa in earnest. The style is unashamedly Russian. The two floors are gracefully symmetrical and surrounded by grey and white birch trees. The garden is in bloom and the walls are painted a soothing pastel green and white. He finds it delightful. When he approaches the gate, he spots the brand new marble plaque on the right pillar. He turns to Vassily with a friendly frown.

'Villa Mandelli?'

'We thought it would be a nice gesture, sir. The owners were thrilled. They are only merchants, not aristocracy. When they heard you were also a count, they insisted on paying for the plaque themselves.'

'I must meet these lovely folks.'

'Oh, you will. They have reserved a box for the whole season. They rushed to offer the villa and the plaque to jump the queue. Welcome to Russia.'

'The queue?'

'You have no idea, Maestro. I really hope you like the house, sir.'

'I already do. And stop shaking, Vassily, I don't bite.'

Once inside the hallway, he finds a finely attired middle-aged man leading a small parade of servants standing at attention. He gently returns the bowing, causing consternation. Vassily whispers in his ear.

'Russian nobility don't bow to servants, sir.'

He stops in front of the butler who proceeds to introduce the rest of the staff: a couple of maids, a cook, a gardener and a young, shabbily dressed valet whom Carlo suspects is more of a boy for errands and heavy chores.

'You will have to relay all of your needs to the butler, sir. He's the only one with a smattering of French. In any case, in Russia no count speaks directly to servants.'

He nods and follows the butler into the drawing room where he's delighted to discover a small but quaint back garden under more birch trees which filter the sun's rays flooding in through the French windows.

Once in the study he plays a few notes on the grand piano, noticing that it has just been tuned.

'We hired the best tuner in town, sir.'

'It's perfect, Vassily.'

The large and comfortable bedroom hosts an oversized four-poster bed and a small balcony overlooking the garden.

Happy with the arrangements he asks the butler if they could have some tea and cakes in the garden.

Once the butler, whose French might be better than Vassily believes, leaves to arrange it, the young man stares eye-wide at the Maestro.

'Me?'

'You… what, exactly?'

The handkerchief is out of Vassily's pocket again, drying the constantly sweating forehead.

'I'm a junior clerk, sir.'

'And clerks are not supposed to have tea with orchestra conductors?'

'Not with a nobleman, sir. Not in Russia.'

'Nonsense. And it will do some good to that shaking of yours.'

Once tea is served, he relaxes and calmly prompts Vassily to brief him on the summer season and the ins and outs of the theatre. The warmer months are usually filled with a light programme: some operettas and a few works by Rossini and Handel. Just as he's about to take a little dig at the lemon drizzle cake on the pink china plate, he notices that Vassily's sponge has already disappeared from the table. He looks up and sees the embarrassed expression but decides to ignore the sudden display of hunger. Vassily stares at the gravel while clumsily trying to explain his voracious appetite and consequent bad manners.

'I… I am a fast eater, sir.'

'That is no problem, Vassily. Actually, would you like another piece? Let's call the butler, what is his name again?'

'Fyodor.'

He has taken to Vassily. The young man seems to be very dedicated and he's pleased when towards the end of the conversation he seems to have managed to calm his nerves.

He promises to sign a programme of any of his future performances for his girlfriend. Vassily almost jumps on the chair when Carlo expresses his firm intention of wanting to meet her.

'Does she like lemon drizzle cake?'

'I believe she does, Maestro.'

'Then we will instruct Fyodor to pack some for her.'

He spends the day at the old Steinway, planning for the opening night. The artistic director has played it safe and gone for Rossini's most feted - and performed to destruction - masterpiece. He knows it by heart, note by note. He has conducted it too many times.

Dinner doesn't involve the dreaded beetroots and in the morning he's almost surprised at having enjoyed a night of serene sleep. The weather allows a pleasant breakfast of coffee, croissants and fresh fruit *alfresco*. This puts him in a good mood for his first day at work.

He told Vassily to cancel the car as he was looking forward to a morning stroll to the theatre. Vassily had immediately panicked and had drawn a carefully detailed map with clear directions for the Maestro, worrying that he might get lost.

'Please, follow the directions, sir. Some parts of the city are not as agreeable as this one.'

Aware that ending up in some dangerous slum would inevitably land Vassily in an awful lot of trouble, he reads the instructions carefully when leaving the villa and slowly ambles along Chaikovskhoho Lane which runs behind the round building of the opera house. He turns and, unable to find the artists' entrance, he carries on until he finds himself in front of the imposing main front doors.

A noisy crowd is gathered by what appears to be the windows of the Box Office. He hears some shouting though he can't understand anything of what is being said. People are waving hands, banknotes and papers. They seem to be protesting at something. Carlo stands to the side. It all seems very light-hearted to him.

'What do you mean it's sold out?'

The young lady behind the window replies in what it seems a great deal of exasperation.

'That is what it means. Sold out. *Finito.*'

Another man, lurking behind some gesticulating ladies, shouts even louder.

'But it can't be! I am Gran Duke Lepyokhin's personal secretary. I must have some tickets!'

Another man shoves him out of what is clearly not a queue but an unruly mob.

'Nice try, *Tovarisch.* You're no secretary. You're just trying to snatch some tickets for yourself!'

Another loud intervention from the back abruptly interrupts the two men's fraught exchange.

'I am friend of the Maestro. I've met him in France!'

'But he's from Italy, you liar!'

'That is what I meant. Italy!'

'You don't even know where Italy is, you scoundrel!'

The cacophony amuses Mandelli who walks nearer to the gathering to see if he can make any sense of the kerfuffle. When he gets too close he's shoved away by an older lady in some rather garish clothing.

'Nice try, young man. Do you think I'm stupid? You're trying to jump the queue! Stand back. We all want to come to the Italian Maestro's performances. Who do you think you are?'

Carlo opens his arms trying to convey that he does not understand a word of what is being shouted. The window above the box office opens up and a terrified Vassily peers over the edge.

'Oh dear God…'

After furiously descending the main staircase of the foyer and slamming the huge wooden doors of the entrance behind him, he snatches Mandelli and leads him away towards the artists' entrance.

'Good morning, Vassily. What was that?'

The usual wiping of the forehead with a clean handkerchief; he must go through a few of them every day.

'It has been the same every day, sir. Since we announced the season with your name on it. We've been mobbed. It all sold out in the first few hours. The phones haven't stopped ringing, the Box Office is under siege. Some men waited for me in the evening and they roughed me up demanding tickets. We don't know what to do. We had to give precedence to the nobility, and there are a lot of them. Then the rest of the public became really angry.'

'I will put in a couple of more performances. I will tell the director tonight. I believe he's invited me for dinner. But tickets only on sale at the Box Office. No aristocracy.'

Vassily is shaking again, his eyes wide open in terror.

'Maestro, we cannot do that. They will tell the Tsar.

We will all be sacked or deported to Siberia.'

'Not if I demand it.'

The dressing room is spacious and Vassily has arranged for some flowers to be displayed by the upright piano.

'Well, that is most charming. Now let's meet the orchestra. I very much look forward to it.'

'They are on the side of apprehensive, Maestro. It will be hard work.'

'We have three weeks before the premiere of *Barbiere*. We will polish old Gioacchino to distraction.'

Vassily, though now much more relaxed by Carlo's friendly attitude, glances at the ceiling with a rather sceptical look.

'It will be hard work.'

When he finally enters the orchestra pit everyone rises to nervous attention. Some of the members bow, shocking Carlo into a questioning frown.

He almost immediately realises what Vassily meant. This is no Metropolitan. With a quick glance he notices that some sections are understaffed. He spots a few instruments that do not quite look their best. He questions Vassily on why everyone is in white tie.

'That is how they rehearse, Maestro.'

'In white tie? That is only for performances.'

'Not in Russia, it isn't, sir.' He opens his arms wide in resignation, his cheeks crimson. 'We are about a century behind everyone else.'

'I see. Quite a few things will have to change here.'

He greets everyone and shakes the hand of the first violin before starting a round of friendly conversations. He asks for first names and some information about their training and life in general. Everyone is astounded. The first violin stares at his hand as if it has been touched by God.

When he turns to Vassily with a second and slightly

more exasperated questioning look, the poor youth finds himself having to brief him again on their customs.

'Conductors do not fraternise with the members here, sir. They rehearse, order them about, do the performance and then leave.'

'With the members bowing to them…'

Vassily nods with his eyes closed, displaying how stupid he also believes these bows to be. Carlo turns to the orchestra.

'Very well. Does everyone understand my French?'

Everybody nods.

'Very good. From tomorrow rehearsals are done in the most comfortable clothing you can find. Do not come in white tie. That is absurd. If you are reprimanded by some of the opera directors, tell them to come to me for an explanation. I can guarantee you they will get one. And no more bows, please. I'm not the Tsar. Now, I don't see any harps. Are the ladies not well today?'

A deafening silence. Vassily sweats profusely, the handkerchief out again.

'Ladies? You mean… women?'

'Well, that is usually what ladies are; and they are very skilled harp players. Where are they?'

'We… we don't have any…'

'Who plays the harps?'

'No one, sir.'

'Very well, hire some.'

'Hire… ladies?'

'What is so extraordinary about it?'

'They can't play, sir. We can't have ladies in the orchestra. It's unheard of. The Patriarch will have a fit.'

'Let him have as many fits as he likes. I want you to find such ladies and provide them with the instruments if they don't possess any. It will be a long conversation with the director tonight, I fear.'

The members of the orchestra sit stunned and turn to

each other in wonder.

'Now, let's start with the prelude. Although I believe Maestro Rossini called them *Overtures*.'

At the end of the piece he understands what Vassily meant by "hard work". Due to the dictatorial proceedings by previous local conductors there is no team playing, let alone spirit. They are all very skilled and willing but seem almost terrified of displeasing the Maestro. Most of them wonder how the best conductor in the world - after Toscanini - has landed in this splendid backwater. Splendid indeed, but still very much a backwater.

He stops the overture halfway and descends the steps of the podium to chat with the first violin. Then he walks around to give individual feedback and further instructions. When he approaches one of the youngest members, he jumps off his stool and stands to attention like a cadet.

'Please, gentlemen. No more of this nonsense. You're not in the army.'

He pats the youth on the arm, inviting him to sit down, and he leans over the score to go through some of the suggestions. He sees the young man trembling but he also detects his sudden pleasure at being mentored on a one-to-one basis. He can see that he eagerly takes it all in.

When they break for the afternoon even Vassily, who's not musically trained, is shocked by the almost immediate improvement. Before resuming rehearsals Mandelli addresses them from the podium.

'I would be very happy to treat all of you to a drink down at the nearest tavern or café. It would be a good opportunity to become better acquainted since we'll have to work together for some years to come. I apologise that our conversations have to be in French for the time being. But I will have one hour of Russian tuition every day and I soon hope to be able to address you in your language.' He turns around. 'Vassily, anything you can recommend? Somewhere with some decent champagne!'

Vassily is too shocked by such a proposition to hear the question. He finally notices the Maestro looking at him.

'Vassily?'

'What? Champagne? What Champagne? Ah, yes. The Dniepr Aurora. They have French champagne, I believe. Though we're partial to vodka here, sir. Too partial sometimes…'

'Everyone at the Dniepr Aurora then. Now, I've already seen some big progress here, keep it up, gentlemen. Tomorrow we will have the singers to contend with and they are always as difficult as they come. But don't tell them I said that.'

He sees smiles and little laughs for the first time. He doesn't know it yet but they already love him.

The singers are not the hysterical *primadonnas* he had to contend with at La Scala and other Western theatres. They are all locals and very eager to follow his instructions. Their spoken Italian is passable and much better in their arias anyway, though he's not entirely sure that they actually understand what they are singing. The bass playing Don Basilio approaches him after rehearsal. The man is a burly local with a bushy beard and an extraordinarily low range. He is by far the best of the cast.

'Maestro. Forgive my curiosity. What brought you to this outpost? We are of course all immensely honoured. Your outing with the orchestra at the Aurora is already in the papers, together with the advert for harp players of the female variety. This medieval hamlet is in shock, I say. Though that has increased curiosity even further. There will be riots if people don't get tickets.' He frowns with benign suspicion. 'But, again, what brought you here?'

'We are the kind of people who sometimes need to leave everything and everyone behind. Because of what we are, Evgeny.'

The grinning smile is unmistakably friendly.

'I thought you might be such. The long-suffering kind. Welcome to Odessa, Maestro. Love its life. And be careful of its dangers.'

Life in the city settles down slowly. He is of course kept busy by the rehearsals but he's heartened at discovering how suddenly committed and enthusiastic everyone seems to be. Perhaps they scent success and acclaim. When he points out to the maddeningly busy Vassily that no one seems to complain about the hard work, the long sessions and the short breaks, the young man chuckles: 'We Russians never complain. Until we do. By killing people.'

The language lessons are imparted by a severe and unsmiling schoolmaster, clearly lured by the opera house's good salary. He is punctual to the second, starts the lesson without much ado and he's definitely not star-struck by Carlo's celebrity status. Mandelli likes him and he kind of enjoys reverting to being a schoolboy. He is reprimanded in no uncertain terms when he gets the nose-bleedingly difficult Russian cases wrong - an everyday occurrence. At some point he's almost afraid that the teacher will haul a ruler from his leather bag and demand his hands on the table when caught daydreaming and lacking concentration.

The now renamed Villa Mandelli proves to be a delightful abode. The gardens are blissfully peaceful and, despite the hard work at the opera, he manages to make progress on the symphony. The staff are attentive with a hint of Russian reticence and deference. Carlo rightly suspects that the assorted nobility here do not treat their servants too well, and they appear more than happy to have been recruited in his service. Vassily regularly visits to make sure that everything is in order and to Carlo's satisfaction. Mandelli is by now convinced that the opera house would crumble without the young man. At one point he heard an animated conversation with the butler, understanding only the words "coffee" and "Maestro". He suspected Vassily of having gone apoplectic at hearing perhaps that the precious commodity was on the verge of running out or something of the sort. He had then seen him running out of the villa and returning carrying some packages in his hands.

When exhausted he naps on the comfortable velvet sofa or goes out for a gentle stroll along the sycamore-lined boulevards of the city, taking in the eastern elegance of the buildings. A few equally elegant gentlemen and ladies recognise him and greet him by slightly lifting their hats or with an almost imperceptible nod of the head.

In the meantime, Vassily is researching the cheapest tailors in the city, trying to find affordable tails and white tie. His girlfriend has enrolled her aunt to mend the best dress in her scarce wardrobe. When he presented Mandelli with the free tickets allocated to him with his usual endearing efficiency, he was left speechless as Carlo gave back two of them for himself and his girlfriend.

'Maestro, I can't accept that. They're in the stalls. I might be sitting next to an Archduke. I might be arrested. I'm only a clerk.'

'And a very good one, young man. You and Paulina deserve it. Come and introduce her to me in my dressing room before the performance.'

'I… I don't know what to say.'

'And no fear. They are not going to deport you to Siberia for sitting next to an Archduke with a valid ticket.'

'You don't know the Okhrana, sir.'

'Hopefully I never will.'

On another of his strolls he sits to rest on a bench, watching the traffic of cabs and cars negotiating the bustling Primorskyi Boulevard. When he peers over to the next bench he recognises a man in a black suit and a bowler hat. He had seen him a few days earlier and again when coming out of the artists' entrance. He's being followed. Again. Like in Weimar. And Carlsbad. And maybe on the *RMS Adriatic*. Maybe they never left him or these ones are indeed the Okhrana, now suspecting him of Bolshevism. He resigns himself to never finding out why all these agents - they seem to be secret agents - keep following him. Equally he feels more relaxed about it. He reasons with himself that if they had wanted to arrest or murder him they would have done it by now.

Together with the tickets he demands a pay increase for Vassily who seems to feel guilty about it since he appears to work even harder.

On the evening of the premiere, the cream and custard of Odessa is present: the ladies' dresses have mercifully arrived from the French capital in time for the grand event. Emeralds and military decorations vie for room in the elegant foyer. Vassily and Paulina are relieved to find that after all they are not seated next to an Archduke but some wealthy merchant who nevertheless glances suspiciously at the fabric of Vassily's tailcoat and the absence of sapphires on his girlfriend's neck.

Three weeks of hard work pay off. Everyone is in great form and Prince Konstantinovich in the imperial box is the first to rise in enthusiastic applause at the end of the performance.

A grand ball is given in Mandelli's honour. Several unmarried young ladies of the local aristocracy are introduced to him in the usual forlorn hope and he's finally beaten when crashing on the four-poster bed in the early hours of the following morning.

He's woken up by an over-excited Vassily, rushing in alongside the butler's trolley with an inviting breakfast display.

After the butler has pulled the curtains open revealing a sunny day, Vassily cannot contain himself any longer and starts reading the front pages of the local newspapers aloud.

'Maestro, Maestro! Listen to this: *"Thanks to Maestro Mandelli, we are now the best opera house in the world!"'* He throws the *Odesskiy Listok* on the bed while opening another broadsheet. 'And.... and this is the *Odesskaya Zhizn*: *"We are now up there with La Scala and the Garnier. No! We are better than them! Make Maestro Mandelli stay forever! Honorary citizenship for Maestro Mandelli! Sign the petition!"'*

Carlo smiles at the deranged Russian passion in the papers while sipping a steaming coffee.

'Calm down, Vassily and have some cakes. It was indeed a good performance.'

'Good? It was the best I have ever attended in my life, sir!'

'You're twenty-five.'

'Ah! But we are the best theatre in the world. Look: the *Odesskiy Listok* says so!'

He has come to nurture a tender affection for Vassily: his stoical indefatigability, his ability to resolve the most difficult situation without too much fuss while never complaining, his loyalty, his almost serene resignation to the maddening idiosyncrasies of his country and the unjustified reprimands by his inept and corrupt superiors. He would adopt him if he could.

The members of the orchestra turn out to be a friendly and easygoing bunch of different ages and backgrounds.

It doesn't escape his eye that some seem to be better off than others.

One of the viola players is a perennially brooding young man. He arrives on time, plays well and leaves without socialising much with the other members.

Mandelli doesn't make much of it. The season is going from strength to strength, summer is around the corner and he feels reasonably happy and relaxed.

However one afternoon he finds several orchestra and choir members distractedly perusing a clumsily cyclostyle-printed leaflet. After being given one, his knowledge of Russian is now enough to understand that it is some kind of Marxist Manifesto summarised in one front page.

Vassily is not far behind, and after quickly reading the content of the paper, he goes around snatching them off the musicians' hands. When he has managed to collect most of the revolutionary material, he stands in front of Carlo with an apologetical expression.

'I'm so sorry, Maestro. Won't happen again.'

'I'm more concerned about the safety of my orchestra. How did that material make it inside the theatre?'

Vassily is reluctant at first, but his loyalty and devotion to Mandelli prevent him from hiding what he knows.

'Oleg, sir.'

'Oleg? You mean the young viola player?'

Vassily nods.

'Is he a Bolshevik?'

'He might not be the only one, but others tend to be more discreet. They are growing in number, sir. There has been some occasional disorder here and there. Not in this part of town though. That is why you haven't noticed.'

'I see. Do you think I should talk to this young revolutionary?'

'Maybe. Won't change his ideas. He's of the militant type.'

'I don't want to change his ideas. I don't want him to endanger my orchestra.'

The conversation turns out to be polite and respectful but on the side of cold and resentful. What he thought to be mild youthful brooding turns out to be rather a spot of angry rage. Carlo's aristocratic stock hardly helps, and he's unsettled by Oleg's last words: 'We're coming for your ilk.'

Vassily reluctantly suggests that perhaps Oleg should be let go but Mandelli is firmly against it.

'That is how you make enemies.'

One day Vassily arrives at Villa Mandelli visibly excited, shaking and sweating more than usual. When Carlo invites him into the garden while ordering his favourite lemon drizzle cake, the young man fishes some papers out of his leather briefcase from which he never seems to part. He can hardly bring himself to announce the news to Mandelli.

'Maestro…'

'What is it, Vassily? You seem more agitated than usual. Has something happened?'

'His… His Imperial Majesty is coming to attend the opening of *Boris Godunov*, sir.'

'I see. You had better have some tea and cakes, Vassily. And try to calm down. It's just the Tsar. He clearly wants to hear some Russian music.'

'Just? The whole imperial family is coming and the director has put me in charge of all the arrangements. What if something goes wrong? I'll be arrested and…'

'Sent to Siberia? Vassily, no one is sending you anywhere. You're an excellent clerk and everything will go perfectly well. Clearly the director trusts you.'

'You think he does?'

'Of course I do. Now. Will I have to attend some ball in honour of His Majesty?'

'Yes, sir. But that is organised by the Imperial Household.'

'It will be fine, Vassily. Make sure everyone receives the score of your national anthem. I will need one too. I'm afraid I don't know it. I guess the protocol will be more or less the same as for all the other kings and queens in the world. Of which there are far too many, I say.'

Vassily is writing everything down with nervous care, still not convinced that he's not going to end up doing hard labour in some icy Siberian quarry.

On a balmy Black Sea evening he leaves Villa Mandelli and walks at pace to the theatre. When through the artists' entrance he's met by a fretting Vassily reporting that everything is going really well and the Tsar and his entourage are enjoying a private reception in the foyer.

'The theatre is surrounded by Cossacks and the local police, Vassily. We are probably safer here than everywhere else. All going well?'

Vassily wipes his forehead with some satisfaction.

'Princess Tatiana told her governess to compliment me on the flower arrangements. Princess Tatiana, sir!'

He pats the clerk on the arm.

'I told you everything would be fine.'

Vassily scrams in a hurry when an usher arrives reporting some trivial issue arising somewhere. Likely Princess Tatiana losing her dance carnet or something dramatically less catastrophic.

He has rehearsed the protocol with the orchestra. He enters the auditorium and stands on the podium waiting for the sovereign and his family to appear in the Imperial Box. When they do, the audience and the orchestra rise in unison and slightly bow their heads. He bows his head further when Nicholas II initiates a deafening applause. When he turns slightly to lead the ovation to his musicians with his hand, he quickly glimpses at the pit and sees Oleg still on his chair, staring at the floor, refusing to stand.

He tries to ignore the youth's reckless gesture but when he turns around and signals with his baton that the anthem is about to start, he cannot help looking again in Oleg's direction, noticing that his viola is still on his lap. The boy is now staring at him, his eyes darting shots of unmistakable hatred.

He tries to convey a severe reprimand to the lad, his expression one of worry about his behaviour. He doesn't pick up the instrument. He refuses to play even a single note of the anthem, and when the orchestra stands up again for another round of applause he remains seated in what is clearly an angry sulk.

Godunov ends with a standing ovation, Nicholas II the first to rise with his hands together.

Once in his dressing room, he splashes his face with cold water, preparing himself to attend the ball in his or the Tsar's honour, he's not quite sure which.

While he's drying his face Vassily slams the door open without knocking, jolting Carlo who turns around in shock. The young man is panting, his legendary handkerchief soaked in a pool of sweat.

'Maestro!… Maestro! Please, come at once. In haste. Please!'

'Vassily, what is the matter?'

'They… they are taking Oleg. Please come now.'

Carlo gets up and grabs Vassily's forearms trying to shake him out of his panicked state.

'Who's taking Oleg? Taking him where? What for?'

'The Okhrana. Four of them. I think there is a chief inspector or whatever they call them.' He's on the verge of tears. 'Please, come at once.'

They rush through the dimly lit corridors of the artists' quarters until they arrive at an even darker recess. He sees Oleg and he's shocked at noticing that he's already been handcuffed with his hands behind his back. He firstly speaks loudly in the only Russian he knows.

'Gentlemen, please wait. What is this? Oleg is a member of my orchestra. Release him at once!'

What Vassily had rightly identified as the chief inspector or something similar approaches while indicating to his agents to hold their prisoner without leading him away for the moment. He's a short man with comical moustaches complementing an already comically round face.

To his relief, he addresses Carlo in surprisingly elegant French.

'Your Excellency has clearly failed to notice one of his members' revolutionary activity. I can guarantee you, *Conte di Castagnino*, that Oleg will no longer be able to put you in danger. You are quite safe.'

'What is this nonsense? What revolutionary activity? Oleg is no danger to me or anyone else. He plays the viola in my orchestra. Release him at once, I say.'

Vassily is shaking in fear; Oleg maintains an unhelpfully challenging expression of disdain, likely to enrage the inspector even further.

'He remained seated for His Imperial Majesty's entrance. He didn't play the anthem either. What further proof do you want, Maestro? A bomb going off in his pocket?'

'He's a youth with a hot head. He's not a Bolshevik, if that is what you imply. Young people like to protest. You are overreacting.'

'That is something we are going to find out with a thorough interrogation, sir.'

At those words Vassily covers his face with his hand,

knowing very well the kind of "thorough interrogation" the inspector means.

Carlo remains calm.

'Well, Inspector, as you so well know my name and title, would you be so kind to inform me of yours?'

'For what purpose?'

'Well, you see, Oleg is one of my best viola players. I very much doubt I will be able to continue my work here in Odessa without a full orchestra. I wonder how pleased His Imperial Majesty would be to hear that the conductor who has made Odessa the world capital of opera has been forced to leave under duress?'

The boasting is not his style but over the past few weeks he has slowly acquainted himself with the very Russian weakness for declamatory hyperbole and he's determined to save Oleg from the notorious Okhrana torture chambers.

'Furthermore, I'm sure my King won't be pleased either at the way I am being treated here. As a fellow monarch, he would have no choice but to discuss the matter with the Tsar, don't you think? How unfortunate it would be for you to be the cause of a diplomatic incident. And all for a boyish stunt. Well, so be it, then. I must get ready. Would hate to keep the Tsar waiting, don't you agree?'

He turns to leave but, as predicted, he's stopped by the inspector's now unsure voice. The tone is now one of simmering impotence.

'I am… I am arresting a Bolshevik, Maestro. It's my duty to protect the Tsar. And you, sir.'

'Shall we let the Tsar decide then?'

The inspector parades himself in front of Carlo, preventing him from leaving. A few seconds of tense and tentative silence ensue.

'Very well. We'll only keep him under surveillance for the moment. I strongly suggest you have a long talk with that young idiot. Next time, he won't have the Tsar saving his skin.'

'There won't be a next time.'

'I'll take the word of a count, sir.'

He nods at his henchmen to release Oleg and leaves the recess in a hurry, shaking his head, followed by the heavy steps of his agents.

Once they have all left, he sees Vassily relaxing just a tiny bit and Oleg standing there in defiance, massaging his wrists.

'Well, quite a stunt you've played there, young man.'

'It wasn't a stunt. Sir.'

'Wasn't expecting a "thank you", but may I ask you to keep your politics out of this theatre? You are endangering all of us with your Bolshevik shenanigans.'

'Shenanigans? For a moment I forgot you're one of them, Maestro. You will never understand.'

'What I understand is that you got away this time but you won't be so lucky the next. The Tsar probably didn't even see you. If he had, the inspector would have called my bluff.'

'Your bluff?'

Carlo is fast becoming exasperated with Oleg and he uncharacteristically raises his voice.

'Do you really think that the Tsar would listen to a word I say? In my Pidgin Russian? And that the King of Italy would go to war or something of the sort because a washed-up conductor takes offence at having one his viola players tortured to death? Seriously? I have never even met my King, you damn fool.'

Vassily politely raises his finger.

'With all due respect, Maestro, you're the best conductor in the world. Hardly washed up.'

Oleg reluctantly relents, comprehending for the first time the risk Mandelli has taken in saving him.

'I'm sorry, Maestro.'

'Well, that wasn't so hard, was it? Look, I am not entirely unsympathetic to your cause - if that is your cause - but please do not place all of us in danger. They could have taken poor Vassily too, as he's responsible for everything here. I understand you want to start a revolution but do you have to murder everyone to do it?'

'That is usually how revolutions work, sir.'

'Go ahead then. Start with me. Why not? I am a count after all. First in line to be shot. Are you going to wait till dawn, or would you like me to walk in front of the firing squad right now? For the good of us all, Oleg, go home.'

He makes for returning to his dressing room to change, but Oleg's voice is firm.

'Would you like to give me a lift home, Maestro?'

Carlo turns around again, puzzled by the strange request.

'What? Take you home? I see you're under shock. I'll get my driver to…'

'We sure can go by car, sir. But I'd like you to come with me. Consider it an invite.'

Vassily's handkerchief is out again.

'No, no, no. The whole imperial court is waiting for you, Maestro.'

But Carlo has his searching eyes fixed on Oleg.

'Why do you want me to take you home?'

'Do it and you'll find out.'

Vassily's panic is palpable.

'Maestro, we have already been in grave danger tonight. Please, don't make it worse. The Tsar…'

Carlo turns to the clerk.

'Tell him I'm not feeling too well. Stomach cramps. I will be going home to bed. Fetch my car.'

Vassily never questions Mandelli's orders and he runs outside to hail the car, by now resigned to be deported to the far end of the Kamchatka peninsula. Once inside the old Yakovlev the driver turns with a surprised expression after glancing at the rear mirror and spotting Oleg beside the Maestro.

'Potocki Palace, sir?'

'Oleg, tell him where we're going.'

'Suvorovsky.'

The driver seems shocked and starts what appears like an argument with Oleg. Then he turns again to Carlo.

'But the ball is at the Potocki Palace, Maestro.'

'They will have to start the dances without me. We're taking Oleg home. Do as he asks.'

He starts the car and slowly drives off.

After driving away from the back entrance of the theatre, it doesn't take long for the surroundings to change into something decidedly less sophisticated. Carlo and Oleg are pensively peering out of their windows without exchanging a single word.

As they venture further and further north of the city, the sumptuous buildings start to give way to more modest ones, albeit still in a reasonable state. The night is still young and quite a few people are out enjoying the balmy evening, blessed by a fresh breeze from the Black Sea. He notices a few modest cafés and taverns and a spillover of inebriated people on the pavements.

After another ten minutes' drive the picture becomes less and less attractive as they continue the drive to the Suvorovsky district.

There are no longer buildings who can reliably be defined as such. The single floor houses are getting more and more ramshackle and Carlo starts noticing that most people are dressed in rags. Almost all the women seem to hurry somewhere, holding woolly moth-eaten scarves on their shoulders or covering their heads with them. A lot of children are still playing in the street, forcing the driver to swerve a few times to avoid hitting the most erratic ones. They are all very grimy, soiled in a kind of permanent way, not the temporary dirt caused by street games. Carlo finally turns to Oleg.

'Shouldn't all these children be in bed at this time of the night?'

Oleg doesn't turn from looking out of his window.

'What beds?'

Carlo is starting to understand the point Oleg might have been wanting to make when he asked him to be taken home.

When they finally turn the corner into the first streets of Suvorovsky, Mandelli's heart sinks with a loud thump. The single storey ramshackle houses have given way to mere shacks. Doors are broken and fires are burning in the street. Quite a few people are cooking malodorous concoctions in rusty cauldrons. A lot of the women carry semi-naked babies on their shoulders, all crying, some screaming. Carlo notices a few dangerously drunken men openly assaulting the younger ladies. The police are nowhere to be seen.

When Oleg tells the driver to stop, Carlo turns, eyes wide open.

'You live here?'

'Welcome to the real Russia, Maestro. I hope you forgot your shoe at the castle. Prince Charming won't be able to come and fetch you without it.'

'Very funny.'

Oleg tells the driver to stay with the car.

'The Maestro will be safe with me.'

They get off and he follows Oleg along a dark alleyway, almost tripping over the bedraggled humanity surviving on the steps of the shacks. Carlo winces at seeing a few rats swarming over the back of a drunkard slumped on the muddy road.

When they reach the end of the alleyway, Oleg opens the door of the only wooden shack that remotely resembles a more solid house.

'No need for a key. There's nothing to steal.'

'What about your viola?'

'I leave it at the opera house. They let me practise in any empty room they have available.'

They climb up a set of rickety steps that lead them to the first floor. A pungent and pervasive stench of cooked cabbage and beetroots hits Carlo's nostrils. Oleg smiles: 'Dinner. Not quite the Dniepr Aurora.'

An old lady is snoozing on a rocking chair; Mandelli stares at the old woman, appalled at how ill she seems to be. Oleg leans over to kiss her cheek.

'Good evening, Grandma. I have a guest tonight: Maestro Mandelli. My boss.'

Carlo bows.

'Pleased to meet you, madam.'

'He was supposed to be at a ball in the Potocki Palace, Grandma. He was going to meet the Tsar.'

Carlo is shocked that the old lady is actually able to utter a few words. When she lifts her hand Mandelli shakes it and gently holds it.

'Would you tell His Imperial Majesty that I pray for him every night? He is the father of us all.'

Carlo glances at Oleg before answering. Oleg nods.

'Of course I will. He will be pleased.'

The old lady pats his hand.

'Oleg, don't be rude and make some tea for your boss. We still have a decent samovar.'

'Yes, Grandma.'

The door that seems to lead to some sort of sleeping quarters slams open and three young children storm into the room, surrounding and hugging Oleg. He introduces all of them to Mandelli despite their lack of interest in a stranger. Then the young man sends them back to bed.

Once they are seated with a couple of cracked mugs in their hands, an embarrassed silence precedes the obvious conversation about to happen.

'I… I don't understand. I thought the opera paid well. You're a qualified musician. This is unacceptable.'

'It is acceptable to a lot of people. It has to be. The ones who don't accept it end up in Siberia, courtesy of the Okhrana. Compared to the inferno you've seen out there my salary is adequate. I can afford the rent for this dump. Most people can't. But Grandma is old and needs doctors and medicines. My brothers and sisters need to eat. School… well, sometimes.'

'What about your parents? Where are they?'

Oleg turns to his grandma, pleased to see her fully asleep.

'In 1905 they thought a revolution was on its way. The *SS Potemkin* crew rebelled and started to fire its cannons on to Odessa. Mother and father went along to the Steps to join the protest. You must have heard of that event even in your faraway country. They were slaughtered by a full regiment of Cossacks and the Imperial Guards. They didn't even let me see them. Enemies of the fatherland, they said. Grandma still thinks that they shouldn't have rebelled against the Tsar. She believes that they committed a mortal sin.'

'I'm ever so sorry.'

Oleg looks out of the dusty window, perhaps to hide the tears.

'Now, Count Carlo Mandelli di Castagnino. Tell me: do you still want me to stand up for the entrance of my parents' murderer?'

Carlo stares into the mug.

'I'm so sorry… I didn't know…'

'No. Of course you didn't. How could you have? Your villa sits in the best part of the city. Your servants accede to your every whim. The Tsar himself throws a ball in your honour. You only see what they want you to see. They've nothing to fear, anyway. You are aristocracy yourself. Why would you turn against them? It's not even your country. You are here for… well… that has been bothering me since your arrival. What are you here for? Can't be the money. The ladies? The boys? Were you bored on the gilded shores of your beautiful lake?'

'That is unfair. And given the circumstances, irrelevant too.'

Now it's Oleg's turn to stare in his mug.

'I was talented and the academy paid for all my studies. I was just a bit luckier than the other boys who are out there stealing, killing or selling themselves to some lecherous prince. I'm not even sure which one is worse anymore. We are desperate and the Bolsheviks are the only ones who give us hope. Maybe, just maybe, we will win.'

'Are you supporting all of your family by yourself?'

Oleg nods.

'I pay the rent and put food on the table. We barely reach the end of the month. Two or three days before payday I stop eating; I don't want the children and grandma to go hungry. But I cannot control what they do during the day as I need to practise. Ekaterina is expecting a baby.'

Carlo feels his blood draining away.

'Your sister? The one who just came in? But… she's a child… what kind of…?'

'…Hell have you walked into? A very special one, Maestro. As I said, I can't look after them during the day. If I lose my job we will starve or freeze to death. You haven't spent a winter here yet. Wait and see. One day she came back with a wad of roubles. She wouldn't tell me how she got them. Despite her resistance I lifted her crumpled dress and I started crying in deranged, angry pain. The blood, the dirt. I didn't know what to do, whom to call. Three weeks later she started vomiting.'

Carlo can barely speak.

'She…'

'She's twelve.'

He shuts his eyes in horrified shock.

'Oh dear God.'

'No. He's not so dear. Not here.'

He walks him back to the car. The driver has been busy shooing off begging children. They face each other while he keeps the door open for Carlo.

'I… I'm so sorry, Oleg. I think I understand now.'

'Yes. I think you do. You're not quite as heartless as the rest.'

'If there's anything I can do? Maybe for the baby?'

'We'll manage. Around here most babies and mothers die during birth anyway. We might be lucky.'

'Oleg!'

'Deprivation begets depravity. Which one shocks you the most, Maestro? It's a start. I mean, to be shocked. We can't afford that luxury.'

He climbs into the back of the car and lowers the window, feeling his eyes welling up.'

'Good night, Oleg.'

'Do you know why Vassily was apoplectic at the thought of you coming here?'

'Vassily always panics.'

Oleg points at a junction not far down the road. A fire is burning on the dirty street, some people in the crowd are angrily shouting at someone else.

'He lives over there. Just round the corner.'

He knocks on the car to signal the driver to set off.

'Good night, Maestro.'

The following days go by in a haze of stunned guilt. Vassily avoids his gaze, possibly guessing that Oleg has revealed the squalor in which he and Paulina spend their lives when away from their workplaces. Perhaps that is why he's always at work: better the offices of the opera house than the slums of Suvorovsky.

He would like to help both of them but he's not sure how to go about it. Merely offering money would be offensive to their pride, though Oleg didn't seem to have much left of that. Gifts perhaps, but it would be too obvious. He negotiated a pay rise for Vassily but he cannot interfere with whatever contract the whole orchestra is under.

With time Vassily, perhaps reassured by Mandelli not mentioning that night, returns to his usual oddly adorable self, running around like a headless little Russian bear, his spectacles steaming up, his handkerchief wiping his sweaty forehead, daily terrified of being arrested and deported to Siberia for anything wrong he might have done. Although he practically runs the show by himself, the director general and the rest of the board keep mistreating him, despite themselves being useless and corrupt to a mesmerisingly grotesque level.

His success in turning around the fortunes of the opera house continues unabated and he's admired and feted by the aristocracy, the bourgeois and the few members of the dispossessed who manage to save a few roubles to pay for a ticket in the gallery every two or three months.

One day he points out to Vassily that he finds it strange, especially after his roaring success, that the board won't pay the staff a bit more. Vassily never laughs at Carlo's naivety out of respect, but he can't avoid a little chuckle.

'They still don't have much money, Maestro.'

'But… how can that be?'

'Princes and dukes do not pay, they get an invite. The rest of the revenue is pilfered by anyone who manages to put their hands in the till. The accountants seem to prosper.'

'I see. And I thought my country was a world-beater when it comes to corruption.'

'I think you'll find that we're on an altogether different level here, Maestro.'

After venturing a bit further away from Boulevard Prymorskyi, he comes across a quaint little café positioned under a pergola and surrounded by a garden in full bloom.

Despite being named *Café Leclerc,* he is stunned to discover that the owner taking his order addresses him immediately in Italian, albeit tinged with such a strong Sicilian accent that Mandelli struggles to understand most of the words.

'*Signor* Maestro, I recognised you straight away. I'm Salvatore. I've been to a couple of your performances. Superb! Absolutely superb! This lot was worse that a tone-deaf village band before your arrival. Great job!'

'Thank you. I am rather shocked to be finding a fellow citizen in this remote outpost. What brought you to these shores?'

'Well, Sicily isn't exactly at the centre of the world either, is it? Now that your northern lot has annexed it without asking, it has gone from bad to worse.'

Carlo, detecting a faintly hostile tone to his northern lineage, demurs and orders the coffee and pastries he had come in for.

'I don't get involved in politics, but I'm glad you have found a place to your liking. I do enjoy living here too. It has its ups and downs, of course.'

He wonders whether the café owner has any idea of the grinding poverty slowly destroying the country. The man is handsome in a Sicilian kind of way. He points to a young waiter with platinum hair, boyish features and crystalline, watery eyes. The Slavic kind.

'Love brought me here. Don't enquire how it happened. Mikhail is a local angel.'

Carlo's eyes open still wider at the new piece of information. And at the reason why the Sicilian man feels so free and confident in revealing it to him. He takes a second look at Mikhail, wondering - and worrying - about his age. Salvatore winks.

'And extremely profitable too, *Signor* Mandelli.'

He jolts. Despite the night of discovery in the inferno of Suvorovsky, he's not yet fully immunised against the depths of Slavic depravity. He coldly urges his coffee to be brought over, fearing the Sicilian is about to offer Mikhail's "services" to him. Perhaps he hides a special menu away with clients' "reviews" of the boy.

But Salvatore laughs at the panicked face.

'You haven't quite cracked the Slavic equation, have you, Maestro?'

He wants to leave.

'The coffee, please.'

The Sicilian host is undeterred. They always are. He comes from a stubborn land.

'No fear. I keep my mouth shut. But I'm no fool. Local boys here will do anything for a piece of bread. How is love treating you in the Pearl by the Sea, Maestro Mandelli?'

Carlo stares at the grass under the table, deeply desiring to be somewhere else.

'If you don't mind my objection, I'd rather keep my personal life private.'

'That means that it ain't happening.'

'The coffee, please.'

'The Taras Shevchenko Park. Before night falls. Best time. More meat that you'll ever find at the local butcher. Ready for slaughter.'

He stands up and collects his hat from the table.

'You will have to excuse me. I am no longer in the mood for a coffee. I have a very busy evening ahead.'

Salvatore laughs out loud. Too loud. Everyone turns and Carlo leaves in embarrassed haste, wondering why anyone would even go near such a place.

After a few days he has almost forgotten about that very unpleasant man and his intrusive manners. He goes through another couple of successful performances before having a few free days which he wants to dedicate to working on the symphony.

But at least on one count Salvatore was right. After the riotous afternoon at the Blue Hammam no love in any form and shape has come his way.

He has been so preoccupied with his work that he has hardly given any thought to it. After all, he reasons, wasn't that the main motive for uprooting himself? To forget about it?

But we can only avoid it for a very limited amount of time. It returns. It always returns; stronger and more urgent than before.

One thing that he certainly can't forget is the name of the park and the recommended time to find a willing crowd.

Evenings are becoming warmer, though a cool breeze persists. The pleasant temperature induces people of all ages and status to venture along the birch-lined boulevards for languid strolls, perhaps an ice cream or a cool drink. Young ladies and lads in the traditional Russian white blouse flirt in shady recesses; elegant couples parade their latest garments, frequently stopping for a spot of gossip with their fellow citizens. He mingles with the crowd all the way to the entrance of the park. Dusk is now slowly turning into a darker night. He walks by the statue of Pushkin before venturing further inside, hoping to discover some sort of meeting place. Salvatore didn't specify any particular spot, mostly because Carlo hadn't given him the time to. He didn't seem to need any encouragement to reveal details of his private life. Heaven knows what he would have found out about young Mikhail if he had stayed. Now he's afraid he might see him here; perhaps with Salvatore counting the notes after every duke or prince on the prowl has made good use of his lover. He pauses his steps for a moment in despondent thoughts: what a world.

He wanders aimlessly, slowly realising that without knowing the exact location it will be basically impossible to find what he's looking for. Although he's not quite sure what exactly he's looking for. But we might give up when we can't find a bank, a bakery, even a pharmacy or a hospital. For this, we don't. We never give up. It isn't that important, they say. But it always is.

He gets to the edge of a thick wood, more of a forest really. When he cautiously steps inside it, what was left of the evening light disappears like magic. Like a mysterious God had switched it off to enjoy the show.

He sees shades of bodies disappearing and reappearing behind birch trees and huge oak trunks. Some are leaning against them, waiting. Some seem to be floating above the thick grass, their steps light and silent. He wonders whether the place is exclusively used for financial transactions or more well-intentioned activities take place here. More meaningful encounters. Love even. After all, where would you go for that either?

The young age of the crowd leads him to reason that hardly anything takes place here without an adequate reward. The older wanderers are not of the handsome type, and the younger ones have no aura of vulnerability. Possibly the opposite.

The night is here, and with it a looser offering of the

boys' wares. Some unbutton their shirts, showing hairless, ripped stomachs. Some trousers hit the ankles revealing an unexpected absence of undergarments.

He needs to make his choice. That is what he came for. But some of them are so young. An uncomfortable thought of Ekaterina passes through his now confused mind.

He stops in front of the only lad who seems to be over twenty years of age. He has the start of a beard, a more worn-out look, one of long-lost innocence. Heaven knows how long ago.

His trousers are down. His open shirt reveals a skinny chest with a vaguely manly fuzz of hair running in the middle, gently wrapping round his tiny nipples.

The young man waves his hand inward to signal his availability. He whispers something in Russian which Carlo fails to understand. The lower classes sometimes have a smattering of French and here it is much needed for the foreign punters like Carlo himself.

The lad understands and switches to French, though he only needs a couple of words.

'*Cent roubles*.'

He doesn't need any further vocabulary. With his hand he indicates to Carlo what is allowed to do. By crossing his fingers over his mouth, he shows him what he's prohibited from doing.

Carlo nods. He's still too young for him to be interested in kissing him and what he's permitted to do will allow him to fantasise about an older, handsome man against the trunk of the oak instead of a boy half his age.

The young man is surprisingly aroused and he seems to enjoy the treatment. He seems to be wanting to go till the end but Carlo moves away when his youth explodes, spilling his seed all over the surrounding grass, bizarrely without even a whisper.

The trousers are up, the shirt is re-buttoned and

Carlo fishes his wallet out of the inside pocket of his jacket.

It happens very fast. The lad snatches the wallet at lightning speed. Carlo tries to protest and he's met by a powerful kick in the leg. So powerful that he falls on the grass. The boy could run away with his bounty but a strange sense of revenge seems to be pervading him. Perhaps he belongs to the opposite tribe but in such dire need of money that any mouth would do. Maybe he needs to show that he is still a man. To whom it isn't clear as most of the other boys scuttle away like rats at witnessing the ongoing robbery.

He kicks Carlo in the stomach before leaning over and snatching the gold watch in his waistcoat pocket. Still angry, he lands his fist on the Maestro's jaw. Carlo retreats into a foetal position, covering his face with the hands, thinking that the young man intends to murder him.

In the frenzy the hustler forgets the poor Russian of his client and shouts something which Carlo doesn't grasp at all. Then he uses the other few useful French words, probably learnt from another victim.

'*Plus d'argent?*'

Carlo shakes his head and he also remembers two or three useful Russian words.

'Please, no kill me.'

The lad spits on him and runs away, disappearing into the bush like a baby deer chased by a predator.

Dazed and afraid, he slowly dusts himself down and staggers to the exit of the park, supporting himself by leaning on the trunks of the trees between steps, not sure if he is about to pass out. His jaw hurts and when he touches his lips with his fingers they come back covered in blood.

He's no doctor, but he guesses that no ribs have been broken by the kick, otherwise he might not even be able to walk.

Once he makes it outside the park, he has to take a

few minutes to re-orientate himself before deciding on the right direction back to the villa.

The night is now very dark. The moon has hidden herself away from the troubles of us humans and he starts ambling along the boulevards, away from the entrance to the park.

After barely five minutes' walk, a black motorcar slowly approaches by his left side. It starts sputtering when the driver slows down to the same speed as his walk.

When it stops a few yards ahead of him, the back door opens wide. He gets closer and peers inside, still holding his ribs with his right hand while wiping blood off his mouth with his left one.

'Good evening, Maestro.'

Carlo lowers his gaze in irritated resignation.

'Good evening, Inspector.'

'Perhaps you'd like a lift back to the villa? Unless, of course, you're planning another stroll in the park?'

They exchange sarcastic smiles.

'No, thank you. I'd rather walk.'

He resumes his steps, but the motorcar follows at a snail's pace, the door still open.

'I was also proposing a little chat in addiction to the lift.'

Resigned to the inevitable, Carlo turns.

'Very well. Since you insist.'

He climbs into the vehicle and sits as close to the window as he can, holding his ribs in pain. The inspector signals to the driver to set off with an almost imperceptible nod.

'Warm summer evening. Ideal for any kind of activity, I'd say.'

Mandelli looks out of the window.

'Cut to the chase. Is there a price to pay for not getting arrested?'

'Oh, you're not under arrest. What for, anyway? But you're the most illustrious guest of our city. We cannot allow anything to happen to you.'

'I see. I'm not giving up protecting Oleg from you, if you're planning to ask me that. Leave the boy alone. And I'm not informing on anyone, before you try to blackmail me into it. I know your methods.'

'How can you possibly? Maestro, I'm just taking you home. You're in quite a state. I suggest you see a doctor, or would you like me to take you to a hospital?'

The friendly tone has a lurid and oily tinge which makes Carlo almost want to jump out of the car.

'Take me home and then leave me well alone, please.'

'Maestro, you want me to cut to the chase? Will do. We do have more pressing issues to deal with than bored foreign musicians venturing into seedy parks to suck young men's cocks. How did it taste?'

He stares out of the window to resist the temptation to punch the vile little man.

'Bolshevism is a tide we are struggling to contain. Yes, even with our methods of which you claim to know so much. I have a classified piece of information for you: they may win. Besides, one thing you don't seem to be aware of is that in Russia noblemen and wealthy individuals do as they please. Attempting to arrest any of them would end my career before the ink was dry on the warrant. If you had any idea of what takes place in princes and archdukes' palaces, you would have attended one of their secret parties, instead of risking your life - and my job - looking for young meat on sale between the long shadows of our splendid birches.'

'I was not…' He waves his hand in disdainful resignation. 'Oh, what does it matter…'

'I will take you home but we cannot stop keeping an eye on you. We can't afford to have you hurt. You're famous and a scandal benefits no one. Please, be careful.'

'I will.'

He darts out of the car once it pulls up at the gate of Villa Mandelli. Fyodor sees the wounds and he's about to enquire about them but Carlo waves him away, running up the stairs to his bedroom.

Two or three days go by in a state of shock. When Vassily turns up with some organisational matters, he freezes seeing the cut on the lip and the jaw and cheekbone now a deep shade of purple.

But this is Vassily, the most discreet clerk in the whole of the Russian Empire, the one who is ashamed of where he lives, ashamed of his poverty, terrified of being deported to Siberia.

He doesn't ask. Mandelli helps the poor man out with the oldest of excuses.

'I fell down the stairs. It was very dark and Fyodor must have forgotten to leave the lights on. I'm well. Only a few bruises. No need to worry.'

Whether Vassily believes the ludicrous excuse is irrelevant. He has a story to tell the opera house to excuse the Maestro from one or two performances, though Carlo protests that he will be able to work. He's recovering well.

Four days later Fyodor enters the garden to announce that there is a visitor for the Maestro, without specifying who he is.

Upon entering the hallway he finds a young cadet in imperial uniform waiting for him, his hat respectfully tucked under his arm.

Seeing the Maestro approaching, the lad stands to attention, putting his gloved hand to his forehead in a military salute. Mandelli is puzzled.

'Good morning, soldier. Anything I can do for you?'

'Imperial cadet Kyril Mikhailoivic Dvornikov, sir. At your orders.'

'My orders? I don't have any. Sorry, my Russian is still not that great. Do you speak French?'

'I do, sir. But not very well.'

'I hope it will be enough to tell me why you're here.'

The boy takes a wallet out of his pocket and hands it over with an outstretched arm.

'Your wallet, Maestro. I believe you misplaced it some days ago.'

Shocked, Carlo grabs the wallet and lays it on the hallway's marble console.

'Thank you. How?…'

'It has all the money in it, sir. Nothing was taken.'

'It has? What… what happened to the boy who stole it?'

'I'm not privy to any such information, sir.'

'No, I'm sure you're not. Thank you, young man. Have a good day.'

He makes to turn and walk back to the garden, but the cadet isn't moving, his hat still under his arm. Carlo turns around again, wondering what else is afoot now. Believing he has understood the message, he grabs the wallet and pulls some notes out with the intention of offering them to the soldier.

'No, sir. There is no charge.'

'Very well. Have a good day then.'

'Sir. With your permission, my superiors have suggested that you would be more than happy to have some company.'

He feels his limbs shaking in disbelief.

'Excuse me? I'm not sure I understand what you mean by that and what it might have to do with you?'

He notices for the first time how strikingly handsome the boy is. A heart-stopping Slavic beauty. The eyes are a crystalline blue, the lips perfectly defined and lusciously crimson, the complexion as white as the sandy beaches of Crimea. The aura of innocence - false or otherwise - is endearing. He's been very carefully picked.

He struggles to contain all the emotions storming through his mind and heart. Anger, disgust, shame. The inspector meant what he said. He will not lose his job for failing to protect Maestro Mandelli di Castagnino from another feral hustler. The illustrious guest will be safer with a loyal and obedient cadet. Never mind that he appears to be twelve years of age. Never mind that he has probably never been in bed with a man. Never mind that he has probably never had his purity ravished. Never mind all that. He's just obeying orders. He feels the need to throw up but he gathers the words.

'Kyril, do you have any idea of what your superior officers, or the Okhrana - I'm not sure which - have asked you to do? You're a child. What makes these monsters think that I…' He covers his eyes with his hand, on the verge of angry tears. 'Dear God, what kind of fresh hell is this place? Have you actually ever done anything like this before? Are you even? I mean… Are you even what I am?'

Kyril, still standing at attention, now stares at the elaborate Persian rug covering the wooden floor.

'Orders are orders, sir. I am sixteen. Old enough. A gentleman of your standing shouldn't have to lower himself to the level of a certain kind of people.'

'You mean like the boy who robbed me? He's probably dead, isn't he?'

'Sir.'

He sits on the armchair by the console, dropping his head in his hands.

'Please, leave at once.'

'Sir. I can't report to my superiors an unsuccessful mission.'

'A mission? Is this what it is? A mission?'

He stands up, a special kind of fury in his soul.

'Then tell them that I dragged you up to my bedroom and ripped your uniform off. Tell them that you gagged on my huge manhood until I forced you to ingest the successful outcome of your skilled tongue and how loud your wailing was when I turned you around and, oblivious to any pain you might have incurred, I violently ravished you until blood was oozing from your backside. Is that want they want to hear? Is that it? Would you care for anymore details?'

He's shouting, the boy now terrified. Did he actually understand what they were asking him to do, Carlo wonders.

'Maybe it doesn't sound so good now, does it? Your "company".'

The cadet is stunned, his voice now unsure. As it would be after the vivid picture painted by Carlo. He gulps. Perhaps all those horrific scenes are parading across his eyes.

'Sir. I have to obey the orders. I will do what you ask.'

'And you really believe I would do those things to you? You really do?'

Mandelli sits back, his elbow on the console, his hand on his half-closed eyes.

'Very well. I don't want you to get into trouble. I will report to the inspector that I was immensely pleased with your company and that your "mission" was accomplished. Have no fear. Now, do me a favour. Just go.'

The young man leaves in relief. Carlo staggers into the study and collapses by the grand piano, now sobbing loudly. Sixteen: that is what they think he's after. And forcing a boy who might not even belong to the same tribe, but he has to obey their villainous orders. He feels sick to his stomach. He keeps crying. Perhaps it has all been a huge mistake. No shore of any part of this world seems to be any different when it comes to people like him. He bangs his forehead against the piano several times, hugging its leg, wanting to expire. He thought he had by now witnessed the lowest circle of the Dantesque Inferno a life on the wrong side of humanity can become. But he had seen nothing. There is always something worse.

VII. Doctor Artyom

Oleg was right. After a pleasant and hushed autumn, illuminated by misty mornings leading to cool but sunny days, the harbinger of November brings the first heavy snowfall of the year. The falling leaves have all but gone, replaced by a thick layer of powdery snow. Once it gets swept up by a small army of ragged recruits, the edges of the wide boulevards turn into a black and brown mess of semi-hardened blocks of ice.

The fireplaces in the villa are stoked day and night, the embers joyously flickering when Carlo sits at the piano, endlessly working on his symphony. Every afternoon Fyodor wheels in a trolley with a samovar and tea and pastries are served promptly at five o'clock: 'Like the English, sir', Fyodor is fond of remarking.

Fyodor reminds him of Amilcare. He is another perfect butler: reserved and discreet. His gaze is bereft of any judgement of what he might have witnessed or not. Mandelli is quite sure that he heard him shouting at young Kyril and all the colourful descriptions in the process. After that fraught encounter, Fyodor had not reappeared until he could be reasonably certain that the Maestro would be in a proper state of mind to see anyone, even his own servants.

His velvet smoking jacket keeps him warm and comfortable during the long afternoons at the piano. He still enjoys the long walks to the opera house, armed with thick leather boots, woolly scarves, gloves and the inevitable furry hat.

With the excuse of wanting to discuss business with Vassily, he often invites him over for tea, knowing very well how much he appreciates the lemon drizzle cakes, which he now eats in a less ravenous fashion.

A few days earlier Mandelli had overheard the director general berating Vassily for things which, in his judgement, hadn't been done or some other made-up issues. He has by now figured out how things work here. To all intents and purposes, Vassily practically runs the venue all by himself: delegating, issuing directives, looking after the artists, sitting at the typewriter preparing documents. The boy works tirelessly for most of the day, only to be regularly reprimanded by some big shot or another in between their lunches and dinners at the best restaurants in town.

But this time Carlo had stormed between them and in his now rather acceptable Russian he had firmly put the director general in his place, ordering him to stop harassing Vassily, while praising how hard the young man was working for the benefit of them all. Vassily, who as an infant had deference for authority mixed in his milk, had stood with his mouth open. Mandelli, who by now had been declared the saviour of the theatre, with even the *New York Times* praising his success in firmly placing the Odessa Opera House on the world map, had had no qualms in using his status as a leverage: 'And, Director, what would happen to your theatre if I decided to return to Milan? I might even take Vassily with me, who knows.' The director had retreated in a sheepish way, full of the praises and excuses craven men deploy when confronted by intelligence and integrity. Charlatans and sycophants are afraid of men. Because men is what they will never be.

He had read the article in the *New York Times* from a cutting sent by his father. He has kept up the correspondence with him, his mother and all the other members of the family. The letters from Ernestina are becoming less frequent and more vague in content, though. He often wonders about the reasons but he has concluded that his mad little sister is always too preoccupied with being the undisputed *salon* princess of Weimar to have enough time to write long letters to her equally crazy brother who has decamped to this eccentric outpost on a faraway sea.

His comfortable life at the villa, the good food and vintage wines in the plush and fully heated cafés and restaurants make him feel guilty though. He cannot erase from his mind that evening at Oleg's house, a charitable way of describing the young man's abode.

And he now knows that Vassily lives in the same neighbourhood too. Every time he's welcomed home by doting servants, who, he suspects, are very grateful to spend their day in the warmth of the villa's rooms, he can't help thinking about the Suvorovsky district. Of course he never returned after his summer excursion, and he shivers at the thought of how life must be in this nose-bleedingly fierce frost.

The Christmas lights do not appear until the middle of December. The city transforms itself into a magical fairytale: cacophonous families with well-dressed children roam the elegant avenues, admiring the flickering bulbs adorning the elms and the birch trees.

The theatre is also all festooned with Christmas displays and a giant tree displaces every other ornament in the foyer.

Unaware of Eastern European traditions, he proposes some works by Rossini for the New Year's Eve performance in a general meeting with the orchestra and the board members. The room falls into an embarrassed silence, everyone afraid of offending the Maestro by explaining that his proposal would probably cause a street riot.

Puzzled and worried about having said something very offensive, he turns to poor old Vassily, who's wiping his forehead with the usual handkerchief.

'Vassily, what's wrong with Rossini? What have I said? It looks like I've thrown a hand grenade in the room.'

Vassily whispers in his ear, using his hand as a screen.

'East of Vienna, sir, it's *Die Fledermaus*. Always *Die Fledermaus* for New Year's Eve. With several performances in January too. Sorry, Maestro, it's a long-standing tradition. The public will take offence.'

Carlo smiles and nods to show he has understood the sensitivity behind the issue. He turns back to the gentlemen assembled around the oversized round table and pretends to shuffle the papers in front of him.

'On the other hand, gentlemen, my ever-valuable assistant Vassily has suggested a splendid idea for the very special evening. What about an operetta? I think we should perform *Die Fledermaus*. What is your thought on that?'

A thundering sigh of relief emerges from the room, heads nod in approval, some of the board members get up and shake Mandelli's hand, Vassily once again relieved at having avoided hard labour.

The New Year's Eve performance is a triumph and so is the following morning's New Year Concert. He organises a merry lunch for the orchestra and the singers at the Dniepr Aurora, making sure Vassily does not invite the directors or any prince or duke. Before the boy has the chance to disagree with such a slight, he shuts him up by grabbing his handkerchief and throwing it away.

'No, Vassily. No one is going to deport you to Siberia.'

Christmas is spent with Vassily and Paulina who could not believe that a count would invite them for such an occasion. He also provides Fyodor with a generous allowance for the servants' supper, which is more than enough to include their close families.

Over a happy Christmas lunch at the villa, Vassily can't help remarking that Mandelli's servants probably wish that he will never return to his native land: 'Maestro, no one treats their servants and secretaries like this in Russia. You must understand, serfdom was only abolished on paper here.'

January brings more severe cold and more ice. The fallen snow now glitters in the crisp morning sun during his now rather perilous strolls to the opera house.

Sledges have mostly replaced motorcars and an ever-worried Vassily arranges for one to be driven by the ever-silent and diligent driver. But he never really travels very far to justify the use of any sort of vehicle.

At the end of Chaikovskhoho Lane, where he needs to veer left to reach the artists' entrance, the pavement gently turns into a fairly mild slope. He has never taken any notice of the change of gradient, and neither does so today, despite the cobbles being entirely covered by a gleaming slate of black ice.

It all happens very fast. His left foot slips first and the right one has no grip to help him remain standing. He starts rolling on his back, losing his stick, hat and briefcase over the brief journey to the next lamppost. His already painful left foot hits the frozen metal base and gives way, causing Carlo to scream in pain. He's finally at the end of the slide and he crouches, holding his ankle while squeezing his eyes.

Passers-by are quick on the scene to help. Although he has also hit the lamppost with his head, the left foot seems to be in worse pain, and despite not having any medical training, he guesses it would be wise not to move or walk.

He manages to explain that he works at the opera, though one or two helpers have already recognised him. He dispatches one of them to call for Vassily, who appears on the scene of the accident almost immediately, believing that the Maestro is about to die.

'Vassily, I am really all right. I need a taxi or a sledge to take me to a doctor. I think it's the ankle.'

'But what about a hospital? I'll call an ambulance.'

'No, Vassily, it's really not necessary. A doctor would do.'

One of the helpers, a well-dressed lady almost drowning in a bush of white fur, comes forward.

'May I suggest the surgery of Doctor Kaminsky? He's my physician, one of the best in the city. His studio is just around the block. If two strong men help the Maestro, he could make it there on one leg. Don't touch the floor with your left foot, Maestro, it's awfully swollen.'

Nods of approval from the crowd are followed by two well-built sailors who had interrupted their stroll down to the docks at hearing the commotion, offering to carry Mandelli to the surgery.

They could easily carry him in their arms as they are almost double his size. Once he's carefully deposited on the sofa of the waiting room, Vassily starts a heated conversation with what appears to be a nurse or an assistant, Mandelli is not quite sure.

'What do you mean, "*the Maestro will have to wait*"? Maestro Mandelli di Castagnino is the chief conductor at the opera. He can't wait, and…'

While clutching his ankle in pain, Carlo tries to intervene.

'Vassily, it really isn't that urgent. I will wait. Leave the lady alone, please.'

'But…'

The lady politely smiles to Mandelli, appreciating the calm and understanding reply. She elects to ignore the panicky Vassily.

'I will see what I can do, Maestro. In the meantime, I

will bring a bag of ice for your ankle. Please, gently raise your leg and lower your sock. I am sure Doctor Kaminsky will find the time to see you shortly.'

She turns to a crimson-faced Vassily.

'There is no need for such unbecoming fretting and shouting.'

After bringing over the bag of ice and offering some very welcome tea, she announces that the doctor will see the Maestro in ten to fifteen minutes. She turns to Vassily again with her hands clasped in front of her in an authoritative fashion: 'All it took was to ask some patients to wait a bit longer. Politely.'

The chastened assistant retreats on the sofa. He sits down sheepishly with his arms crossed, muttering his disapproval.

'The Maestro shouldn't have to wait…'

While waiting, and despite the pain, Carlo can't help but admire the fine decor of the room. Besides being clean and tidy, it features some well-executed paintings hung on papered walls. A small fireplace keeps the temperature at a very pleasant level. Some of the patients peruse French magazines neatly laid out on the coffee table, itself an exquisite antique piece. To his surprise none of the gentlemen smoke, a very rare occurrence at this time and place. Perhaps Doctor Kaminsky has forbidden the activity. A daring decree indeed, Carlo reckons.

The high windows are framed by long silk curtains. They are tied up at the sides, allowing the patients a good view of the street. Carlo notices that it has started to snow again.

While he is falling into daydreams, trying not to think of the pain, the same lady opens the double doors and announces that Doctor Kaminsky is ready to see the Maestro.

He leans on Vassily's shoulder and once in the studio, he tells him to wait for him in the sitting room.

The doctor helps him climb on to the examination bed. Then he offers his hand for a shake.

'Honoured to make your acquaintance, Maestro Mandelli. My name is Artyom Nikolaevich Kaminsky. I understand you had a fall on one of our ever-treacherous pavements.'

'Pleased to meet you, Doctor Kaminsky. Yes. I wasn't paying much attention and my foot hit a lamp-post. I hope it's not broken.'

'We will have a look. I doubt it. You would be in excruciating pain.You seem to be holding up well.'

He helps Carlo to lie on the bed and gently removes his shoe and sock, revealing a swollen ankle. He touches a few spots before lifting his leg up and performing several other checks.

'Did you hit your head too?'

'Yes, but it feels all right.'

'Nevertheless, let me check your eyes with my torch.'

He performs the check and after walking to the basin in the corner to wash his hands he approaches the bed again.

'As I suspected, your ankle is only sprained. They have a Roëntgen machine at the main hospital but I don't think it will be necessary. You'll have to rest for a few days with your leg up and lots of ice. It will gradually return to normal. No harm done. How will you get home?'

'I'm sure my loyal assistant Vassily is organising some kind of imperial escort for my journey.'

The reply elicits a benign little laugh from the doctor.

'Ah, yes. My sister mentioned a very pushy young man demanding to jump the queue. She is very strong on rules and propriety, I'm afraid. Your assistant was never bound to get very far with undue insistence.'

'I must apologise on his behalf. He means well and he's indefatigable. He holds me in a rather excessive esteem. He would do anything for me. Forgive him. He's a good egg.'

'Oh, I thought as much. Do not worry. I do get berated by my sister too for not acting my age sometimes. She's younger than me but much more level-headed.'

A sudden pause in the conversation follows, and an unexpected and deeper exchange of gazes happens. Their eyes vaguely search for some inexplicable clues. Carlo feels a slight pang. Doctor Kaminsky's deportment appears uncertain, as if trying to find the right words to continue the exchange. But, strangely, the atmosphere is full of elation. What for, neither man seems to know.

He takes advantage of the pause to look at the doctor: a thin, wiry gentleman possibly nearing or just over fifty years of age. The eyes are a splendid deep blue, a pair of very Slavic diamonds. The complexion is smooth and pale. The fastidiously trimmed blond beard and moustache appear very clean and soft. The smile is always genuine and engaging. Reassuring. When his soft hands were examining his foot and leg Carlo felt an unexpected shiver in his body, despite the non-sexual nature of the touching.

Doctor Kaminsky politely asks him to remove his shirt to listen to his lungs and heart: 'I always perform a routine check on all my patients. You would be amazed at the ailments I find this way. But you look in good health, and I am sure all will be fine.'

The shivers come back when the physician lays the stethoscope on his chest and his back. The tips of his fingers inadvertently touch Carlo's left nipple when listening to his heart.

More exchanges of intense gazing ensue before Doctor Kaminsky instructs Mandelli to button up his shirt.

'I will check up on you tomorrow afternoon. You

have hit your head and I want to make sure that nothing else changes during your recovery.'

'I will be honoured by your visit, Doctor. I can attempt some small conversation in Russian now.'

'Very impressed. But I don't want to try your strength too much, Maestro. I look forward to seeing you again tomorrow.'

They shake hands, Carlo once more elated by the soft and gentle grip.

As expected the sledge is waiting outside, partially covered by the now heavy snowfall. Wrapped in his coat, scarf and coat, Carlo slumps into the fur-lined seats with Vassily at his side furiously trying to arrange the blankets to cover Mandelli.

Before setting off he raises his head towards the large windows on the left-hand side of the big wooden entrance door, without realising that those are the rooms where the studio is located. It's still early afternoon, but daylight is already fading, and the floor lamp by the window is already switched on.

He sees him by the ledge: his hands behind his back, that confident and reassuring deportment, the stunning handsomeness of his face blurred by the reflection in the windowpanes.

And their eyes clock once more, almost without wanting to, as if led by an unexpectedly unleashed force of nature. Their reserve makes them want to avert the embarrassing stare but they seem transfixed and are unable to.

Once home Vassily reassures the Maestro that he will speak to the director general and that he will be able to skip a few performances. Maestro Dimitri Alexandrovich Solokov will stand in, probably causing a riot and the burning down of the theatre by an angry mob - Russians do love a good fire - before the inevitable demands for refunds even start hitting the box office.

'That bad?' Mandelli enquires with a restrained guffaw.

'Worse,' replies an already panicking Vassily.

He bids goodbye to his loyal assistant with the instruction to Fyodor to supply the long-suffering lad with some extra lemon drizzle cake for his tea.

Two thoughts disturb his sleep that night. The painful ankle and the pervading intensity of those blue diamonds during the slow departure of his sledge. They seemed to beg him not to leave. To stay. Forever.

Every single moment in Doctor Kaminsky's surgery is re-enacted in his heart and mind, making his head turn left and right in sudden spasms.

After breakfast he finds himself counting the hours to the appointment with the doctor. After lunch he's down to the minutes. When the bell rings, he lifts himself up in bed and adjusts his nightshirt to make himself presentable, though he immediately chastises himself for believing in what is obviously a misunderstood dream. The handsome doctor is clearly only interested in his wellbeing, as doctors are. He just happened to take a break from the daily routine and look out of the window. His soft fingers - how soft they were - landed on his tiny, defined and turgid nipple by mistake. He is a doctor and he must have known that its firmness was due to the frozen temperature outside and not brought about by his casual though sensual touch.

He promises himself to not let anything slip out. This is a huge mistake, he thinks, and if he dares even a little flirt, Artyom will report him to the Okhrana and the oleaginous inspector will be back for another tiresome berating.

Artyom? Has he just thought about him by his first name? Has he? That cannot be. He reminds himself to be more respectful when he arrives to examine him again. Those soft yet manly hands are going to touch him again. Those hands. The same ones he now imagines slowly caressing his cheeks. Before kissing him.

'Good afternoon, Maestro?'

'What? Ah, yes, good afternoon, Doctor. So pleased to see you.'

'I think I've caught you in a spot of daydreaming, haven't I? Anything pleasant? I hope so.'

'Very pleasant. But, how are you? So pleased to see you, Doctor.'

'Yes, you said that. Have you been repeating yourself with the servants over the past few hours? Remember, you hit your head.'

'No, no. I feel really good. The ankle is still a bit painful though.'

'It will take time, let me have a look.'

And those soft hands gently encircle his foot, checking the toes, then moving over to his shin. The shivers in Carlo's body are back in force.

'All good. As I said, it will take time.'

Fyodor walks in with his trolley, the samovar and a freshly baked lemon drizzle cake.

'Oh, that is very gracious of you, Maestro.'

'I don't want to keep you for too long, doctor. You must have some other patients waiting for you.'

'It's late afternoon. I cleared my diary.'

Another long pause while Fyodor pours the tea and arranges the cakes. The same intense gazing. The same unsure pleasure from the stares until their eyes finally avoid each other.

'I didn't have the time to inform you that I am a great admirer of your work, Maestro. I have attended some of your performances. You have transformed the city's house.'

'Most kind. I've done my best. They are great musicians but they were not appreciated by my predecessor. I fear they were mistreated too. I love working with them.'

Doctor Kaminsky pulls out a piano score from his leather briefcase.

'I am a little embarrassed to ask you this. My sister and I are trying to encourage my young nephew Sergey to be more dedicated to his piano lessons. The lad is rather unenthusiastic, though admittedly he's only just turned eleven. Perhaps a little note on one of his scores with your name and signature will revive his passion.'

'With pleasure. Are you sure that he actually likes playing the piano? He might prefer another instrument.'

'Yes, we have thought about that too. It just happened that we had a piano in the sitting room and I thought he might take to it.'

Carlo grabs a pen on the side table and opens the score on the first page.

'To young Sergey then?'

'Seryozha. That is the diminutive for Sergey here.'

'I'll try it in Russian. Ask him to forgive the grammar and spelling mistakes.'

While Mandelli scribbles on the score, Doctor Kaminsky distractedly peruses the room, possibly to avoid staring too intensely at his handsome Italian patient.

'Maestro, forgive my forthrightness. I wonder if you would accept an invitation to dinner at our house when you are recovered? My sister will be immensely pleased to make your acquaintance in a less formal situation. I swear she will not make you wait in the reception room. And young Seryozha is a well-behaved, sensitive young man, though not on the talkative side. To put it mildly. I have taken both of them to a couple of your performances and they seemed to enjoy them a great deal.'

'I am honoured and I accept the invitation with great pleasure, Doctor Kaminsky.'

After a little more small talk, the doctor stands up,

ready to leave. Or not. Once on his feet and about to shake Carlo's hand, he suddenly realises how much he's enjoying his company: the sunny smile, the humble self-deprecation about his talent, the sudden yet gentle stares.

Their handshakes seem to be lasting longer than propriety would warrant. This time, while holding Carlo's hand in his, Doctor Kaminsky wraps it with his left one. The softness and warmth cause Mandelli to startle.

When alone again he slumps back onto the fluffy pillow, his eyes transfixed on the windowpane, the snow still falling, his heart pumping so fast he fears an imminent explosion.

In less than two weeks he's back on his feet. He's still limping, but the driver diligently ferries him between the villa and the opera house, Vassily relieved to have the Maestro back on the podium.

'See, Vassily, Solokov wasn't that bad, was he?'

'Depends who you ask, Maestro. Grand Duke Mikhailovich invited his mistress to the matinée of Onegin and thereafter he threatened to have me executed if I didn't bring you back in time for his next attendance. And his next mistress.'

'But he can't do that. And it's not your fault, anyway.'

'That didn't stop Prince Ivanovich's aide-de-camp holding me by the throat when his master learnt that you were not on the podium. He said he was going to strangle me if I didn't bring you back.'

'Oh, Vassily, I'm ever so sorry. These people must be mad. They must start to show some respect for you.'

A resigned snort.

'There's no chance of that happening, sir.'

On the evening of the invitation the snow has almost completely melted. The streets are clear and Mandelli proceeds at a leisurely pace towards Doctor Kaminsky's house.

His sister opens the imposing wooden door and greets him in imperfect French but with affable and polite manners. Once in the hallway she takes his coat, gloves and hat before showing him into a tastefully decorated drawing room, warmed by a flickering glow in the fireplace.

Another long handshake ensues before he is being introduced to young Seryozha, who has entered the room holding his mother's hand. He bows without uttering a single word. His mother ushers him out of the room before coming back with two glasses of Russian champagne. Without any malice he can't help noticing that there are no servants, the liquid in his glass isn't French and the doctor's sister is clearly doing the cooking as she disappears in earnest after having served the drinks.

'Forgive my nephew. He's very respectful and well-brought up. But he doesn't talk.'

Carlo nods.

'Not that he can't. He doesn't want to. Not to people. In the garden he converses with birds. They land and perch on his hand for longer than they would with any other human being. And then he talks to them. Sometimes I hear what he's saying.'

They both take a sip.

'You're probably wondering where my brother-in-law is, Maestro.'

'I don't want to intrude, Doctor.'

'Of course not. You're a real gentleman. And I won't bore you with a rather unpleasant story. That would be bad manners. Let's say that he isn't a good man. My sister had to marry him as she found herself expecting Seryozha. But a marriage rarely changes a bad man into a good one. It just makes his wife suffer. I make sure he's well kept away from the boy.'

‘Sorry to hear this, doctor.’

‘I took them in and it has been a genuine pleasure to look after both of them. I have no family to speak of, you see. I love them dearly and I will protect them to the end of the earth if necessary. Despite his silence, my nephew is a bright boy and doing well at school. My sister is of great help with the practice and the day-to-day running of the house. She insists on not allowing me to hire servants. I had to put my foot down to have at least a cleaner coming every day. But I am boring you now. No more of that.’

‘On the contrary, Doctor. I am also interested in other people’s stories. One learns so much.’

After few more exchanges and a little refill of Russian champagne, they are called into the dining room by Yelena. Before exiting the drawing room Doctor Kaminsky turns to Carlo, their faces close.

‘I wonder if you would like to call me by my first name. Of course I would never dream of offending you by reciprocating, given your lineage.’

‘I would be most pleased if you did exactly that. I have very little time for my inherited title. Actually, no time at all. I find it an encumbrance.’

The eyes are twinkling, perhaps with some mysterious expectation. Doctor Kaminsky points at the door leading to the dining room with his right hand.

‘Welcome to my home, then… Carlo.’

‘I am immensely honoured… Artyom.’

Over a pleasant and friendly dinner he starts to understand more about his host and his unusual family arrangements. They clearly lead a comfortable existence without the excesses of the aristocracy. The fare is of reasonably good quality, and Artyom’s sister proves articulate and charming. Seryozha is, of course, silent for the whole evening. But he nods affirmatively or negatively every time is asked a question. From time to time Carlo catches him shuttling his gaze between him and his uncle, perhaps wondering why this stranger has been invited for dinner. Without us noticing, children watch. Then listen. And in the end they understand. They won't tell you. But they do.

With young Sergey safely in bed and Yelena toiling in the kitchen, Artyom invites his guest back to the drawing room for a nightcap. Carlo catches himself pensively staring at the back garden while sipping his neat vodka.

'I'm glad to see that you're surrounded by loving relatives. At times I do miss not having a family around me.'

'But you told me about your sister and your uncle. They sound like lovely people. And you still have your mother and father. I appreciate the circumstances you have relayed to me are not ideal, but still…'

'Yes, of course. But it's not quite the same.'

'Indeed. Perhaps there are situations in which a traditional family cannot happen?'

Carlo turns, and the stare is the most intense so far. It isn't a question. It's a probe.

'Perhaps.'

At around midnight they both feel ready to retire. Once his coat, hat and gloves have been brought over by Artyom's sister, she bids goodnight to both and closes the door behind her with slow care.

'I had the most pleasant of evenings, Artyom. I would like very much to reciprocate. Including your sister and your nephew, of course.'

'It has been a great pleasure to have you here, Carlo. And I accept your invitation with great enthusiasm.'

Once ready to shake hands they find themselves very close to each other, their faces only a few inches apart. They can smell a whiff of vodka on each other's breath.

The silence is full of doubts. The fear of making a mistake. The nagging worry in their heads that it's all a big misunderstanding. That they might not be what they think they are.

But one more look by Carlo seems to convince Artyom that he has correctly understood the message. His hand tenderly wraps around Carlo's neck and pulls his head forward until their lips meet with a light touch, their eyes shut.

Artyom almost immediately lets go of Carlo's neck and lowers his head in embarrassment.

'I am ever so sorry. I shouldn't have taken this kind of liberty. Forgive my mann…'

Carlo's arms are wrapped tight around his waist, the kiss now deep and passionate. The shivers through their bodies are now real and unprecedented. Artyom grabs Carlo's head with his hands, gently kissing his forehead.

'Dear God, I never thought I would meet anyone as handsome as you.'

'I can safely say the same about you, Artyom.'

'How sweet my name sounds on your lips. Lips I am about to kiss again and again.'

'I implore you to do that until we have no breath left.'

After a long kissing spell, Carlo drops his head and hides his face into Artyom's shoulder, almost weeping because of the strong emotion. Artyom hugs him tight, gently running his fingers through his hair, landing small kisses on it from time to time, refusing to break the embrace.

When they do, Artyom takes both Carlo's hands in his, the eyes sparkling with anticipation.

'It is late.'

'So it is.'

'And you haven't called your driver.'

'I have no intention of doing so.'

'Despite my age, Carlo, I have very little experience of… well… this.'

'Which will make it more heavenly. I know it will.'

'Am I being presumptuous by asking you to stay?'

'You don't have to ask.'

Confident that everyone has retired to their rooms, he leads him upstairs. When he opens the door of his bedroom, they start kissing again with a special passion neither of them has ever experienced. There is something different to it. And when they disappear under the covers, a wave of repressed emotions seems to overwhelm them. Because when one finds it, one knows it. It happens almost in an instant. And it's real. In the mind and in the flesh. In the blissful heaven.

'Hold me.' Carlo pleads. 'And never let go of me.'

He leaves by the back door. With Yelena busy preparing breakfast while opening up the surgery and Sergey already on his way to school, he's back in the street unnoticed and strolling home in a haze.

The following days go by in fretful expectation. He has never experienced such emotions. Anatole and the Blue Hammam were raw, almost feral experiences, dipped in exotic charm and under the tacit agreement that they would end with no consequences the moment the last drop of seed left the last man standing.

But this is very different. He can hardly think about anything else and during the afternoon rehearsal for the imminent opening of *Lohengrin*, he sees Artyom sailing in and jumping off the *papier-mâché* giant swan to come to his rescue. To love him beyond the never-ending Russian eternity.

He only awakes when the first violin coughs and mildly rises his voice to shake him out of his reverie.

'Maestro? Maestro?'

'Yes, Artyom?'

The old man frowns.

'Who's Artyom? I'm Solonov, sir. The first violin?'

'Yes, yes. Of course you are.'

Before heading to the dining room, Seryozha is instructed by his uncle to show his progress with a few sonatas by the greatest composer of all time, causing Carlo to choke on his champagne while thinking how to rescue the finely tuned instrument from the boy's angry fingers.

Yelena, a lady of a very matter-of-fact nature with a surreptitious intuition for awkward situations, asks her brother to accompany her for a stroll as she claims to be enchanted by the pristine white canvass another heavy snowfall has bestowed on the back garden.

As soon as they leave Seryozha stops playing and turns to Mandelli with a stony face. Perhaps inquisitive, perhaps upset by his own untalented performance. Carlo hasn't yet learnt how to read the boy's facial expressions. There never seems to be enough anger or happiness to make them self-explanatory.

'Has Meister Mozart done anything specific to you? You hardly made any mistakes but I fear Fyodor will have to collect some of the keys off the floor tomorrow morning.'

Sergey turns to the score in front of him but, as expected, not a word is uttered.

'Not everyone has to love music. It isn't compulsory, Sergey.'

The boy's face lowers and he stares at the recovering keys.

'I'll take a guess, young man. It isn't the music, is it?'

Seryozha shakes his head.

'It's the instrument, isn't it? Your uncle just happened to have a piano and you got lumbered with it. But you hate the thing. I can tell.'

Sergey nods. His affirmative nod is almost enthusiastic. He clearly never had the courage to inform his uncle of his deep hatred for the only instrument in the house and the nods come as a liberation.

Carlo smiles with some affection.

'I hope there is one you'd like to learn. I'm very pleased that it isn't the music.'

Seryozha nods and then lifts his hands in front of his mouth, flicking the lithe fingers in front of it.

'I see. The sound of the birds?'

The boy earnestly nods. His dear friends. Perhaps the only ones.

'I will look into it. Better call your mother and uncle back in, they must be freezing.'

He stands up and slowly walks in the direction of the garden. When he opens the French door he's stopped abruptly by Sergey's voice. Perhaps his imminent liberation from that instrument of torture has given him the strength.

'*Spassiba.*'

Carlo turns in shock. The voice is light and soft but firm. An incredibly pleasant, angelic sound.

'You're very welcome, young man.'

Before he can turn to exit into the garden he sees Sergey's face turning around. His tiny sapphire-like eyes are staring, with neither a boyish joy nor a pervasive angst in the gaze.

'Are you my uncle too now, sir?'

He freezes and he's at a loss as to how to reply. The Russian was very clearly enunciated, and he has understood every single word of it. In a very short moment he recalls how much he understood when he was Sergey's age. How much he guessed. Children know. When you're not allowed to talk you stay silent and observe even the most fleeting of looks, the most imperceptible of signs. And you see everything.

Carlo stares at the rug to find a proper answer, if there ever was one.

'I… I am a very good friend of your uncle, Seryozha.'

He bites his lips after having used the diminutive for the first time. It sounds overconfident, like demanding acceptance in the family.

Sergey nods and returns to the chair where he originally perched before being called up to the gallows. He slips his hands under his thighs and stares into a void, Mandelli unable to figure out what kind of reaction, if any, his reply has generated in the taciturn lad.

On the next dinner at the Kaminskys he presents Seryozha with a leather case and everyone is pleasantly surprised to see the boy smile, perhaps for the first time in his short life.

'After a conversation with your uncle, I've arranged the lessons too. One day you might end up in my orchestra! Who knows?'

He hasn't revealed Sergey's abrupt questioning to Artyom as he rightly believes that the boy is the type who resents his very few words being reported to others.

One morning, when he leaves the doctor's house after another night of heavenly bliss in Artyom's arms, he feels as if he is being sucked into a vortex of deep thoughts. He stops halfway down Rishelievska street and turns back. Then he stops again. No. He shouldn't do this. But then he turns back again and with brisk steps he reaches the front door of the house very quickly. He rings the bell and, to his surprise, Artyom answers the door.

'I saw you walking back in a hurry, Carlo. Is everything alrigh…'

'I love you. That is what I came back to say. That is all. Perhaps that is not right and proper. We are men.

Two men. And I know we shouldn't do what we do. I know I shouldn't lie in your arms while you kiss my hair. I know I shouldn't look at you the way I do. I know that maybe we are monsters. Well. So be it. I am a monster. But one who is in love with you. And I have never felt this way before. I have been in many places and things have happened. Of course they have. I don't want to lie to you. I can't. Because I love you so much that I could no longer walk back home without telling you.'

He stares away, merely to regain breath.

'And maybe I'm making an almighty fool of myself. But if don't, I know I will regret it for the rest of my life. You cannot kiss me here. We cannot kiss. Because we are monsters. And I'm not demanding an answer right now. It would be unfair. You're already in your gown, your stethoscope is around your neck and your first patient is waiting for you. I don't want you to answer me now. But I needed to do this, otherwise I would have exploded, right there in Rishelievska Street.

'Your surgery closes at five. I will be waiting for you at the Dniepr Aurora with two small glasses of vodka on the table. If you decide against the deranged madness I'm proposing, I will love you still. And I will understand you. The world detests us. But we can love each other. Who needs the world? Goodbye Artyom.'

When the clock on the wooden wall of the Dniepr Aurora strikes five, he turns to the window. Grabbing the edge of his jacket's sleeve he wipes the steamed up glass and sees a slim, tall gentleman standing on the pavement opposite. He's in a black coat, grey scarf and gloves, and he seems to gaze intensely at the windows of the Dniepr Aurora.

He sees him walking slowly and coming through the door. He hears the voice of one of the waiters directing the new guest to Carlo's table. He stands there, without taking his coat and gloves off. He purses his lips, the crystalline eyes twinkling, the striking handsomeness devastating. He hangs his hat on the coat hanger and slowly takes his gloves off. Then he shakes the last speckles of snowflakes on to the worn-out rug.

'Is this the table usually reserved for monsters?'

Carlo remains silent. His hand offers the seat in front of him to Artyom. He then lifts his small tumbler of vodka and stops mid-air. Even the other punters can hear the beats of his exploding heart. He lifts the glass even higher, inviting a toast.

Who needs the world?

Spring brings a fresh breeze from the Black Sea. Public and private gardens are in bloom, cafés *dehors* teem with young students raucously debating politics.

The new season also brings the news that Sergey's tutor has selected him for a solo flute performance for his students' summer concert at the boy's school. Artyom is over the moon.

'He practises in the garden. The birds perch on the flute sometimes. And on his shoulders. Then he asks them how he played the piece. The tutor says there is real talent there. He's happy, Carlo. I have never seen him so happy.'

He no longer needs to leave by the back door. Yelena has taken to him for making both her brother and her son visibly happier.

Sergey will never reveal anything that could place his newly formed family in danger. Every time Carlo visits the house he drags him to his room to listen to his progress with the flute, eager to take in every suggestion or correction.

An almost oppressive heat descends on the city at the start of July. The opera house shuts for the two hottest months of the year and Carlo is delighted to hear a proposal from the man he loves.

'We have a small dacha by the sea near the town of Lebedivka, a few miles south. Nothing luxurious. Yelena and I inherited it from our parents many years ago. We try to keep it in good repair though it isn't easy. It has two good size bedrooms though and Seryozha is more than happy to sleep on the couch in the hallway. Just as well as he's an early riser. He darts for the beach for an early morning chat with the seagulls. We will have time for ourselves too. There are some splendid coves and secluded beaches.'

'I would come even if it were a cave.'

'Well, you've been warned.'

The slow train gets the party to Lebedivka in time for dinner. However, it takes some time to open the house, Artyom complaining about newly discovered items which need repairing. Carlo loves it at first sight. It is quite remote, though Artyom has hired a phaeton for the duration of their stay to allow them to shop for groceries and other things they might need.

It is quite a large bungalow. Larger than Carlo imagined, in fact. Perhaps Artyom was trying to lower expectations. Over the past few months Doctor Kaminsky has learnt a lot about his lover's past and at times he finds his wealth intimidating. He's a respectable city doctor but neither a count nor a world-famous conductor. His finances are in good shape though far from the wealth of some of the Romanovs' acolytes. But he realises gradually how little Carlo cares for his fame and lineage.

When Artyom opens up their bedroom's shutters, a breathtaking view of the Black Sea leaves Carlo awed.

'I hope you like swimming. I know a few isolated spots where cumbersome bathing suits will not be needed.'

In the splendid isolation they embrace and kiss until

they are recalled by Yelena who has already set up the table and prepared dinner. Carlo pats Artyom on the chest.

'What would you do without your sister?'

'She has really taken to you, you know?'

Before heading for a day of solitary bliss they spend a couple of mornings playing with Seryozha on the beach-front. Not before his morning conversation with the local seagulls, of course.

After having tidied up the house and driven to Lebedivka to shop for groceries, Yelena enjoys a well-deserved rest, snatching a light nap on the armchair under the parasol set up on the sandy shore by the now three men in her life. A life that has long ceased to seek or plan for a fourth one. One drunken and violent husband was one too many.

In the afternoons, while Sergey and Yelena enjoy a siesta, Artyom reads novels and some new medical papers to keep up with all the discoveries in science.

The dacha has no piano but Carlo has brought his symphony along to continue all the progress he has made since meeting Artyom. The burst of new energy in his life has been enormously inspiring. He reckons he might be completing it soon.

'Am I an inspiration for this work, Carlo?'

'Only for the most beautiful passages.'

'You Italians. You just can't help it.'

On the third day they set off on the phaeton to a beach cove which Artyom discovered when holidaying here in his youth. After enjoying the uneven coastline during the fifty minutes' journey, he reveals to Carlo the most enchanting of spots: secluded, sheltered and solitary.

'No one ever comes here as it's a long journey. Also children like the sandy shores of the city. This is a bit rocky and the sea can be rough. But it's all ours. Just for us. We can be monsters here.'

Once the picnic is safely away under a recess in one of the rock formations and the long towels have been laid on a wind-swept sheet of basalt, Artyom kisses him on the forehead.

'Now for a swim, my beautiful man.'

They strip and dive into the deep and warm waters of the cove. After a few athletic strokes, Artyom leads him around the rocky bend where the water becomes shallow, allowing them to stand on their feet. Carlo feels the muscular, lean arms encircling his waist. Artyom's lips start to kiss his neck, his manhood seeks an opening between his cheeks. Then his lips move to his ear.

'I love you, Carlo. I loved you from the very first time you came into my practice with your sprained ankle. I could not believe such a Greek god had been dispatched by Zeus into my house.'

Carlo smiles.

'Now. Who's the hyperbolic Italian?'

'We Russians have hot blood too.'

His hands caress his nipples under water. His teeth now gently sink into the soft, tender skin of his neck. He positions his thumb between Carlo's lips before entering him with nervous, loving care. For him to bite. To ease a pain that doesn't exist. Their hands are everywhere, their lips soon run out of flesh to kiss and they start all over again: the armpits, the ears, the noses, the nipples. The shallow depth allows Artyom to be forceful, the thrusts pounding and tender at the same time. Until love leaves their manhoods, seeding the Black Sea and Carlo's trembling body.

When he turns around, seawater is dripping from both their foreheads, making their sealed kiss salty.

There are no words until they are well dried. Still as Mother Nature created them, they lie on the towels, blessed by an approving eastern sun. Spent by the thundering act of love, they briefly fall asleep hand in hand.

When they come around from their slumber they kiss again. Artyom holds Carlo's face in his soft hands, knowing he loves it to distraction. Then they lie back again, Artyom's forearms now behind his head.

'I have never been this happy. What generous god sent you to this forsaken corner of the earth? But I'm fearful too. Fearful of losing you.'

'Losing me?'

'You come from a faraway country. And the reasons why you came here are still a wonder to me. This backwater won't appeal to you forever. It only really appeals to locals.'

'You're wrong. I had doubts before I met you. Of course I had them. Who wouldn't? You can be a really maddening lot. The things I've seen. Poor Vassily. In Germany he would have been promoted to Director of the Imperial Opera by now. Here he's harassed and berated by drunken and corrupt aristocrats.'

'Yes. Your account of Vassily fits with the whole narrative here, I'm afraid. And that is why I'm fearful. That you will tire of all of this. And there are dangers coming our way.'

'There are?'

'The most loving trait of all your adorable ones is your detachment from politics. Your music is everything for you.'

'That is incorrect. You are.'

'Trouble is coming for Russia, Carlo. And you have no stake in what it might happen.'

'Perhaps. But I'm not completely blind. There is a kid in my orchestra. Oleg. He's a Bolshevik, or so he says. After a very dangerous stunt of his, he took me back to his house. Well, if one can call it that.'

'Where does he live?'

'Suvorovsky.'

'I see.'

Carlo sits up with his hands waving in righteous rage.

'How can the Tsar keep his people living like that? We do have our share of poverty, we are not saints. But what I saw was…was…'

'Depraved?'

'Yes.'

Artyom sits up too and hugs Carlo's waist.

'The Tsar and his fellow aristocrats have no awareness at all of what it's brewing under their feet. They believe their divine right to rule will last forever. Until, of course, it will not. Every Wednesday I do a round of the Suvorovsky district myself. For free, of course. What would I charge anyway? These wretched souls haven't got a kopeck to their names. I start at six and finish twelve hours later. I carry medications that I pay for. Not that they are anywhere near sufficient. Sometimes there is no illness to contend with. They are just hungry.'

'I skipped a ball given in my honour by the Tsar himself to go there.'

Artyom turns.

'You did what? Brave man!'

'Oleg took me there.'

'I'm worried all of this will come to a boil. And there will be war. I'm keeping a journal of Sergey's medical issues. They are of course mostly psychiatric; the lad is as fit and strong as an ox. But I don't want them to take him. Conscription starts at sixteen. Only four years to go.'

'They can't possibly enrol Seryozha. It would be madness. Who would do that?'

'We would. Soldiers are cannon fodder here, Carlo. Just meat.'

But that world is far away from here for the moment. They embrace and wrap the towels around their naked bodies, ready to love again.

Officially non-existent (they're monsters), their relationship grows more and more stable. The afternoons and evenings spent at Artyom's house are an endless source of love and merriment. Yelena and Seryozha's affection slowly wraps itself around Carlo more and more every day.

The first Christmas at the Kaminsky residence finds the household descending into frenzied excitement. Carlo insists on paying for a richly decorated Christmas tree and raids the shops of the city for presents.

Vassily and Paulina are invited and the merry group spends the afternoon playing games and over-indulging in cakes and hot chocolate with an increasingly smiling Sergey. From time to time, while seated around on the soft rug, Artyom fires long and intense looks at his wonderful lover.

In the early evening their games are suddenly interrupted by unidentified chattering coming from the boulevard. A few minutes later the buzzing noise intensifies and is followed up by some shouting. They also hear the sound of horseshoes on the paved thoroughfare. Carlo stands up.

'I wonder what that might be. I'll go and have a look.'

But Artyom forcefully grabs his arm to prevent him from walking to the door. He briefly stares at Vassily before speaking to him.

'No. Don't open the door. Stay on the floor.'

Then he turns to his sister.

'Yelena, take Seryozha and Paulina upstairs and close all the shutters. Vassily, draw the curtains and turn all the lights off. If anyone knocks at the door, do not answer. We're not at home.'

After the house is plunged into darkness, Artyom leads Carlo near the window and opens the thick velvet curtains by just about an inch.

A wall of men, women and children in dirty rags and carrying torches is marching down the boulevard. Some are singing, some have their left fists raised up into the air. The ones who appear to be the leaders shout what are perhaps orders. Carlo's face turns the opposite way and he sees the Tsarist troops on horseback deployed at the other end of the boulevard, swords drawn, their horses neighing restlessly. A dusting of snow has started to paint the paved road white. Vassily whispers to the others.

'Red bands on the arms, sir. Bolsheviks. This isn't good.'

Artyom draws the curtain close and turns to Vassily.

'You and Paulina will sleep here tonight. This is no night to be in the streets.'

'Thank you, Doctor Kaminsky.'

Carlo turns to his beloved with a shocked expression.

'I don't understand. It's Christmas Eve.'

'When there's no food on the table, Christmas Eve is a night like any other, Carlo.'

Mandelli grabs Vassily's arm while on their way to the bedrooms.

'Do you think Oleg might be out there?'

'I'd be surprised if he weren't, Maestro.'

'But he might get hurt.'

'That is how revolutions work, Maestro. Remember his words?'

Artyom shows the guest bedroom to the young couple and while walking to his bedroom he keeps staring at Carlo. A fearful stare. Mandelli stops and chides him.

'I won't leave you, Artyom. All the Bolsheviks and Tsarists in the world will not make me leave you.'

Kaminsky turns, hugs him tight and without further words opens the bedroom door. Who needs the world?

VIII. Livadia

The following months seem to revert to some sort of peace. Sporadic demonstrations are repressed with ever-increasing violence, but the city - at least its beautiful centre - appears to carry on as normal.

Carlo does notice a few changes, though. When the snow melts away in mid-March he informs Vassily that neither car or sledge will no longer be required as he will revert to enjoying his mid-morning and early evening walks to the house.

He's met by an uncharacteristically stern reprimand from the young man. The car will continue to ferry him between Villa Mandelli and the theatre. The tone of his voice is surprisingly one that demands compliance.

'The protests are increasing, sir. Please, do not walk alone. And not in white tie for the evening performances.'

In May the weather takes a turn for the better and a series of sunny days pushes Artyom to propose a short break of four or five days in Lebedivka.

Everyone is happy to leave Odessa and get away from the fraught political climate.

Once the train leaves Central Station, a middle-aged couple enter the first class compartment and take the two empty seats by the door opening onto the corridor. While Seryozha continues reading the book in his hands, Carlo notices their impromptu fellow passengers' ragged clothes, their unfriendly stares and, above all, the red armbands on their sleeves.

He exchanges looks with Artyom whose expression counsels calm and no reaction.

When the guard opens the door of the compartment,

Artyom shows him their tickets and reservations. Once he demands the same from the couple they both cross their arms on their chests and look at each other, wilfully ignoring the poor man who had noticed their armbands as soon as he had slid open the door.

He might be braver than Artyom and Carlo think.

'This is first class, sir. Your tickets and reservations?'

The two remain silent and do not change their challenging body language. Understandably all the guard wants is to reach Lebedivka alive and, given his low-paid position, he might even be a sympathiser. Although he wouldn't dream of showing his political leanings in the presence of well-attired and fare-paying travellers. He slides the door closed behind him and leaves without further challenging the pair.

Once in the phaeton on their way to the bungalow, Artyom sort of mentioned it first.

'From now on we should dress in a less conspicuous way. I'm not suggesting we shop for red armbands, of course.' He smiles to Carlo. 'Will you be able to give up your suits and shirts arriving directly from Paris, my dear Carlo?'

'Naturally. Anything for the cause.'

They laugh at the mildly dark humour. And yet the sudden danger slowly seeping daily into their lives, lives which had finally converged to unexpectedly create an unconventional yet so loving family, hangs heavily on their thoughts. It takes another sunny morning playing with a smiling and happy Seryozha on the sandy shore to lift their spirits.

A few days after their return, Mandelli arrives at the theatre for a rehearsal of *Macbeth* on a cloudy afternoon. He's met outside by a fretting Vassily, his world-famous handkerchief back in his hand, wiping his sweaty forehead.

'What's wrong, Vassily?'

'A letter from Livadia, sir. For you. It states your full title: *His Excellency, Carlo Alberto Mandelli, Count of Castagnino*.'

'Livadia? Who's writing from Livadia?'

'You had better look at the seal and the coat of arms, sir.'

Mandelli turns the envelope and notices the double head of the imperial eagle and a wax stamp hermetically sealing the envelope.

'Is it from?…'

Vassily nods while holding his forehead with the palm of his hand.

'Dear God, I hope we haven't offended anyone, sir. The other day Grand Duke Mikhailovic was back with a new mistress and…'

'Vassily, stop. We haven't done anything. And that prince of yours is clearly more interested in his selection of mistresses than me being on the podium or not. He probably draws the curtains of his box as the operas start. And heaven knows what happens behind them. Would you calm down?'

They're still standing on the pavement in front of the artists' entrance and they have to keep turning their heads to greet fellow musicians or workers walking in and out of the door.

Carlo leads Vassily to his dressing room and makes him sit in the armchair to calm him down while he grabs a letter-knife to open the envelope.

He starts reading it but it must be very short as he lifts his head almost immediately with a mild expression of surprise on his face.

'The imperial family is gathered at Livadia for their holidays. I am invited to join them for three days.'

Vassily's relief is brief, his paranoia returning almost immediately.

'What if the Tsar wants to complain about the house?

He might want to talk to you because you're the chief conductor and a count. He might want to shut down the theatre or… it might be me. Yes, I know it's me. I must have offended someone and…'

'Vassily, again, please stop. It's nothing of the kind. I didn't attend the ball in my honour and they want to meet me. That is all. Stop that brain of yours running away with crazy theories.'

In the evening he informs Artyom of the invitation over dinner. Seryozha's eyes widen at the mention of the Tsar and Yelena crosses herself. Carlo is not sure why. Artyom surprises him with a gentle smirk before fishing a folded paper from the inside pocket of his jacket.

'And this is the one I received.'

Carlo is stunned.

'The same invitation? Is it for the same days?'

'Even better. We have been booked on the same train. The same first class compartment and - such a coincidence - opposite seats. The efficiency! I wouldn't expect anything less from the Secretary of the Imperial Household.'

'I struggle to understand, how?…'

'No amount of precautions and discretion will beat the Okhrana, my dear fellow. They know everything, of course. We have been followed, possibly photographed. Do not worry. They won't use it against us. They must know that we're not Bolsheviks. They are most likely listening to our conversation right now, who knows. But we're not a threat. You're their peer and from a foreign country. And one that is constantly annoying the Austrian emperor with its demands for a chunk of his empire. That must be pleasing old Nicholas no end. And I'm a doctor. We are held in high esteem in this country. Perhaps because we all seem to become writers at some point. Bizarre, I know.'

Two different motorcars are dispatched to take them to the station the day of their departure. Artyom kisses Seryozha on the forehead and Yelena on the cheek before leaving. He tries to reassure her too.

'I know we shouldn't hope and it isn't morally right, but meeting His Majesty might come useful when they come for Seryozha. I won't allow them to take him, Yelena.'

This time there is no danger of menacing Bolshevik couples gatecrashing the compartment they are booked in. It must have been booked just for them as no one comes in at any stops along the way and two Cossacks armed to the back teeth are stationed at each end of the carriage. When they decide to decamp to the dining car, the soldiers follow them discreetly, repositioning themselves at the entrance of the restaurant. Artyom smiles while perusing the menu.

'They won't take any chances with their guests, I guess.'

'Who would want to harm us anyway?'

'Friends of the Tsar are the people's enemies, Carlo.'

'Friends? I don't even know the man!'

'Your shocking lack of deference is so amusing. But it's also normal. Everyone is deferential to you; why would you be awed by just another monarch? I daresay that for you they are probably all the same.'

Artyom starts a light commentary on the various places the train is travelling through. The old steamer chugs along at a snail's pace. At Kherson the wait for the service to Simferopol is rather lengthy, though they are ushered through the first class waiting room by a fawning railway attendant who's obviously been told where the two gentlemen are expected. Once on the second leg of the journey Carlo remarks how comfortable and luxurious the new train appears to be.

'The routes used by the imperial family and their entourage are well maintained and the rolling stock is of the highest quality. I suspect the St. Petersburg-Moscow line is also spotless. The rest of my vast country makes do with whatever is left.'

There is no connection waiting for them in Simferopol when they arrive in the early evening. Hotel rooms have however been booked for them and they enjoy a pleasant dinner in the best and possibly only restaurant of the small city. They also notice that the two shadowing Cossacks are replaced by a fresh pair who escort them discreetly everywhere they go.

'Is this really necessary, Artyom?'

'I'm not the Okhrana. They clearly think it is. There have been a few assassination attempts on minor noblemen and you are one. And invited by the Tsar in person. And from a foreign country, albeit a friendly one. A revolutionary coup and a diplomatic incident all in one. Attractive proposition for these Bolshevik youngsters, don't you think?'

He notices the worried expression of his naive beloved and smiles under his blond moustache.

'Do not worry. I doubt we are that important. Let's savour Simferopol's renowned cuisine. Now, that is definitely of some danger.'

On the final leg between Simferopol and Livadia they can finally enjoy the Crimean coastline and take in the splendid views, basking in the blinding morning sun filtering through the carriage windows. Some of the villas on the hilly shores are surrounded by cypresses, taking Carlo back to his childhood in Mandello del Lario. Artyom doesn't fail to notice his brooding.

'You never seem to mention your country, Carlo. Only a few Russians have the chance to ever visit it. But the reports never fail to mention how beautiful it all is. You must miss it.'

Carlo keeps staring out of the window.

'It doesn't have you in it. It never had. Someone like you doesn't exist there.'

'Nonsense. What about your family?'

'I love them. Of course I do. But no, I don't miss it. You are my family now. All of you.'

At their request the driver waiting on the station square reluctantly opens up the cover of the black Bugatti. Not before getting a wary nod of approval from the two Cossacks who board another motorcar parked behind. Carlo turns to the driver, determined to show off his improving Russian.

'I'd like very much to enjoy the sights.'

The man nods without replying, though once in the driving seat he opens the glove compartment, grabs a loaded revolver and lays it on the passenger seat. He then scans the surroundings before turning the engine on and driving away. Carlo and Artyom turn and stare at each other in worried wonder.

'A Bugatti Cabriolet? It must have cost a fortune.'

'We're going to see the Tsar, Carlo.'

'Well, he could spend some of the money on the Suvorovsky district.'

Artyom notices the sudden anger on Carlo's face.

'I would strongly suggest that you do not enter this kind of debate with His Majesty or any other member of the court. For them Suvorovsky doesn't even exist.'

'I know, I know. You don't have to worry. I left my red armband in Odessa.'

They laugh while the small motorcade hugs the winding road to the palace.

Once they are let through the gates, the car climbs on a short hairpin and the sight of the imperial palace reveals itself in all its grandeur. Its white walls shine with the reflection of the midday sun.

Carlo notices the immaculate gardens and the small army of men attending to them. Once in front of the main entrance, a butler and what appears to be the imperial secretary are waiting for them.

They are led to their separate and elegantly furnished bedrooms. In the long corridor they are addressed by the secretary after a light bow.

'His Imperial Majesty and his family are spending the afternoon at the beach. You will be able to enjoy a light lunch in the Orangerie. Afternoon tea is served on the terrace. Guests often comment on the rather splendid views. An intimate dinner is given in your honour in the ballroom tonight, Maestro. Cocktails at seven, sharp.'

After briefly feeling the firmness of the four-poster bed, he opens the French doors and walks out on the small balcony. After taking in the sight of the zephyr-blue sea he turns to his left and sees Artyom on the adjacent balcony. They both smile.

'If we were… Well, if we could marry, we could enjoy this extraordinarily romantic view together. On one balcony. Your arm around my waist. Holding me. Telling me that you love me.'

'I think we can consider ourselves lucky that we are not being murdered and thrown in a common grave like we have leprosy, Carlo. What you are saying is absurd. We are men. We cannot do any of those things. At least officially. But one thing is true: I do love you.'

At cocktail time they are finally - and of course separately - introduced to the Tsar who in turn introduces all of his family to them. The Princesses are giggling and fawning over Carlo, showing a knowledgeable appreciation of his talent. The Tsarina offers a cursory and slightly sulky nod before walking away in impolite haste.

A Tsar cannot possibly apologises for his wife's

rudeness but he smiles to Carlo nonetheless.

'Her Majesty has a natural aversion to social events. And she doesn't take to music either, I'm afraid. The Tsarevich is very much like her too.'

Carlo nods.

'He was nevertheless looking forward to meeting you, anyway. He wanted to ask you a lot of questions about your country. He likes your bicycles and motor-cars. We actually have a few right here at Livadia.'

'Yes, Doctor Kaminsky and I had the most pleasant of drives from the station in a Bugatti convertible.'

'I ordered it to be used to collect you, Maestro. To make you feel at home.'

'Thank you, Your Majesty. I do feel at home. I look forward to meeting the Tsarevich and telling him all about Italy.'

Mandelli is surprised to see the Tsar's face lowering and his eyes staring at the polished marble tiles of the sumptuous reception hall.

'He's not well tonight. Maybe another time.'

'I am so sorry to hear that, sir.'

'Let us join the others. I must warn you Maestro, a lot of the guests will be sinfully boring ministers and fellow noblemen. I suggest a conversation with their wives if you want to avoid falling asleep over dinner.' He then gently grabs Artyom's arm to lead him away from Carlo and the other guests.

'Doctor Kaminsky, would you be so kind to join me in my study tomorrow morning at ten? No need to tell anyone else. A very private meeting.'

An astonished Artyom can barely find the words.

'Of course, Your Majesty.'

'Please. Not a word to anyone.'

The "intimate" dinner is just shy of two hundred guests. And the Tsar was right: they all bore both of them to distraction. When just past midnight they retire to their bedrooms they are beaten by the rich fare, the wine, the vodka and the never-ending inane conversations. Carlo walks out on the balcony and holds the bannister with both hands, staring at the full moon and the gardens in bloom. Then he turns to the left.

'I knew you'd be there.'

Artyom smiles, hands in his pockets, staring at the moon's wake.

'Likewise.'

He approaches the left side of the balcony and stops to stare at Artyom's handsome profile.

'How close these balconies are. Only a few inches. I say one could easily jump over and barge into the adjacent room unexpectedly.'

Kaminsky doesn't turn around.

'The youngest and the fittest should do the jumping, I think. The night is still very warm. I think I will leave the door open.'

He walks back in. Carlo carefully scans the gardens for guards or other attendants walking by. When sure that the coast is clear he climbs on the bannister and lands safely on the adjacent balcony. He enters the room and finds Artyom lying on the bed, his shoes off, his white tie undone, his shirt opened to his navel. He jumps on him and, before kissing him, holds his face an inch away from him.

'I have never been so in love. You're everything I always wanted. You've always been the man I was looking for. I don't want this ever to end. It will not end. Swear it to me.'

'I wonder if the Okhrana is watching us from one of those spyholes they plant in fake paintings.'

Carlo turns around to look at the wall by the window.

'The gondola on that Canaletto looks rather hollow…'

A laugh from Artyom.

'Let us give them something worth watching then.'

He feels Artyom's soft hands encircling his head, stroking his hair, the kissing almost violent in the thundering passion. He will have to jump back on to his balcony before the butler arrives in the morning. No. They aren't married. They cannot be. But they are much, much more. Monsters in love.

He's ushered into the study and finds the Tsar signing some documents at his desk. He's taken aback by the friendly and informal welcoming. When the young guard leaves, he stands up, walks around the desk and greets him with a handshake.

'Doctor Kaminsky, please take a seat.'

'Your Majesty.'

'I'll come to the point quickly. A very busy morning ahead. I have reports which confirm your outstanding record as General Practitioner, your pro-bono services to the less privileged and, above all, your seriousness and… discretion.'

'I'm very honoured by such a compliment from His Majesty.'

'We have, of course, several physicians and surgeons in the Imperial Household, however, they tend to be afraid of relaying the truth to me or the Tsarina.'

'The truth?'

'Yes. About a specific diagnosis of a member of the household.'

'I see.'

'You do?'

'Rumours are difficult to stop, sir.'

'I'm aware of that. Would you care to examine the Tsarevich for me? In private. No one must know. I believe I can trust you.'

Kaminsky nods and the Tsar presses a button under his desk instead of using the bell cord by the long velvet curtains. A false door in the bookcase opens up and a sailor appears. He bows to the Tsar before standing at attention.

'Doctor Kaminsky, this is Master Dorovienko, the sailor in charge of Alexei. His main task is to make sure the Tsarevich doesn't do anything which could aggravate his condition. He will take you through to his bedroom. It is a good time for an examination. My son is in the middle of one of his recurrent bouts.' He turns his face and looks away with a sudden sadness. 'He's in terrible pain.'

'I am so sorry to hear that, Your Majesty.'

'I will wait for you here. Dorovienko will escort you through.'

When he returns to the study he finds the emperor in contemplation at the window. The midday rays now filter through the open balcony door.

'In this case the imperial physicians haven't lied to you, sir. It pains me to confirm that the Tsarevich has inherited haemophilia, for which there is no cure. The remedies for the pain prescribed by your doctors are the right ones but they won't cure your son. I must stress that there are doubts about the effectiveness of aspirin, though it won't have any adverse effects, anyway. I am truly sorry, Your Majesty.'

The Tsar nods.

'When will he die?'

'Cases vary a great deal but most boys pass away in their twenties. There are no records of patients living longer than that.'

The emperor turns.

'I appreciate your honesty. Not all my doctors were truthful. Some suggested the possibility of a long life. Albeit a painful one.'

Kaminsky stares at the Persian rug covering almost all of the study.

'No, Your Majesty. That is not going to happen. I have a nephew of the same age. He's not my son and not the heir to the throne. But I understand your and the Tsarina's tragedy. Suffering for the boy must be acute.'

'What is his name?'

'Sergey. Seryozha.'

'Give him the emperor's personal greeting.'

'He will be honoured, sir.'

'One more thing. The Tsarina seems to think that some spiritual people with mysterious healing powers will be able to cure or at least alleviate the boy's pain.'

'With all due respect to Her Majesty, there is no scientific evidence for such kind of therapy having any chance of success. I would not recommend raising hopes.'

'I thought as much. Doctor, is anything I can do for you? Please feel free to ask anything.'

Kaminsky hesitates, Seryozha suddenly jumping into his thoughts. He stares at the vast blue expanse of the Black Sea through the open door.

'Doctor?'

'Your invitation to join you in Livadia was such a great honour, I couldn't possibly demand any more favour from our Tsar, sir.'

'It was reported to me that you and Count Mandelli were real gentlemen.'

'Sir.'

Knowing that it is time to leave he walks backward to the door and turns the knob. He stalls and turns around. The Tsar is already walking back to his desk.

'Forgive me, Your Majesty. You seem to be in possession of a considerable amount of information about Count Mandelli and myself. Are we being watched because of our…friendship?'

The Tsar seems unfazed.

'No.'

'Any other reason?'

'My dear doctor, even the Tsar is not allowed to reveal the Okhrana's secrets. They would probably arrest me too.'

Taking advantage of Artyom's summons to the emperor, Carlo heads to the music room, a pleasantly decorated studio whose French doors offer a full view of the coastline. He spreads the pages of the score on the grand piano and works on them all morning, inspired by the beauty of the place and his love for Artyom.

At about midday a valet knocks at the door and enters with a message on a silver tray.

After a light lunch and a restorative nap he changes into an elegant cream-coloured afternoon suit and strolls along the long white stone terrace, still sizzling from the midday heat.

He reaches a round alcove in a shaded corner and finds a small table set up for afternoon tea.

He doffs his hat, bows and kisses the right hand of the elderly lady at the table. He's struck by the dignified yet welcoming and friendly pose. She gestures to the empty chair. While he takes his seat two valets are fast around him with napkins. They then stand at attention waiting for orders.

'Earl Grey, please. No milk. And just a small piece of lemon drizzle cake, if available.'

The valets leave after bowing to a smiling Empress Dowager.

'How very English, Maestro. We were informed of your impeccable manners. The Okhrana never fails. That is probably why we are all still alive. Well, after all, they have nothing else to do but follow unsuspecting gentlemen. And Bolsheviks. But you aren't one. We know that too.'

An approving smile by Carlo.

'Your Majesty.'

'You have no idea of how pleased we were on hearing of your invitation to Livadia. We nagged our son no end to send you one. When we mentioned that he could also invite your dear friend Doctor Kaminsky, he immediately called for his secretary. He was keen for another opinion on our grandson.'

'I was told the Tsarevich was not well. I hope he feels better today.'

The old Dowager stares pensively at her teacup.

'He doesn't. And he never will.'

Carlo wisely elects to stay silent.

'Maestro, we are very grateful that you have accepted our invitation to tea. The conversation at this court is on the side of catastrophic. We have attended some of your performances. What you have achieved with your musicians at the Odessa Opera is quite extraordinary. Heavenly. We were very much looking forward to meeting you in person.'

'Thank you for your kindness, ma'am.'

'Let us keep to French. I know you've learnt the local language, and so have I. Hardly a good reason to have any intelligent conversation in it, don't you think? And your own language. So musical to the ear. We Danish struggle to learn it but I am in awe when I listen to the singers in Italian operas.'

'French it is then.'

The tea and the lemon drizzle cake gently land on the table and both take a sip of their infusions. Mandelli cuts a small bite of the cake and cautiously tastes it.

'Dear Carlo, can I call you Carlo, Maestro? In return I will drop the ludicrous formality of *Plurales Majestatis*. My son becomes frightfully upset when I forget to use it in public. He turns apoplectic when I enquire with my personal maid about her family. The Russian aristocracy still believes the abolition of serfdom never happened.'

'Of course, Your Majesty.'

'Dear Carlo, I understand you have found a happy accommodation with your friend, Doctor Kaminsky? Another gentleman of unquestionable integrity, I am informed.'

Carlo reddens while taking a sip of the tea.

'Yes. We are… we are very good friends.'

A benevolent grin appears on the Dowager's lips.

'No need for embarrassment, my dear young man. I was born in Denmark. I was only sent here to marry the old Tsar. I knew my duty but my own country is about a century ahead of this medieval backwater. I haven't known love, no. That is never what royal marriages are about. But I can recognise it. I can see it. Doctor Kaminsky is a delightful gentleman but there is a reason why I have you invited you alone.'

Carlo nods, inviting the Empress to continue. Suddenly her gloved left hand gently grabs and holds his right one on the table. Her diamond ring sparkles under the blinding sun.

'Have you and Doctor Kaminsky considered leaving Russia?'

'Leaving Russia?'

'My dear Carlo, the Tsar might be my son but he's also an incompetent fool. And currently egged on by my daughter-in-law, a gullible and bitter lady of no intellectual standing whatsoever. It might sound harsh but that is the reality. They want a war. They are preparing for it and there will be one. And they will lose. All they have is naive young men and old rifles against the Reich's mechanised brigades.'

'I doubt Artyom will ever consider leaving Odessa, ma'am. And he has…we have a small family too.'

He feels her hand lightly squeezing his.

'I thought as much, but worth a try. The Danish ambassador has asked me to pass on a message from the

Copenhagen Opera. They will welcome you with open arms. And Doctor Kaminsky could practise too. I so hope you two gentlemen will think it over.'

'I promise Your Majesty that we will.'

'I am making preparations for departure myself. I cannot be sure which hurricane will hit us first: the Bolsheviks or the Kaiser. Possibly both at once. My son will be defeated and he will drag this unfortunate land down with him. Please, consider my proposal.'

'The kindness of Her Majesty greatly moves me. I promise I will talk to Doctor Kaminsky.'

The Empress nods and let go of Carlo's hand.

'Let's talk about your wonderful music now. More tea?'

They are silent on the way back to Simferopol, Kaminsky in deep thoughts about his meeting with the Tsar and his odd request for another opinion on Alexei's condition. Mandelli is equally reminiscing about his conversation with the Empress Dowager. An exchange full of foreboding, albeit a very pleasant one.

The arrival at Simferopol station is chaotic. They find themselves almost trapped in the carriage as a protest march seems to be taking place on the platforms.

From the window of their compartment they witness formations of Cossacks pushing the demonstrators back. The shouting is deafening, the angry chants from what appears to be Bolshevik agitators come across as threatening yet powerless.

Once the crowd is pushed back from the concourse they manage to find a porter and make their way to the same hotel as they used on their way to Livadia.

The hotel has now been fortified by a wall of sandbags. A few Cossacks behind them aim their rifles at the open space of the square through a narrow opening through the bags.

They're asked for their papers before the guard has

the time to notice the two soldiers escorting them back to Odessa. They elect to have dinner in the hotel restaurant. The concierge suggested it for its cuisine but also pointing out the safety aspect of it. The first words come from Mandelli.

'The general situation seems to be worsening.'

He merely receives an acknowledging nod for his comment.

The morning seems to be quieter, and once on the train to Kherson, they are able to relax a bit more. Asked about his meeting with the emperor, Artyom cannot help but slip in the only bit of information he's allowed to divulge.

'As I've always suspected, the Okhrana knows everything about us. But our "friendship" is not the reason why we are under their constant surveillance.'

'What then?'

'The Tsar didn't feel at liberty to tell me.'

After a long and awkward silence Carlo can't help displaying a certain annoyance.

'I'm not hiding anything from you. You know I'm not political and take very little interest in all of this. I mean Bolsheviks, Tsarists and all. If the Italians had wanted to send a spy, trust me, I would have been the last to be picked.'

'I do believe you. And I trust you. I just cannot figure out what it might be. In any case I'm not sure for how long we will be able to stay detached from all of this.'

He turns to check that the curtains of the compartment are still drawn before leaning forward and taking Artyom's hand in his.

'I'm not leaving Odessa without you. I never will, unless you decide to come with me. That is settled.'

'I have Yelena and Seryozha to think about and… and…'

He stares out of the window in what it seems to be a bout of impotent anger.

'Artyom?'

'I couldn't ask him. I thought it would be too demeaning. The Tsarevich is ill and he asked me to examine him. I can't say anymore. But asking for a military exemption for Seryozha would have been in bad taste.'

'He would have probably granted it. To thank you.'

'We'll have to think of something else.'

His inclusion in Artyom's unconventional family unit now seems complete. And he loves them dearly. Doctor Kaminsky's honesty and integrity prevent him from bypassing an already vastly corrupted system to save Sergey from a conscription which would probably kill him. No such compunction for Count Mandelli.

'I hail from the land of corruption. The Romans possibly invented the very thing. Seryozha will not serve.'

Artyom squeezes his hand, the hand of his extraordinary lover.

Back in Odessa they try to get back to what has now become their normal everyday routine. Carlo works hard on his symphony and spends blissfully quiet evenings at Artyom's house, checking upon Seryozha's progress with the flute, sometimes playing games with him on the large soft rug in the sitting room. This is something Sergey seems to greatly enjoy as he always leaves the dining table in a rush to retrieve game boxes and then nudging Carlo to follow him.

When they are alone the boy talks to him. He keeps this development from Artyom to avoid hurting his sensibilities. He's the real uncle but Sergey still keeps completely silent with him and his mother. With Carlo he cracks jokes, laughs and slips effortlessly into a trusting behaviour, unexpectedly leading Carlo into fatherly love.

He continues to have success after success at the opera house but a few chairs in the stalls now remain empty.

Some of the boxes have the curtains drawn for the whole performance and when he asks Vassily if anyone is sitting behind them, the young man disconsolately shakes his head.

'No, Maestro. A lot of the aristocracy have fled abroad. The merchants and the haute bourgeoisie are afraid of being seen in public. The price of bread is shooting up. We have had demonstrations outside the theatre. Times are changing.'

'I haven't seen any of this. Are you keeping it from me?'

Vassily's face turns its usual embarrassed crimson.

'We're afraid that you will leave.'

'I will do nothing of the kind. This is my home, Vassily.'

The visibly relieved young man regains his normal pale complexion.

'On another subject, Vassily, tell me: is by any chance the Head of the Odessa Military District an opera goer? This opera I mean.'

Vassily almost stands to attention, always eager to help Mandelli as much as he can.

'Grand Duke Alexandrovich, Supreme Commander of the Odessa District. He has a permanent box on the second row. He regularly attends your performances with his wife and young children. Occasionally with his aide-de-camp.'

'I see. Let me take a wild guess. Is this "aide-de-camp" young, charming and on the side of unbearably handsome?'

'He could be described in those terms, yes.'

'Clearly an opera lover? So enraptured by the music that he prefers to listen to it with the curtains drawn?'

'He's indicated to me that he would love to meet the greatest conductor in the world.'

'After Toscanini.'

He pats the young man's upper arm and winks at him, something which always makes Vassily very proud.

'I'll leave it to you'

Spring brings about an unexpected calm. There is hardly any unrest. The revolution might be inevitable but it turns out to be a slow-boiling frog, hindered by the constant squabbles between the Mensheviks, the Bolsheviks and the party of the Cadets. All of them under close surveillance by the Okhrana.

Artyom and Carlo's relationship slowly and gently gives way to a less carnal passion, helped by the loving presence and approval of Yelena and a blossoming Seryozha, who cherishes his brief and secret conversations with Carlo.

He overrules Artyom's protestations against his offer to help with the maintenance and refurbishment of the dacha in Lebedivka. It becomes a place of refuge and occasionally a love nest, due to Yelena deftly declining to join them because of some clearly invented chores which cannot be postponed.

They shop together for new furniture and linen. Carlo commissions a local handyman for a complete redecoration of the interior. He also finds a local musical instrument dealer, and an old and hilariously out-of-tune upright piano is delivered to the house.

They spend an afternoon being greatly amused by Carlo playing extracts from his symphony in between diving into the poor old instrument with a tuning key, desperately trying to correct the screeching noise.

They have lazy mornings. Artyom gets up and makes coffee for both of them after opening the now redecorated shutters, revealing a morning sea, whose surface glitters with floating jagged reflections of the eastern sun.

The serene days are enough to make them forget the

crumbling world around them. In any case it is crumbling too slowly to save some of the peasants from dying of hunger and too fast for the remaining nobility, still believing that their excesses will never lead them in front of the firing squad.

One morning Carlo returns from the postmaster's office with an envelope. He places it in front of Artyom's glass of milk before their late breakfast. Once he sees his questioning look he smiles and kisses him on the cheek.

'Merry Christmas.'

Artyom sits and calmly opens the envelope. He sees him crying for the first time. He thought he would never see Doctor Kaminsky's tears.

'Oh, Carlo. How…?'

'Didn't cost me much. A lunch with Grand Duke Alexandrovich's aide-de-camp or… cat-a-mite, depending on the time of the day, I guess. And a tour of the artists' quarters at the theatre. A rather pleasant lad. Not quite a rough trade from the street. But I suppose in these times he needs to make a living too. By the way, I know you are not partial to jealousy but he's only twenty years old. Not my taste. I told you to trust me. When it comes to corruption we Italians give you a good run for your roubles.'

Artyom is between laughter and tears. He stands up and takes Carlo's face in his hands. A long, intense kiss follows, Kaminsky still holding the exemption in his hand.

'You won't need it for another three years. Keep it safe and ready to use when they come knocking at the door. Perhaps it's better not to inform Seryozha. All boys go through a phase of fascination with military life. You know: the shining uniforms, the parades, the glory. Sergey is an intelligent lad but he might not be immune from all that nonsense and he might feel he's not good enough to be conscripted. Even I had a brief period in awe of my brother. He looked so dashing and martial in his cadet's uniform. I was so proud of him.'

'I find it hard to believe that.'

'It was brief. Very brief. I soon wised up, believe me.'

In June they escape to Lebedivka once again, this time taking a happy Seryozha and a grateful Yelena with them. Kaminsky's sister can't stop thanking Carlo for the refurbishment of the house and the kitchen which is now more user-friendly for the indefatigable lady.

As they do almost every morning, Carlo and Sergey head for the beachfront with a ball for a healthy dose of sunshine, exercise and a spot of their secret conversation.

It has become a tradition for Artyom to head into the village centre to purchase a copy of the *Odesskyi Listok* from the local newsagent who also serves him with his second coffee of the day.

Carlo and Sergey wave when they see his silhouette slowly approaching from the promenade. Once closer they notice the serious, worried expression. He hands the crumpled paper to Carlo with a sigh.

'Archduke Franz Ferdinand has been assassinated. He was the heir to the throne of Austria-Hungary. The Austrians are furious. There are talks of mobilisation and war. A small mob of young hotheads has assembled in Pushkin Square calling for the Tsar to show Slavic fraternity and protect Serbia. A peasant student fanatic fired the shot. Gavrilo Princip, I believe, is his name. His picture is on the front page.'

He sees Mandelli pick up the paper and quickly turn white.

IX. Red Dawn

Yelena and Seryozha have walked up to the promenade for his late morning ice cream, strictly allowed only after a vigorous swim, leaving Artyom and Carlo sitting pensively by the shoreline, their feet splashing in the water.

'It was a few years ago, Carlo. You weren't even aware of the smuggling, and the chances are that it wasn't the pistol that Princip used for his assassination. It's nonsense.'

'I know. But the mere thought of it gives me the shivers. Having met him, that's all. He seemed to be such a harmless young man.'

'I'm more concerned about the reaction of our government and the European ones. Sazonov, our foreign secretary, is an unrepentant German-hating warmonger. We have enough troubles at home without looking for more abroad. But then, this country is just one trouble after another.'

Between strikes and chaotic demonstrations often leading to violent unrest, life continues more or less unchanged. When Russia declares war on the Central Powers, Artyom goes into his study every day to check that Sergey's conscription exemption letter is still there. As always Carlo tries to reassure him.

'He's still too young. Your army cannot be that desperate.'

The performances at the opera dwindle to one or two a week. He can't help noticing that some broken window panes are left unrepaired and that the pavement around the theatre is often unswept. Weeds have started to grow through the limestone. In the autumn the mounds of leaves almost reach the window sills. Mandelli worries about his musicians being paid less or not at all. Lunches and dinners with Artyom or some of his colleagues at the Dniepr Aurora go from a weekly occasion to a monthly one, until one day they find the venue closed down and the entrance door boarded up with no notice or explanation.

Fyodor now rarely opens the windows facing Boulevard Primorskyi and Vassily appears one day with a chain and a lock for the gate.

Almost a year goes by with less of the good things and more of the worrying ones happening. The opera house is now an unsightly fortress surrounded by the almost ubiquitous sandbags. What seems to be a full regiment of Cossacks defends it on performance evenings, soon outnumbering the fewer and fewer brave punters.

At his next rehearsal Carlo notices that Oleg is missing. When he enquires about his welfare the orchestra members fall into a dissembling silence. Heads turn left and right, as if to establish who will break the news. Solonov, the ageing and loyal first violin sighs before speaking.

'Oleg has left, Maestro.'

'Left? Why? You're the best orchestra in Russia.'

'Not for another orchestra, sir. He's joined the Bolsheviks. Not before doing a very forceful round of recruiting in the pit. I won't rule out more defections, Maestro.'

During the brief car journeys back to the villa he notices for the first time how deserted the streets have now become. The harbinger of spring doesn't seem to bring any joy, despite the blossoming of the flower beds lining the silent boulevards.

Vassily is now daily braving the black market to keep Villa Mandelli fully stocked, helped by Carlo's healthy financial situation. At least the Narodny Bank is still able to clear his money wires from Milan. It gives Mandelli a good excuse to reward him with a substantial fee for his efforts, the young man always very grateful and obliging.

But when he doesn't turn up for a few days, Mandelli frantically walks from one office to another to find out what has happened to him. No one seems to know his whereabouts; they just report what they know, which is that one evening he left after clearing his desk.

He's consoled by an equally dejected Artyom. He had grown attached to poor Vassily. Perhaps because he was always so mistreated by everyone else. And he was so polite and loyal. He feels like he has lost a son.

A few days after the sudden disappearance Fyodor enters the music room, apologetically interrupting Mandelli's time for composition.

'Someone is at the door, sir.'

'Who?'

'I would recommend coming to the door yourself, sir.'

When in the hallway he freezes.

'Vassily?'

He sees Vassily and Paulina standing in the door frame, holding hands. His eyes fall on the ill-fitting dark green uniforms, the rifles on their shoulders, the ammunition rounds belts crossing their chests, the armbands on the sleeves. The flat berets bear a shining red star above the visor. Their expressions are sombre, but Carlo detects a hint of either pride or freedom, possibly both.

'I must apologise for my sudden disappearance, Maestro, but some decisions are more difficult to take than others. I needed time to think. My commanding officers insisted that I should leave without coming to say goodbye, but I stood my ground.' Vassily smiles with an endearing and self-deprecating snort. 'Vassily standing his ground! Could you believe that, Maestro?'

Mandelli is on the verge of tears.

'I understand why you and Paulina have taken such a decision, Vassily. And I am so proud of you. So proud of your courage.'

Vassily reddens, his eyes on stalks.

'You are?'

'I've been proud of you from the moment we met at the embankment. I cannot thank you enough for all that you've done for me, Vassily.'

Vassily's eyes are misty, his hand now ready for the farewell shake. Carlo takes it.

'Look after yourself, young man. Try not to get killed.'

'But that is how revolutions work, sir. Remember? No more sweaty handkerchief.'

'No more handkerchief, no.'

He sees them walking away, still holding hands, in love and possibly heading straight to their deaths, leaving a craven existence behind forever. That is indeed how revolutions work.

In April 1915, as soon as Artyom reads in the *Odesskyi Listok* that Italy has entered the war, Carlo sends a telegram to Mandello del Lario. He's soon informed that Vittorio, finally a captain, has been sent to the Carso plain for his first war engagement. He can't help crying in Artyom's arms.

'Everyone seems to be wanting to fight a war or a revolution. I don't understand why. What is wrong with these people?'

'That is why I love you so much.'

* * *

The opera house eventually closes down. The daily clashes in the adjacent streets make it too perilous even to attempt to attend a performance. Stray bullets are an everyday occurrence. Villa Mandelli is now a bunker, surrounded by the ever-present sandbags, the shutters always firmly closed. Fyodor and the other servants have taken to sleep on camp beds in the basement and the kitchens. Mandelli refuses to leave his bedroom on the first floor with the excuse that it overlooks the internal garden. He's reprimanded by Artyom as usual.

'As if that would stop the Bolsheviks or the Whites. I'm no longer sure who will be knocking at our doors first.'

Fyodor is on daily missions to the remnants of a rapidly dwindling black market, using Carlo's roubles to stock both Villa Mandelli and the Kaminsky residence.

They now walk between the two houses, keeping close to the walls, the collars of their black coats up to their noses, their black hats so low as to impede their view of the street. On Carlo's last car journey to see Artyom and his family a youth with a red armband had suddenly appeared out of a corner and had thrown a brick through the back window, luckily missing Carlo who was sitting crouched on the opposite side. He had then banged on the roof of the car with a metal bar, shouting revolutionary slogans. Carlo, terrified, had expected a mob to form and had almost resigned himself to a lynching but the unhurt driver had slammed his foot on the throttle and had sped away, not before the youth had the time to throw the bar at the back of the car, luckily hitting Carlo's head with only a spent force.

An eerie and uneasy calm falls on the city over the following winter, allowing them to have a black market-filled Christmas lit by a few candles and with the shutters closed. Fyodor still manages to find wood for the fireplaces but they have to ration the hours of the day in which to keep them burning. Artyom's surgery is still visited by the remaining people able to pay and he bravely still performs his rounds in the Suvorovsky district, where the Okhrana or the Cossacks no longer venture.

When he reaches the edges of the borough he adjusts the red armband on his sleeve and walks around undisturbed, trying to attend to what is now evident malnutrition. Carlo finds him often at his desk, his head in his hands.

'I doubt the Whites will ever come for Seryozha now. Odessa will soon fall to the Reds. But we don't have an exemption for the Bolsheviks. They are going house to house.'

'We'll pay them, Artyom. That's all I can think of. They must need money for their revolution.'

After Lenin's triumphant arrival in Petersburg the general situation becomes more and more chaotic by the day. Odessa finally falls and neither Carlo nor Artyom can fathom why their respective houses have so far not been requisitioned by the Soviets now in control of the city.

Expropriations start in earnest and for that very reason they opt to remain in their separate residences, at least officially. Mandelli takes in the servants' families, hoping that the crowding of the villa will show that some kind of "revolutionary" rearrangement has already been put into action.

But neither Villa Mandelli nor Artyom's house are requisitioned when the Bolsheviks finally establish a local government.

On a freezing winter morning a small contingent of Red Army soldiers appears at the gate and surrounds the building, though they leave quietly after assigning four fully armed young men guarding the perimeter. When Carlo walks to the gate wrapped in his worn smoking jacket and woolly scarf to demand an explanation and ready to prove that his villa has already been "reallocated" to the people, the lad who seems to be in charge shrugs.

'Orders, Comrade Mandelli.'

'Am I under house arrest?'

'No.'

They are equally surprised that Artyom's surgery remains untouched, though the space available is admittedly much less than Villa Mandelli. Artyom is asked to prioritise wounded Bolsheviks - all the Whites have now left - and the local Kommissar is pleased by his further offer to visit their barracks to assist where he can.

'I will understand if you requisition my dacha in Lebedivka, Kommissar.'

'The orders are not to.'

Carlo now has to accompany Fyodor on his daily journeys to the ever-shifting black market spots. Artyom objects to the danger but Mandelli has no time for his concerns.

'We have to eat somehow, Artyom. Fyodor is an old man and you need to look after the Bolsheviks. We need to remain in their favour if we are to survive. We cannot send Seryozha on such errands, they might stop him and ask him why he hasn't enrolled in their ranks. They might take him away. We need wood for the fire. And bread.'

'There is one thing I cannot understand, Carlo. Members of the aristocracy, merchants and other wealthy individuals are executed daily, their properties confiscated. Why are they leaving us alone?'

'I really don't know. I haven't paid anyone. I'm not hiding anything, Artyom.'

They head for a hidden alleyway at the back of the now renamed People's Square. But when they are about to cross the esplanade by creeping along its walls full of bullet holes, Fyodor grabs Carlo's arm and pulls him back, both now hiding behind the small entrance to a rundown tenement. Fyodor raises his finger to his lips, intimating silence.

'Reds.'

He sees him in handcuffs, the younger and angrier members of the platoon hitting him on the head or in the spine with the butts of their automatic Fedorovs. His nose and right eyebrow are bleeding. Despite - or because of - the nail-biting frost, he's been stripped to his underwear. They see one of the soldiers savagely kicking his face. They can almost hear the tinkling noise of his teeth falling on the cobbled stones. After he's collapsed on the ground, the commander pulls him up by his remaining hair and drags him to the wall next to their hiding spot. In their vengeful, homicidal frenzy, they fail to notice the pair in the doorway. Carlo manages to recognise him: the round, savagely beaten face, the short stature, the dirty moustaches. Fyodor pulls him back while the squad organises itself into formation. Hidden away in the recess they can only hear the crack of the rifles and the soft but clear thump of a falling body.

After the commander has kicked the body a few times he leaves a placard sticking out of the underwear. The blood from the bullet holes slowly seeps on to it.

When the coast is completely clear, and against the advice of Fyodor, Carlo ventures out and kneels by the body.

He had seen him only twice, when he was trying to save Oleg from the clutches of the Okhrana and on his ride back from the Taras Shevchenko park. He lifts the placard with his hand. He has to wipe the blood away with the other in order to read it.

NICOLAI KULESHOV
INSPECTOR OF THE OKHRANA
ENEMY OF THE PEOPLE

* * *

By July 1918, the civil war is raging. The city now resembles an army garrison. The stocks in the black market are down to a few rotten oranges and worm-infested bread. Artyom can only venture into the Suvorvsky district with an armed detail of Soviet Guards for his protection. Hunger has made the liberated resentful of their liberators.

They are still inexplicably left alone by the Soviet of Odessa, now in complete control of the city, despite the war against the remnants of the Whites still raging east of the Dniepr.

On the 18th of the month, Artyom returns from his round of the Soviet Barracks with a copy of the *Pravda*, now the only newspaper available. He hangs his jacket on the stand in the hallway and enters the room to find all of his loving family setting up the table. Seryozha and Carlo are eagerly helping Yelena with her kitchen chores.

For a moment Carlo fails to notice the dark and worried expression on Artyom's face.

'Fyodor and I had a good day at the market. We manage to secure some salmon. Salmon, Artyom! And cheese! Celebrating tonight, and…Artyom, are you all right?'

He removes one of the chairs from under the table and sits down. Then he throws the *Pravda* on the centrepiece, its gloating headline clearly visible.

'They have murdered the Tsar. And young Alexei. The whole family. Everyone.'

X. The Choice

The first days of September bring a fresh breeze and a tentative return to some sort of normality. The Narodny Bank reopens under a hammer and a sickle banner and Carlo is once more able to draw from his financial reserves, his employment contract with the opera house now not worth the paper it is written on.

Seryozha attends a reopened school, though Artyom and Yelena notice with dismay that most of his homework material is now nothing less than crude and grammatically challenged Bolshevik propaganda with big chunks of history rewritten altogether. Alexander I is no longer the man who defeated Bonaparte but a foppish womaniser who exploited the Russian peasants. In all truth he did both with remarkable guile. As his silence continues unabated, they remain in the dark about whether the gigantic nonsense is making inroads into his still raw adolescent mind. Carlo, still the only human being he talks to, tries to reassure them without revealing his special relationship with the young man.

One day, unprompted but alert to his adopted uncle looking over to one of his school assignments, he speaks softly and without lifting his head from the open book on his desk.

'This isn't the time for me to start talking to people. Nor to let them know what I think.'

When the autumnal winds start lashing the leaf-strewn boulevards of the much changed city, a visitor appears on the doorstep of Villa Mandelli.

Once in the music room he greets Carlo with a vigorous handshake while declining his offer for some tea from the bubbling samovar.

A few stars adorn his epaulettes and the now ubiquitous dark green uniform seems to be in better condition than that of many of his fellow comrades Carlo regularly meets along the way to Artyom's house.

'I'm the Chief Kommissar for Cultural Development of the Soviet of Odessa, Comrade Mandelli.'

Over the past two years he has become increasingly pleased at being addressed in that way, all that *Maestro* and *Your Excellency* stuff washed away by the Revolution. He found himself laughing at it first. Then he started liking the simplicity and straightforwardness of it.

'Pleased to meet you, Comrade.'

'I'll come straight to the point. We are re-opening the opera. It is safe enough to do so. Well…sort of.'

'That is good news.'

'We are asking you to resume your position, Maestr…Comrade.'

He smiles at the Freudian slip.

'Asking or ordering me? Not that he makes any difference. I will be delighted.'

'You will? We…we can't pay you the original fee. All contracts under the Tsarist regime have been rescinded and are void.'

'Are you going to pay my musicians?'

'The people's pay, sir…Comrade.'

'Then that is what you'll pay me. All on the same wages. I think it's fair.'

The Kommissar's eyes open wide in astonishment.

'You do?'

'Why the surprise?'

'You are a count.'

'I was. I am a Comrade now, am I not?'

He's reassured by the huge smile under the Kommissar's fluffy moustache.

'I'm glad you consider yourself such, Maestro.'

'You mean *Comrade…*'

'Yes…of course. Comrade. I think I will have some tea now, thank you.'

They sit down for tea, the Kommissar relaxed at the thought of what appears to be a genuine conversion.

'There will be no white tie. The orchestra will be in Red Army uniforms and tickets will cost a nominal amount. Also…only works containing regicides or portraying the Church and the aristocracy in an unfavourable light. These are Moscow's directives.'

Carlo sips his tea with a light guffaw.

'Practically almost all of them then. You'll be surprised what composers had to go through to slip their works through various royal censorships. They were craftier than you think. Thank you again for the opportunity. I'm looking forward to being back in my position.'

'You are?' The Kommissar stares into the now empty cup. 'We thought you wouldn't want to work for us.'

'You were wrong.'

When the dark green, buttoned-up uniform and black boots are delivered to Villa Mandelli, he tries them on, rolls the red band up the left sleeve, positions the flat cap on his wavy hair and walks to Artyom's house.

Seryozha opens the door and bursts into a loud laugh at the sight, slightly annoying Carlo. Artyom and Yelena can't help a giggle or two either when he turns around in the sitting room showing off his new People's Conductor uniform. He checks himself in the mirror of the wooden sideboard.

'Stop laughing you two. I think I cut a rather dashing figure, don't you think, Artyom?'

'Only an Italian could make such rags look dashing, Carlo.'

'In all truth I don't miss the white tie. This is quite

comfortable. And people waved at me in the streets!'

Solonov, the loyal and now visibly aged first violin is moved to tears when he shakes his hand.

'Maestro. We are so pleased to see you again.'

'It's *Comrade Mandelli* now, my dear Solonov. We live in a new world.'

Solonov lowers his head while picking up his violin from the chair.

'So we do, Comrade. So we do. But for us you'll always be the *Maestro*.'

Carlo nods with a reassuring smile.

'Let us play for the glory of the Revolution. Shall we, Solonov?'

The performances are a success. Old sets are hauled out of storage and singers are allowed to use the old costumes. Only Carlo and the orchestra must stay in Bolshevik uniforms. The Kommissar is a regular and greatly satisfied that the renowned conductor is now performing for the enjoyment of the working people.

The long winter nights are spent under the covers, holding and kissing each other, secretly hoping that somehow everything will be all right at some point in time.

Far too often exchanges of heavy artillery can be heard in the distance, and at times they shake the buildings of the city, reminding them of the civil war on their doorstep.

Yelena can now buy some groceries at a local *Committee-approved* market and Seryozha is made Young Pioneer of the year at his school. His new Headmaster, a former cobbler from the Suvorovsky district, has pompously declared the flute a "*very proletarian instrument for the cultural development of the masses*". Though Sergey's apparent compliance with any new onslaught of unhinged propaganda makes Artyom angry, Carlo is well aware of the lying. When he had come home with the red-starred award, the now teenage boy had looked at Carlo with a mischievous grin, allowing him to read his thoughts: '*The way I am playing these fools.*'

One sunny morning, harbinger of the imminent spring, Carlo is in the bathroom shaving and trimming his beard. He has adopted a full Bolshevik beard and moustache, leading Artyom to remark that he is starting to vaguely resemble Comrade Trotsky, making both of them laugh.

The knocks at the door are heavy and incessant. The sound of desperation. He has no time to ask Fyodor to attend to the call. Suddenly Seryozha is beside him, his red-starred hat in his hand, his jacket unbuttoned, the cheeks strewn with tears.

Carlo turns and grabs his arms with worried strength, looking straight into his crying eyes.

'Seryozha? What's wrong? What's happening? Why are you crying?'

Between the sobs he almost shouts at Carlo.

'They're taking Uncle Artyom. You must come now. Please. They're taking him!'

'Who's taking him? And where? Why?'

'The Reds. Please, come to the house.'

While still in his pyjama trousers and white vest, he gets to the first pair of shoes he can find. He wipes away the shaving foam still on his neck and he runs with Sergey to the house as fast as he can, bumping into some passers-by and almost knocking them onto the pavement.

Once they turn the corner they abruptly stop. Carlo holds back Seryozha with both arms.

A small platoon is positioned in front of the house. A middle-aged man who's possibly some kind of officer sits on a black horse. A few feet in front of him a young officer seems to be talking to Artyom. Yelena stands on the doorsteps, holding her apron in front of her mouth, her cheeks covered in tears.

Carlo pushes Seryozha in the direction of his mother who hugs him tight. Then he walks towards the officer and Artyom.

'May I know what this nonsense is all about, Comrade? Surely there must be some mistake. Doctor Kaminsky is…' He squints his eyes and shelters them from the sun with the palm of his hand. 'Wait a minute… Oleg?'

'Good morning, Comrade Mandelli. When I saw young Sergey running away, somehow I knew we were about to meet again.'

'Well, you can start with explaining all this misunderstanding.'

The tone is angry and tinged with a touch of the old aristocratic entitlement. Artyom grabs his arm.

'Carlo, don't make it worse.'

'What shouldn't I make worse?' He turns to Oleg again. 'Doctor Kaminsky hasn't done anything. He has been of invaluable help to your cause.'

'No one is arguing the contrary, Comrade. But the Whites are on the offensive and we are taking casualties. We have a lot of wounded men. We need doctors.'

Artyom looks at Carlo with an expression of mild rebuke.

'Carlo, I have to go with them. The order is from the Soviet of Odessa.'

He sees the panic on his lover's face.

'But you can't. What about Yelena and Seryozha? They need you. What about…' He lowers his voice. 'What about me?'

Oleg intervenes, trying to be reassuring.

'Nothing will happen to them. They will continue to live in your house. They will be safe.'

Carlo shouts at Oleg.

'You can't take him!'

'Maestro. I mean… Comrade. You have been spared the fate which has befallen most of your fellow aristocrats as you're not Russian and you haven't agitated against the Revolution. But it's time for Doctor Kaminsky to come with us to the front.'

'Spared? You've surrounded my house with soldiers. You might as well have arrested me from the start. You're taking away Doctor Kaminsky and I have been spared?'

Oleg's still young face is darkening into an angry expression. His head turns left and right with impatient rage.

'Yes! Spared! What we couldn't spare was a round-the-clock guard of four to five men stationed at the villa to protect you. We need those men but we had to assign them to your protection, sir! I mean… Comrade.'

Carlo looks back and forth between Oleg and his lover, now visibly confused.

'Protection? What protection? Those soldiers are there to protect me? Why? Why would the Soviet of Odessa want to protect an Italian nobleman?'

Oleg stares for a second at the dirty pavement, almost as if counting the stones to remain calm. Having regained some composure, he turns his head around to meet the Kommissar's eyes, as to seek permission for what to say next. The Kommissar, perhaps tired of Mandelli's posturing, shrugs before a nod of approval. Oleg faces Carlo again.

'Your sister.'

The silence is deafening, interrupted only by the neighing of the Kommissar's horse. Carlo and Artyom exchange shocked looks. Then Mandelli moves nearer to Oleg, literally a few inches away from his face.

'My…my sister? What has my sister got to do with

all this? How… how do you even know I have a sister? What is all this?'

'You might as well learn it from me. Comrade Ernestina is our top emissary in the Reich. She's been an invaluable agent for the Revolution. She single-handedly organised the logistics of the train journey which took Comrade Lenin to St. Petersburg, I mean… Leningrad. She has ordered that you receive full protection. I, for one, wouldn't like to incur her wrath if something were to happen to you. She's in daily contact with Comrade Trotsky.'

He feels Artyom's hand on his bare biceps, trying to comfort him.

'My sister a Bolshevik? That isn't true. You're lying, Oleg. Ernestina runs a *Salon des Artistes* in Weimar. My sister is no Bolshevik. This is all a lie! Tell him Artyom! It's a lie!'

'Well, spies need a cover and that bourgeois *"Salon des Artistes"* she's running is a pretty good one. In any case, Comrade, why on earth would I lie to you? And you are right: how else would I even know that you have a sister? But I would add that you should really be proud of her. She's possibly our best agent. Well, we can't delay any longer. You, Yelena and Sergey will continue to enjoy your sister's protection. If you want to leave the country, you're free to go. You're a subject of the Kingdom of Italy. There's still a steamer service to Constantia every three days. Soldiers will escort you to the docks on the day of departure and see you off safely. But Doctor Kaminsky must join us, Comrade. I'm sorry.'

He stares for a few seconds at his beloved, on the verge of perhaps losing him forever. Then he turns to Oleg, his eyes now squinting in anger, a sudden rush of courage running through his veins.

'No!'

Oleg cocks his head as if pretending that he hasn't heard properly.

'No?'

'Only if you take me too. Alternatively, you'll have to kill me. That won't please Comrade Ernestina one bit, won't it?'

Oleg lowers his voice to a whisper.

'Maestro, have you taken leave of your senses?'

'Not in the slightest. I will help. I have no medical training, that is true. I will learn. And you need to boost the morale of your fellow comrades, don't you?'

'Well, yes, but…'

'Do they sing? I mean, Bolshevik anthems? Popular songs? I will teach them. Get them together. I will come with you. It will lift their spirits.'

'Maestro, the battles on the eastern front are savage. The fields are covered with bodies. This isn't a game. War is not a game for…'

'For whom? Why don't you say it, Oleg? Why can't you say it? You think your war is savage? So are our lives. You've just started your fight; we start from the moment we are born. Against practically everything. Against the relentless hatred which rolls with menacing thunder in our direction all of the time. Like your enemies of the moment: the Whites. But we don't have "moments". All our lives are a fight. You take your breaks, we never stop. Because if we do, there's is a good chance we get murdered. I will come with you and I will help you. Don't worry, I will report to my sister that it was my will and you couldn't stop me. Trotsky will not have you shot.'

'Maestro, this is madness.'

'Yes. Of course it is. Can't you see it? It's all around you.'

Oleg turns again to the Kommissar. He has been listening in a mildly interested way. All he wants is another doctor to saw one more leg off without anaesthetic. Who comes with whom hardly bothers him. He shrugs and nods again, perhaps exploring new possibilities. A Red Army Choir. Boosting morale. Oleg resigns himself to what he rightly judges sheer lunacy.

'Very well. If it is so important to you. Welcome to the Red Army, Comrade Mandelli. I will see if I can find a horse for you.'

'If everyone else marches, I will march too.'

Oleg smiles, nods and makes for turning but he's stopped by Carlo's voice.

'One more thing. I want a few minutes to pick up some important stuff from my house. Passport and some other documents. Don't worry, I'll leave my French suits behind. Artyom will come with me. You know we won't run away. Where to anyway? But you can send an escort with us if you prefer. Won't be long.'

'Well, you can hardly join the Red Army in pyjama trousers and vest, Comrade. Why do you want Doctor Kaminsky to come with you?'

He throws a sideways glance at the young man.

'Not all artists are that stupid, Comrade Oleg.'

In Villa Mandelli Carlo hurries to gather the score papers of his symphony. He then frantically pushes them into a leather briefcase. He opens a safe and fetches his passport together with some rouble notes.

'I doubt we'll need those.'

When he has finished Artyom grabs him by his bare biceps as he's still in his vest.

'This is pure madness, Carlo. You shouldn't have done that. You'll be in immense danger.'

'So will you. If you die I will die too. I will not leave you. Sergey and Yelena will be safe. I will get in touch with Ernestina and she will make sure they will be looked after. Soviet agent or not, she still loves me enough to dispatch a Red Army platoon to protect her crazy brother. Oleg seems to think she's a big shot. I mean… Trotsky?'

Artyom has no words. He can only kiss him and embrace him but time is short. The soldiers are waiting outside and they don't want them to suspect that they are trying to flee.

The farewells to Seryozha and Yelena are heartbreaking. When the lad is in his arms he whispers in his ear.

'Look after your mother. I know that you can and I know that you will.'

Knowing that his uncle cannot hear him, he whispers back.

'*Dyadya* Carlo.'

In the end all the medical personnel and Carlo are allocated to an old truck as Oleg explains that they cannot be too tired when the first wave of casualties hits the field hospital.

The journey to the east of the city isn't very long. Oleg was right: the Whites have advanced and their counteroffensive, though patchy, has been successful.

Over the rather tedious journey on the benches of the truck Artyom has the time to start a basic medical training for Carlo and he's surprised by his nervous attention and willingness. Notwithstanding their predicament he finds the spirits for a spot of humour.

'Whatever the subject, I've always suspected you to be the most diligent of schoolboys.'

The truck struggles with the muddy roads and a few times they have to alight to help the strongest of soldiers to push it out of a deep hole. When they reach their first camp the booming noise of heavy artillery exchanges awakens them to their new reality. A real war is very different from a spoken one.

All the medical staff and Carlo are allocated to a single big tent and without much ado they proceed to the operating tables. While walking, and without turning to

Carlo, Artyom, already in his white scrubs, stares pensively at the uneven path towards the field hospital.

'I'm no surgeon. Never been. This will be a fast learning process. Well, more of a full deep end than a process, considering the shortage of morphine. If it hits you too hard, head for the door as fast as you can. There is no shame.'

'I think I'll be all right.'

The first wounded soldier is carried into the tent by a pair of inexperienced young men who weren't able to establish that once the interiors of a man are dangling out of his abdomen leaving a long, gruesome wake of blood and mashed remnants of his intestine, his chances on the operating table might be just about zero.

Before Doctor Kaminsky can wave them away while shaking his head in disbelief that anyone couldn't realise that the poor man had been dead for some time, Carlo cannot avoid taking a good look at the almighty mess on the stretcher. He runs outside and empties his stomach while holding on to one of the poles of the medical tent.

He wipes his mouth with his sleeve. He is breathing so hard he thinks he's about to suffer a heart attack. He feels like crying but he resolves not to. He can't. They might send him back. Away from Artyom.

Once he reappears inside the tent, Kaminsky is busy attending a much less dramatic injury. While he bandages a young man's arm, a nurse carefully wipes blood and detritus from his face. He turns to Carlo with a worried expression.

'I did exactly the same when I attended my first autopsy at the Odessa Medical School. It's more than normal. How are you?'

Carlo grabs a cloth and wipes his lips further, his face still white, his forehead still sweaty.

'I… I am well. What can I do?'

Artyom smiles. A smile full of love for his brave boy.

'Comrade Safronova will show you what to do.'

The Whites are in retreat and the regiment is shortly on the march again towards Rostov-on-Don. The summer brings scorching days. The smell in the medical tent becomes unbearable, though Carlo has now toughened up considerably and, always a fast learner, he is of invaluable help to both doctors and nurses.

He is determined to keep his promise about forming a choir and the young soldiers volunteer with a surprisingly hefty dose of enthusiasm. Artyom is quick to explain: 'We Russians love a good choir.'

Mandelli doesn't know any of the old and new patriotic songs but he quickly rises up in the Kommissar's and Oleg's esteem by opening the rehearsals with a booming rendition of the Socialist International. Artyom can't help a quip.

'The irony of having an Italian count conducting the anthem of the proletariat.'

It's one of their regular evening talks in front of the fire. Their dirty metal bowls lie aside, the warm beans and beetroots already eaten. They sip cheap vodka from their flasks, their only escape from the unrelenting hell of war.

'Well, you'd be surprised to learn that I think that it's a rather good tune. And I'm supposed to be the best conductor in the world. After Toscanini.'

'Not surprised at all. I always suspected you to be more of a socialist than myself, Comrade Mandelli.'

After their mutual laugh, Carlo's face lights up by the lively fire.

'I'd love so much to kiss you right now. I want so much to be held by you. Will we ever be able to do that again?'

Artyom takes another good sip from the flask. He needs it badly. He doesn't even remember how many young men he's seen dying on the table today. When he knows that all is lost he just calls the first nurse available and asks her to hold their hand while their life slowly seeps away. When one of the nurses had mildly protested that she was rather busy, he had chided her: 'In the last moments they might believe you are their mother or girlfriend.'

'We're not their enemy right now,' Artyom retorts while nodding to some officers walking by. 'But after they've defeated the Whites, we will be. Again. It's how it goes. They always revert to their fear and hatred. When they no longer need us.'

The Red Army advances at the cost of huge losses and the field hospital never stops. Supplies are scarce and Carlo has now grown inured to the screams, the sudden deaths, the stretchers carrying out lifeless bodies. He sees men who have been rehearsing in his choir returning from the frontline without limbs or sometimes disappearing altogether. Collection of battlefield casualties is not a priority in the raging, inhuman inferno of civil wars.

One night, before Artyom can join him in front of the fire, Oleg perches himself on the empty munition box next to him.

'Maestro.'

'What happened to *Comrade Mandelli?*'

Oleg laughs with his lips closed.

'No one can hear us here. How's your daily ration of oysters and caviar tonight, sir?'

Carlo scoops another spoonful of gruel with pretended relish.

'Delicious as usual, young man. Compliments to the chef.'

Oleg is silent for a while, staring at the fire and drinking perhaps too heavily from his flask.

'For the life of me I would have never believed you could do this. All the doctors and nurses are full of praise for your work. And the lads. They love the choir. They love you. You're a better leader than I will ever be, Maestro. And I envy you.'

'You envy me?'

'Giving up all you have to follow the man you love. Possibly to your death. Your title, fame, money, position, career. None of them crossed your mind when you were begging me to let you join us. I could tell. I will never have that. That kind of love.'

'Nonsense. You will find the girl of your dreams. If you have such dreams. And you will love each other. It happens, Oleg. It happens.'

'I'm not that confident I will survive this. Commanders are supposed to lead by example at the front. And I do. By the way, your sister sends her love. She can't contact you directly but we've let her know of your invaluable work for the cause. She must be proud of you. The letter to the Odessa Soviet regarding Yelena and Seryozha had Trotsky's signature on it. They are safe.'

'Thank you, Oleg. I'm so grateful. Mad lady, she is. I have wanted to ask you for quite some time about your sister Ekaterina. Did she have her baby? Do you know where your siblings are?'

Another long sip from the flask, noticed by a now worried Carlo.

'We were lucky.'

'Oh, Oleg. I am so sorry.'

'The baby was born dead. The malnutrition and the poor hygiene saw to that. There were no midwives available and we couldn't even find any hot water. Ekaterina survived for a couple of hours before the room became a pool of blood. Just in time for me to say goodbye.'

He notices the first tears in Carlo's eyes. Oleg seems to be visibly drunk. After a pause for thoughts he points his finger at a small tent some hundred yards away from the fire.

'That is my home, Maestro. As a Deputy Kommissar I get one all for myself. There is hardly anyone around. Without getting noticed, get in there and wait. All I ask is to keep it as quiet as you can.'

'You don't have to do this, Oleg.'

'But I want to. You saved me from the torture chambers of the Okhrana, Maestro. I owe you one.'

He pats Mandelli on the knee and stands up in an unsteady way, throwing away the empty flask. Then, without looking back, he slowly ambles towards the medical tent.

When Artyom enters Oleg's tent they don't exchange a single word. The kisses are violent, as they always are when lips are starved of them for such a long time. When they start almost ripping their clothes off each other, Carlo stops for an instant and takes Artyom's face in his hands.

'You do realise that we haven't had a bath for days?'

'They can smell us a mile away. Do you care?'

'We could be dead tomorrow.'

The march towards Rostov-on-Don continues with great difficulties over a rainy autumn. The roads are increasingly muddy and treacherous, the random shelling more and more dangerous. Artyom and Carlo continue to help as much as they can. The incoming flow of dead and wounded men never seems to stop.

But one evening, while returning to their lodgings, they hear a long and menacing whistle from the east. Some soldiers shout orders to everyone at the top of their voices. The sky lights up, and before they can run and take cover, the world around them goes dark and silent.

* * *

The first thing he notices when he wakes up is the low ceiling above his bed. At least he thinks it's a bed. He's not sure. He lifts his hand to his face and touches his bandaged eye. The other one can only vaguely discern a white and blue apron at his side. Perhaps a nurse. Everything is foggy and unclear and the sounds are muffled. His hearing seems to have been impaired by the explosion. Then he notices the rolling. It's a gentle one but it is a rolling. He touches the walls surrounding his bed. They are made of wood. It's not a tent. This is a berth. This is a ship.

The nurse wipes his unbandaged eye with a warm cloth and he starts perusing the surroundings with more clarity. Yes. It is a ship. He becomes agitated and utters his first words.

'Where am I?'

The nurse places her soft hand on his forehead and tells him to wait in French. Why not in Russian? Why is he on a ship? Why is this nurse not Russian? Where is the field hospital? Oleg? The Red Army? His choir? Artyom?

His ramblings in Russian seem to worry the young lady who opens the door to go and fetch someone. Carlo angrily punches the side of the berth.

'Where am I? Why am I not marching towards Rostov-on-Don? Where is Artyom?'

Despite the shouts, the officer enters the room calmly, politely telling the nurse that the Maestro will be fine on his own for a little while. Carlo turns and his good eye blinks in disbelief.

'Vittorio?'

Vittorio sits on the stool by the berth previously occupied by the nurse and pats Carlo's arm with restrained affection.

'Good morning, little brother. Finally awake.'

'What…what are you doing here? What are you doing in Russia?'

He takes his captain's hat off and leaves it on the small desk in the cabin.

'We are not in Russia, Carlo. Not anymore. We're on the *SS Iliescu*, sailing across the Black Sea. We should be docking at the port of Constantia tomorrow morning, weather permitting. Then we'll head home.'

'My home is in Odessa. Why are we going to Constantia? Why am I here? Where is Artyom?' He now finds the strength to raise his voice and grabs Vittorio's arm with desperate force. 'Where is Artyom?'

Vittorio calms him down by patting his shoulder and trying to lead him back to his pillow.

'Doctor Kaminsky is alive and well. I believe your comrades are on their way to Rostov-on-Don as we speak. You took a big hit during the shelling of your camp. The Whites must have got hold of your coordinates somehow. Spies. You know, they are everywhere these days. Sometimes closer than you think.'

Carlo turns to the wall of the berth. Angry.

'You know about Ernestina?'

'We all do. Except mother, of course. A philandering husband in Boston, a son trying his best to get killed in a foreign war and a Bolshevik daughter in Moscow. The old lady is becoming too old and frail to countenance this relentless array of betrayals. At least you've always been rather transparent in your shenanigans.'

'Moscow?'

'Weimar was no longer safe for Ernestina. She's rumoured to be Trotsky's mistress now. Won't surprise me. I hear that the man is famously partial to attractive ladies. It hasn't been fun for Uncle Giulio and myself either, if you'd care to ask. We have been summoned countless times to the *Ministero degli Affari Esteri* for clarifications. I'm not entirely sure they believe that we are not Bolsheviks ourselves. Do you and your sister ever consider anyone else when embarking on your dangerous adventures?'

'Why have you taken me away from Artyom?'

Vittorio hauls Carlo's leather briefcase from a recess under the berth. Then he calmly lays it on the blanket.

'I haven't. He gave me your briefcase. I believe your symphony is in it. And a letter. You still have one good eye to read it. Don't worry, you haven't lost the other. Just shrapnel wounds. It will heal but you might need strong spectacles. I also suggest you stop being so agitated. Your left leg is broken and it's in a cast. Where Doctor Kaminsky managed to find a cast in that mayhem I would never know. I will leave you now. I will send the nurse back in later.'

He slowly opens the case. The score papers are all there, albeit in a rather disorderly manner. He sees an envelope.

My dearest Carlo,

With the best of luck, at the time of reading this letter you will be safely sailing home.

We were hit by flying debris after a sudden heavy shelling of the camp. You were thrown on to the ground unconscious and I carried you all the way to the field hospital on my shoulders. The Red Army artillery fought back and soon the Whites gave up their bombardment.

Your eye is badly wounded but I believe you will not lose it. Perhaps your sight won't be as good as before though. Your leg is broken in several places though and you might end up with a slight limp. I sent someone to get some plaster from our supply. Heaven knows how he found it. All the soldiers were begging me to save the Maestro. I heavily sedated you and as I went back to attend the other casualties, Oleg came in to tell me that your brother Vittorio had just arrived, escorted by a small contingent of soldiers from Moscow. He had moved heaven and earth to come and find you. You hadn't told me that you had stopped writing home. But then perhaps it was too difficult a thing to do given our circumstances. He had been dispatched by your uncle Giulio.

I'm asking you not to be angry with your brother. His mission wasn't to take you home but to ascertain whether you were still alive. Your family was ever so worried about you. Through Ernestina they had learnt that you had enrolled in the Red Army. My God! They must have thought that you had really lost your mind this time.

Italy is not at war with Russia and your brother had a safe-conduct obtained for him by your ambassador in Moscow. But he still risked his life to come and find you. Bear that in mind when you berate him as I know you will.

The person you should be angry with is me. I'm the one who begged Vittorio to take you home. There was no need to explain our "arrangements". Somehow he knew what we were. He said that if he had ever wished for his little brother to find a soulmate, I would have been the one. Your brother is a honourable gentleman, Carlo.

He was the one to remark that perhaps you didn't want to be separated from me but I insisted. He did predict you would be furious with him but he said you've always been so anyway.

I kept you sedated because I knew that you would have refused to leave. You'll probably wake up in safety, sailing towards Constantia.

I want you to live, Carlo. And here you will die. I love you too much to see you die in my arms. You have a chance. Here you don't. The brotherly hatred which fuels civil wars is of a special kind. There are no rules of engagement, no prisoners taken, no justice. He who wins, rules. And lives.

I know you will remember me forever and so will I, if

I ever get to live that long. No one will ever love you the way I do. Perhaps you'll hate me for doing this for the rest of your life. But I will die happy in the knowledge of having saved you from a terrible end.

Six years ago we walked into each other's lives to discover how happy two men could be together. I am so very sorry that in the end it wasn't to be. After all, has anyone ever fought cruelty such as this and won?

Farewell, my beautiful boy. You are the only one I will ever love.

Artyom

The tears turn into uncontrollable sobbing, the letter on his shattered heart. Sometimes we kill the ones we love. And sometimes we save them.

Wrapped up in a thick blanket and now able to be pushed about in a wheelchair, he's surprised to see Timoteo opening the door of the now aged and rusty Mercedes once they've negotiated the ramps of Stazione Centrale. The drive to Mandello del Lario is long and tedious, the thick fog preventing Timoteo from speeding. He has barely spoken to his brother for the whole journey. The crossing of the Otranto Strait was rough, fevers and chills further debilitated his still weak constitution. In the car, while keeping their sights firmly out of their respective windows, Carlo finally feels he ought to say something.

'I suppose I owe you an apology.'

'Accepted. Though the list of slights is rather long.'

'I still can't believe you've risked your life to come and find me.'

'These nasty pesky brothers. You have no idea of what we are capable of.'

'Life is over for me anyway. I might as well be nice to you and Mother.'

Vittorio pats the leather briefcase between them.

'Over?'

Carlo turns, his eye still bandaged but improving.

'What is a symphony when you've lost everything?'

'Doctor Kaminsky did the right thing and you know it. And that is why you're still so angry.'

'What will it take you to call him Artyom?'

'He's a fine gentleman. Will it suffice?'

'No, it will not. He's not just a "fine gentleman". He was…he is my lover!'

Vittorio's eyes dart in Timoteo's direction, begging his brother for discretion. Exasperated, Carlo violently turns his gaze back to his window, feeling a few bones cracking because of the sharp movement.

'What do I care! It's hardly a secret anymore. And why should it be anyway?'

Once in his old room, he's left to rest under the soft covers of his old bed. Amilcare has stoked the fire and its glow is reflecting on the patterned wallpaper. A good foot of snow has accumulated on the ledges of the windows.

In the morning, to the dismay of the visibly older yet still loyal butler, he doesn't touch any food and remains still in a foetal position for hours, staring at the winter landscape of the lake.

He's silent during his mother's visit, except when she's about to leave and has already opened the door. Then he suddenly turns, as if remembering the discreet suffering of the old lady.

'I'm sorry, Mother. I really am.'

Uncle Giulio's visit brings some life back into his shattered bones. The bandage on the left eye is off and the scar running from the top of his forehead almost down to his jaw is clearly visible. When he gets up to allow Uncle Giulio to help him with his dressing gown, he limps to the French doors.

'I wouldn't go out, Carlo. We are below zero degrees. But opening them to allow some fresh air is a good idea.'

He takes a deep breath and returns to sit on the bed, his hands together between his thighs, gazing aimlessly at the rug covering the parquet.

'I fully understand your pain, dear nephew. I'm not sure what advice I can give. But we're not holding you prisoner. If you wish to go back and search for Artyom when fully recovered, I will help you as much as I can. I have contacts.'

'You always had "contacts", Uncle Giulio. Where would we all be without your contacts? Perhaps I would still be in Russia? With Artyom?'

'That is unfair. Vittorio's orders were to find out whether you were still alive. He wasn't meant to take you back. Artyom saved your life. First by carrying you to the field hospital, then by entrusting your safety to Vittorio.'

'Is one of your contacts still Ernestina?'

'No. And for good reasons. Our letters are read and our movements watched. The very idea of your brother or myself suspected of being a Bolshevik is utterly preposterous. They should have worked it out by now. All the same, we're still under surveillance. Either they aren't very bright or they're just trying to justify their employment. Like almost everybody in need of an income, I guess.'

'Welcome to my world, dear uncle. I was followed from the time I left Italy. And now I know why. The Germans, the Austrians, the Okhrana, the Reds. Quite a crowd. Everyone on my heels. What a waste of time and resources. No wonder they are all at each other's throats. They seem to have nothing else to do.'

Uncle Giulio picks up the leather briefcase and takes a passing look inside. Then he turns to his nephew.

'There is a way to honour his memory, Carlo.'

'He isn't dead, you know.'

'No, I don't. And neither do you. But this is the only way you can be with him without risking your life.'

He throws the briefcase on the bed before embracing his sobbing nephew while caressing his uncombed, messy hair.

He survives on soup, now craftily laced by Amilcare with strips of meat and small cubes of pancetta.

After a week or so, after drinking his coffee, he picks up the briefcase and opens the door to check that no one is on the landing. With the coast clear he walks down the staircase barefoot, still in his pyjamas and dressing gown. He then quickly locks himself in the music room. He opens the piano and he is relieved to hear that it is still reasonably well tuned.

He sharpens a few pencils before positioning some of the pages on the music stand and others on the long sofa by the wall.

He picks up from where he left off a long ago. When still in Odessa. When alive.

In the evening he's still there. Amilcare and his mother have turned the knob on the door trying to gain access, but he shouted them away.

In the morning he's still locked in the room. He has slept on the uncomfortable sofa, curled up again in a foetal position, Artyom and the symphony the only two thoughts in his mind. He hears Amilcare knocking at the door.

'Sir, I have some breakfast for you here.'

'Leave it outside. I will pick it up.'

He retrieves only the pot of coffee and the cup. He furiously goes back to the piano. The pencil scribbles frenetically, correcting, crossing out entire passages. His forehead feels feverish and he's drenched in sweat. His now hollow eyes are circled by deep purple rings.

The next day he retrieves his usual coffee but still no food. He's dropped the dressing gown and the jacket on the floor and frantically paces the room in his pyjama trousers and dirty white vest, sharpening his pencils every hour, the pages of the symphony scattered on the floor, on the piano, on the dresser.

More and more days. No food. Only black coffee. The beard now covers his neck, the lips are cracked and bleeding. Amilcare and his mother are still trying in vain to gain access.

He runs around the room conducting an imaginary orchestra, talking to an imaginary first violin. He shouts at himself, hitting his face with closed, angry fists: no, the fourth movement won't do. It is wrong. It could be better. It must be better. The pencil breaks on contact with the paper. He screams. A scream full of rage. He sharpens it again and lies on the parquet floor, correcting the fourth movement again. He punches the floor and cries. No, it still isn't right. It has to be perfect. For Artyom. He leans on the keyboard, snot hanging from his nose. Another note. For Artyom. Another tune. For Artyom. This is all for Artyom. And he knows he's listening to his symphony. And that is why it has to be perfect.

Every night he runs barefoot into the back garden, the snow up to his knees. He then falls on the frosty ground and screams his lost lover's name at the top of his voice, begging the starry sky for an impossible miracle. The loss. The unbearable loss. Why? Why him?

After a relentless week he sits back after correcting the last note of the finale. Half-naked and exhausted by the all-consuming madness of creative energy, he lays the pencil down on the piano and closes his eyes, recalling how it all started. Then he collects all the pages and places them in order on the stand. He takes out Artyom's letter from his pocket. It never leaves him. He reads it for the umpteenth time, touching the writing with his fingers. He leans with his feverish forehead on the score and shuts his eyes.

Then he picks up the pencil again. A title. A name. That is all that is missing.

XI. The Kaminsky Symphony

The crowds form quickly. Everyone tries to get closer to the posters while the men are still in the process of glueing them onto the walls under the porticos. The thick winter fog and the dim lights of the lampposts make them difficult to read. Witnessing the small but growing posse, more and more punters approach, wondering what the excitement is all about. Then the last roll of glue allows the announcement to be visible to the now large gathering.

Teatro alla Scala

Milano

17 Dicembre 1919

Sinfonia Kaminsky

Op. 1 in Re Maggiore

PRIMA MONDIALE

Maestro Carlo Alberto Mandelli di Castagnino

The bulbs on the side of the mirror highlight his still visible scars. The bigger one, the one along the left cheek, bestows a rugged aura on him, more of a rough and tumble unruly sailor than a refined composer of music.

The knock on the door startles him. He still goes

through these moments of complete stillness of the mind, Artyom's image floating in front of his eyes. Eyes still searching, now veiled with a constant sadness, hopes fading further and further as the days go by.

'Come in.'

'Maestro, I only wanted to wish you good luck and congratulate you on such a great work. It's a masterpiece.'

'Nonsense, Alessandro. But I'm so glad you like it. Of all people yours is the opinion I value most, you know that. And this is?…'

'Jean-Pierre, a student at the conservatorio. Cello.'

'Splendid choice of instrument, young man.'

'We are… well… we have started a special friendship, Maestro.'

A brief, tender smile of approval, genuinely happy for his former admirer.

'So happy for you boys. Jean-Pierre, do you have a seat for tonight?'

'In the gallery, sir. The only one available. And the only one I could afford. But I wouldn't have missed it for the world.'

'I hope you'll enjoy the concert. I have departed from the usual conventions. Hopefully it won't be too hard on the ladies' delicate ears. This city can be awfully conservative in its tastes. There are some interesting cello variations. They'll be useful for your studies.'

Alessandro's words come out sounding like a gentle warning.

'Schoenberg and Strauss are in a box on the left-hand side, Maestro.'

A little smile greets the news.

'I thought they couldn't resist the temptation to insult me a little bit more. They are probably salivating at the prospect of a highly melodic work to deride and belittle in the press tomorrow. How disappointed they are going to be. I'm counting on the violas to be outstanding tonight, Alessandro.'

'We will be, sir.'

He opens the leather box and gently grabs the baton with his gloved hand. He opens the door and walks slowly from his dressing room to the orchestra pit, carrying his light limp with all the dignity he can muster, occasionally adjusting the white tie. Stage workers and various assistants part and bow as he progresses along the tunnel. He doesn't turn or acknowledge anyone, but not out of rudeness. Millions of words swirl in a vortex across his mind. And he still hasn't decided what to say. And what not to say.

A roaring applause greets his entrance. He steps onto the podium and turns towards the audience. He then bows respectfully to the King and the Queen standing and joining in the applause in the royal box.

When the applause withers he doesn't turn back towards the orchestra but he calmly stares at the floor before finding the courage for words. Words that may break him. He waits until an expectant silence falls on the house.

'Your Majesties, ladies and gentlemen. You might have found it rather odd that no programme was published for my work. That was my wish.'

He lowers his gaze and spots Uncle Giulio and Edine in the first row, gleaming in their white ties, gazing at him with glowing, misty eyes. He takes a deep breath. And a sudden courage surges through his still wounded body.

'This work is dedicated to Doctor Artyom Nikolayevich Kaminsky of Odessa.

'Doctor Kaminsky attended an injury of mine in 1913 and upon that encounter we became very close friends. He was the kindest gentleman I ever met. We spent the most blissful of years together. Upon the breakout of the civil war, one day the Bolsheviks came and ordered him to follow them and enrol in the Red Army. They had plenty of wounded soldiers and they badly needed doctors.'

He stares again at the red carpet in front of him.

'If any of you had seen what I have. The carnage. The senseless, savage carnage.'

He pauses to clear the knot slowly forming in his throat.

'They offered me an escape route. As a subject of the Kingdom of Italy, a few guards would have escorted me to the port where some sort of safe passage would have been arranged for foreigners fleeing a burning country.'

He pauses again and looks up. Proud.

'I refused. I asked to follow Artyom and help him as much as I could to save the few lives which could be saved. In all truth, not many. I also formed an amateur choir with the recruits. Mainly patriotic and Bolshevik songs. They were rather good singers and I felt so moved by their efforts.

'But one day we came under heavy artillery fire and a blast threw me onto the ground unconscious. I woke up in a berth of a steamer on the way to Constantia, rescued by my brother who had been bravely searching for me among the chaos and destruction.'

His eyes see Artyom in the audience. Those blue, thinking diamonds.

'I don't know what has happened to Artyom and perhaps I never will. Whether he's injured or safe. Dead or alive. There is simply no way to know. My letters receive no replies. Phone lines are blocked or down.'

He draws breath and finds the courage to look at the audience without blinking. The extraordinary courage of a battered tribe.

'I know many of you will find such love distasteful,

perhaps even offensive. But I know of no other. This symphony is for Artyom and for him only. You are under no obligation to listen to it. If such love is unacceptable to you, please leave.'

He stands still, waiting for a verdict. A judgement. A condemnation.

Murmurs and confabulation ensue until Queen Elena stands up, causing a rush of bows and curtsies while restoring a stony silence in the auditorium.

She joins her gloved hands in the most dignified of poses before speaking in her broken Italian, the words oddly elongated by her heavy Montenegrin accent.

'My husband and I are looking forward to hear the Kaminsky Symphony, Maestro Mandelli. You will play. Even if I am to be the only one left in this house.'

The King stands up and lifts his wife's hand in his, the applause deafening. So loud that no one can hear him muttering between closed lips: 'Thank you.'

A modern, thundering score shakes the house, followed by moving, melancholic movements, the audience enthralled. In a first floor box two bespectacled men whisper in each other's ear while attentively listening to what they can immediately recognise as a masterpiece.

Just west of Rostov-on-Don, Oleg, recently promoted to the rank of Kommissar, is supervising the last preparations for the imminent offensive. The Whites are on the other side of the long ridge across the plain. Intelligence has reported that they are short of ammunition and have only old rifles left. Their ranks are desperately reinforced with terrified teenage boys and diehard old fools. Artyom and the other doctors wait not far behind, ready to collect the wounded. The collection of the dead is the job of prisoners of war, the only chore preventing angry revolutionaries from executing them.

They wait in a deathly silence, hiding behind the high grass, the warm rays of a crisp winter sun making them sweat.

The fourth movement is laced with a special poignancy, masterfully executed by the violas. Alessandro looks up to follow Carlo's lead. He loves the symphony so much. He has learnt it by heart, note after note. He stares and notices the sudden sadness in Carlo's expression. They catch each other's eyes. There is a cold wind suddenly blowing in the Maestro's heart. The cold wind of the steppe west of Rostov-on-Don.

Oleg rises and skilfully loads his Fedorov. He then gives the command by lifting his arm to signal the attack. His deputy blows into a makeshift wooden whistle to incite their troops to the fight.

And a wave of young men surges between the high stems. Behind, even younger men, boys really, stand up and wave giant red flags marked with the hammer and sickle. They shout at the top of their voices, giving each other courage to defeat the last remnants of the Romanovs' White Army.

A small tear marks Maestro Mandelli's left cheek. The cold in his heart is now frost, the foreboding seizing his shaking limbs. He still waves the baton and the commands are still perfect but Alessandro keeps looking at him, worried.

The intelligence was false. Possibly the work of treason and disinformation. They don't have old rifles. They are not old, deluded fools and silly boys playing soldiers. They have machine guns and grenades.

Oleg realises all too soon that they have been deceived and he's at a loss as to what to do. Perhaps he should order a retreat. He looks at his deputy on the left, only marginally older than his twenty-four years. But he has no idea about what to do either, the legendary impervious omnipotence of youth crumbling in front of the impending terror, their eyes wide open in horror, now afraid to die.

The fifth movement is grandiose, the huge orchestra used to the full: the drums, the tubas, the cellos, the horns. A giant and overwhelming silvery wave awes Schoenberg and Strauss. The ladies and the gentlemen in the audience look at each other in stupefied wonder: the perfect score, the haunting passion, the immense sadness behind the sound of the tubas and the clarinets.

And more tears.

The boys with the red flags are the first to fall. The huge drapes slowly flutter downward, covering their lifeless bodies. Oleg sees his comrades trying to counter the machine guns with their weapons and falling one by one in a pool of blood, their limbs hacked off by the incessant rounds.

He shouts to order the retreat. They start running back while trying to shoot at the enemy now pursuing them. The first round enters his right shoulder blade, forcing him to drop his rifle on the ground while emitting a piercing scream. The second one smashes his knee. He tries to carry on walking on one leg, hampered by the muddy terrain, the pain unbearable. He sees his deputy mowed down by a hail of rounds.

Another shot hits him right in the back and he falls lifeless. Not far behind the front line Artyom sees Oleg's body in the mud. He shouts his name in pain and anger before running to retrieve him, the other doctors desperately trying to hold him back.

He somehow manages to get to Oleg and attempts to

drag him back to the infirmary, knowing anyway that he's already dead.

But the guns haven't stopped. One round hits him straight in the right leg and he falls, still holding Oleg in his arms. He looks up and sees the scornful and vengeful grin of a White Guard, his revolver pointed at him. He hugs Oleg tight and kisses his hair before the shot.

Doctor Artyom Kaminsky. Your symphony.

The finale blows the house away, leaving Strauss and Schoenberg speechless. Carlo slowly lays the baton on the lectern and looks down without wiping the tears off his cheeks. Some land on the last page of the symphony. Life ends in many ways.

Queen Elena stands up and initiates what turns into a louder and louder applause, Strauss and Schoenberg shouting *Bravo!* on their feet.

Alessandro and Maestro Mandelli stare at each other, their lips sealed in mutual sadness, understanding everything, somehow acknowledging a far away fate.

Despite the applause and the roaring success of the Kaminsky Symphony, the invitations to dinners, parties and *soirées* have all but gone. The polite Milanese society still greets him at Cova and in Galleria but they're no longer interested in his company.

The Kaminsky Symphony is making him and Amedeo even richer and more celebrated around European *salons.* Except that the ladies running them conveniently forget to invite its composer.

Uncle Giulio's words of wisdom were, as always, redolent of resigned truth: *'Our fellow Italians will never send us in front of the execution squad. But they will never allow us to be in the squad either.'*

His new solitude is though both welcome and soothing. He reads and goes to bed early, after a good supper prepared with care and affection by Cecilia. Tonio seems to be happy to attend to the Maestro again.

He has stopped sending letters to Odessa or trying daily telephone calls. The lines are always down and nothing comes back. The news on the *Corriere della Sera* reports a country in chaos, ravaged by violence and famine. Embarking on a search would be sheer, pointless madness, and he has stopped considering the idea.

One day, while re-reading his diary, he finds a name and a number. He sits at his desk, pondering for a long time whether to call or not. It's late afternoon, probably the most appropriate time for a call.

'Good afternoon, Miss. Could you connect me to this number in Berlin, please?'

'Yes, sir, please wait on the line.'

'Thank you.'

He's no longer sure if he wants this call anymore but he waits.

'Guten Abend, Residenz Kimmich.'

'Kann ich mit Herrn Walther Kimmich sprechen?'

'Ich bin Herr Walter Kimmich.'

He's surprised at the absence of a butler answering the phone. Perhaps he's out.

'Können Sie Französisch sprechen? Mein Deutsch ist nicht gut.'

'Yes, of course. How may I help you?'

The voice is warm, the spoken French almost perfect, the tone welcoming.

'I am… I am Carlo Mandelli, the Italian conductor.'

A short silence follows his introduction. He's not sure whether to worry about it or not.

'Honoured.'

'You might be surprised that I have your number, Herr Kimmich.'

'I'm not, Maestro.'

'The reason for my call is, well… you see, in Carlsbad I had the pleasure to get acquainted with your nephew Walther. A charming, intelligent and good-hearted young man. He gave me this number and made me promise to get in contact at some point. Regrettably it hasn't been possible until now. Let's say my circumstances have prevented it. Lately I have been wondering how he is. When we met he was recovering from tuberculosis and making good progress. I hope you don't find my enquiry impertinent, Herr Kimmich.'

This time the silence is longer.

'Herr Kimmich? Are you still there?'

'Forgive me, Maestro. Walther came back from the sanatorium in good form. He was convinced that he had beaten the disease.'

'Convinced?'

'The doctors had actually advised him against leaving Jánské Koupele, but you know the exuberance of youth, they are afraid of nothing.'

'Yes. Walther is a bright and very brave young man.'

'Maestro, Walther didn't survive the disease. He worsened after a few weeks and he passed away three months after returning.'

The tone of the voice is flat and emotionless, but not because of coldness. Tragedy has become an everyday fact of life for Walther's uncle.

'My nephew did tell me of your friendship, Maestro. He admired you greatly and he treasured the time spent with you in Carlsbad. He was hoping you would visit him in Berlin one day. I daresay he loved you.'

'I see. I understand he had three brothers.'

He detects a sigh of pain behind yet another silence.

'You have to forgive me for not contacting you before, Maestro. Times have been hard for our family. His three brothers were strong and healthy and were conscripted into the Imperial Army. They were dispatched to the front line in the offensive of the Marne. None of them have returned.

'The family's finances have suffered a great deal of losses during the war years. I'm not much of a profiteer I'm afraid, and we are a defeated country. If it's of any consolation, when Walther returned I actively encouraged him to get in contact with you and perhaps even join you in Milan or even Odessa. I believe he would have been happy at your side, Maestro.'

'Thank you, Herr Kimmich. It means a lot to me. I am so deeply sorry for your losses.'

But Herr Kimmich has no more words, exhausted by the constant pain of the years gone by.

'Good day, Maestro.'

He hasn't touched any food. When he retires upstairs he feels his head exploding with thoughts. After all, he concludes, there isn't much left of all these years. Not even a single picture. Only a letter. The one and only person he ever loved is gone forever and life goes on as life does. More of the same. He is preparing himself for the next chapter, where only memories will fill his now long, lonely nights.

He tiptoes down the stairs and dons his coat and hat. Tonio has heard his soft steps anyway and follows him into the downstairs hallway.

'You forgot your gloves, sir.'

'Oh, thank you, Tonio. With a bit of luck, I won't be long.'

Tonio nods in an unhappy and worried way.

'Sir.'

He pulls a wad of notes out of his pocket and weighs them in his now gloved hand.

'I'm in the dark regarding the ongoing rates. Two-hundred Lire?'

'It isn't just the rates. Times are changing too, Maestro. For a while now we've had these young men in black shirts roaming the streets day and night. Bad eggs. They shout and beat people up. Some of the boys have been roughed up. It would be wise to steer clear of these thugs. Let me handle this for you, sir.'

'I'll take the risk. Besides, I no longer have a reputation to defend, my dear Tonio. I destroyed it with my own words. Do you know what they call me now? The bent composer. And that's the most gracious of the array of insults. I know you hide away the scurrilous notes which land on our doorstep. I've caught you scrubbing out the graffiti which appear on our door in the morning. All the money in this wretched world would not buy their respect. And I'm not even sure I wish for it anyway. I committed the ultimate sin in this most peculiar of all lands: I have revealed to them what they already knew and that is unforgivable. I have stopped lying and that won't do. Not in Italy.'

He pats the old butler's shoulder with the usual affection.

'You're not getting any younger and I now understand how insensitive and dreadful it was of me to ask you to undertake such a task. I humbly hope for your forgiveness. Are the Gardens still the spot?'

Tonio lowers his head, nodding in quiet resignation.

'Still they are, sir.'

'I thought they would be.'

Author's Note

"Those who make peaceful revolutions impossible will make violent revolutions inevitable"

If heeded, John Fitzgerald Kennedy's famous quote could have prevented both the French and Russian revolutions, whose foundations lay in the simplest analysis of such complicated events: people had simply had enough.

Naturally, they both imploded badly as revolutions do, causing a possibly worse mayhem than the status quo. But that doesn't necessarily mean that the status quo was tenable. It wasn't. There is a breaking point when talking to your exploiters and persecutors becomes meaningless as you realise that they will never listen. Killing them *en masse* is then your only option.

France, of course, has fared better than Russia but that might have something to do with another famous quote.

Knowing full well that Emperor Bonaparte's days were numbered, Talleyrand couldn't resist a good quip to Tsar Alexander I during a reception at the Winter Palace: 'Your Majesty, you are the most culturally refined sovereign ruling over millions of ignorant peasants. For France, of course, the reverse is true.'

As I write Russia is more or less back to where it has always been. Ruled by a murderous tyrant put in charge by a compliant, fearful and sheepish population. When the mob rises again (as it always does in Russia), violence will change everything before everything reverts to exactly the same. The country is basically stuck in a loop of nostalgic imperialism and delusions of faded grandeur.

As eloquently explained by the historian Sean McMeekin in his account of the causes of the First World War, it has always been a myth that Russia was an impoverished country in the years leading to the October Revolution. Its economy was actually booming. The issue was that due to its grotesque, almost feudal system, only an elite of aristocrats and wealthy merchants shared the proceeds while enjoying living standards as good as the ones in Western Europe. By taking a good look at some of today's societies one could be forgiven for believing that truly some things never change.

When it comes to culture though, we should remember that almost all of Russian artists have always been very critical of whatever vicious and utterly ghastly regime might have been in place at their time. They loved their country but thoroughly detested their rulers.

Tchaikovsky suffered greatly at the hands of the authorities because of his homosexuality. His fame as one of the greatest composers in history didn't save him from persecution and a miserable life.

There is no proof that Richard Strauss and Arnold Schoenberg were so ferociously contemptuous of 19th century melodic compositions. They probably didn't detest pompous Italian opera either. This is historical fiction and I made it all up. The timelines and the characters might have to be accurate but what famous people did or said doesn't have to.

Carlo Mandelli, his uncle Giulio and Doctor Kaminsky belong to that restricted tribe of reasonably wealthy people who understand that your wealth shouldn't come at the expense of your fellow human beings. Leaning neither left or right, they rightly sense that some kind of social justice must figure in the grand scheme of life and that without it the results are invariably dire.

There aren't many of them as most people tend to side in the most forceful way with the array of classes and castes they more or less belong to (or pretend to be part of).

When a family friend of the Mitford sisters knocked at the door of their home, he was let in by one of the famous siblings with a sharp and peremptory question demanding an equally decisive reply: 'Are you a fascist or a communist?'

The puzzled man calmly replied that he was neither. The young lady stormed off leaving him in the hallway, hanging onto her dismissive comment of such a reluctant answer: 'Wet.' There are times when it is just too difficult to be grey.

Well, most gay men are possibly "wet" and justly proud of it. We intensely dislike wars and revolutions. Beside exterminating beautiful men on both sides as they do - *'The waste, my dear boy. The insane waste!'* - most conflicts are unnecessary shows of brute arrogance and force started mainly by powerful and toxic men (and it is always men).

We love beauty, and wars are unspeakably ugly, full of butchery, hate and misery. For Carlo Mandelli what happens around him is repugnant though he obviously understands the necessity of it. He dwells on Artyom and his symphony: love and beauty; the rest of humanity is just too busy massacring each other and still claiming to call themselves "human".

Life ends in many ways. The physical one is merely one aspect of our demise. Once back in Italy, Carlo's dreams are over and he's preparing himself to survive on memories, possibly hoping that the real end will come soon. It happens more often than we would like to believe.

The lives of others, in particular the ones who love

you, matter and when they disappear your existence becomes meaningless. It is when you die inside. Ghosts are ghosts.

And perhaps at that point you hope for a blade to flicker in the Gardens of Porta Venezia; to do away with what has by then become a life full of nothing, the sound and fury which destroy our lives while simultaneously keeping us alive all but gone. A crystallised silence randomly interrupted by syncopated, haunting noises. And the dreadful people who make them. You leave the world to the next young fellow who will search for what you found and lost. The hope of finding it will be the same. And his inevitable failure will be just another tale. By another idiot. Signifying nothing indeed.

Acknowledgements

As with my previous works, special thanks go to my wonderful partner David for the editing and his invaluable help with timelines and historical authenticity.

I would also like to thank Andrew and his team at Spectrum Books for their encouragement, support and help.

Printed in Dunstable, United Kingdom

75870297R00154